P9-CDH-863

Bank Strategies and Challenges in the New Europe

Also by Edward P. M. Gardener

COMPETITION AND REGULATION OF BANKS (*with Christopher Barclay and Jack Revell*)

CAPITAL ADEQUACY AND BANKING SUPERVISION

CREDIT INSTITUTIONS AND BANKING: The Single Market Review (*with Philip Molyneux and Barry Moore*)

EFFICIENCY IN EUROPEAN BANKING (*with Philip Molyneux and Yener Altunbaş*)

EUROPEAN SAVINGS BANKS: COMING OF AGE? (*with Philip Molyneux, Jonathan Williams, Santiago Carbo and others*)

INTEREST RATE RISK AND BANKS

INVESTMENT BANKING: Theory and Practice

SECURISATION: History, Forms and Risks (*with Jack Revell*)

STRATEGIC CHALLENGES IN EUROPEAN BANKING (*with Joe Falzon*)

STRUCTURE AND REGULATION OF UK FINANCIAL MARKETS (*with Philip Molyneux*)

THE FUTURE OF FINANCIAL SYSTEMS AND SERVICES (*editor*)

UK BANKING SUPERVISION: Evolution, Practice and Issues

Bank Strategies and Challenges in the New Europe

Edited by

Edward P. M. Gardener
Professor of Banking and Finance
Institute of European Finance
University of Wales

and

Peter C. Versluijs
Training and Development Consultant
ABNAMRO
Harderwijk
The Netherlands

palgrave

Editorial matter and selection © Edward P. M. Gardener
and Peter C. Versluijs 2001
Chapter 12 © Yener Altunbaş, Santiago Carbo
and Edward P. M. Gardener 2001
Chapters 1–11, 13 and 14 © Palgrave Publishers Ltd 2001

All rights reserved. No reproduction, copy or transmission of
this publication may be made without written permission.

No paragraph of this publication may be reproduced, copied or
transmitted save with written permission or in accordance with
the provisions of the Copyright, Designs and Patents Act 1988,
or under the terms of any licence permitting limited copying
issued by the Copyright Licensing Agency, 90 Tottenham Court
Road, London W1P 0LP.

Any person who does any unauthorised act in relation to this
publication may be liable to criminal prosecution and civil
claims for damages.

The authors have asserted their rights to be identified
as the authors of this work in accordance with the
Copyright, Designs and Patents Act 1988.

First published 2001 by
PALGRAVE
Houndmills, Basingstoke, Hampshire RG21 6XS and
175 Fifth Avenue, New York, N. Y. 10010
Companies and representatives throughout the world

PALGRAVE is the new global academic imprint of
St. Martin's Press LLC Scholarly and Reference Division and
Palgrave Publishers Ltd (formerly Macmillan Press Ltd).

ISBN 0–333–94936–6

This book is printed on paper suitable for recycling and
made from fully managed and sustained forest sources.

A catalogue record for this book is available
from the British Library.

Library of Congress Cataloging-in-Publication Data
Bank strategies and challenges in the new Europe / Edward P.M.
Gardener and Peter C. Versluijs.
     p. cm.
Papers presented at the 1997 annual seminar of the European
Association of University Teachers of Banking and Finance in
Amsterdam.
Includes bibliographical references and index.
ISBN 0–333–94936–6
    1. Banks and banking—Technological innovations—European
Union countries—Congresses. 2. Electronic funds transfers–
–European Union countries—Congresses. I. Gardener, Edward
P. M. II. Versluijs, Peter C., 1954– III. European Association of
University Teachers of Banking and Finance.
HG2974 .B353 2001
332.1'094—dc21
                              2001021873

10 9 8 7 6 5 4 3 2 1
10 09 08 07 06 05 04 03 02 01

Printed in Great Britain by Antony Rowe Ltd, Chippenham, Wiltshire

Contents

List of Tables   ix
List of Figures   xii
Preface   xiv
Notes on the Contributors   xvi
Synopses of Contributions   xxii

1   The Bank is Dead, Long Live the Bank   1
     Ray Shaw
     1.1   Introduction   1
     1.2   Changing functions and processes   1
     1.3   Impact of technological change on costs for the UK
           clearing banks   3
     1.4   The architecture of future electronic banking   7
     1.5   Developing payment systems on the Internet   9
     1.6   Specialist corporate network services   12
     1.7   Will the banks survive?   15

2   Technical Change in European Banking   19
     Yener Altunbaş and Philip Molyneux
     2.1   Introduction   19
     2.2   Methodology   20
     2.3   Data and results   26
     2.4   Conclusions   28
     Appendix   32

**3   Competitive Advantage Based on Information
     Technology in Banking**   46
     Esteban Fernández, José M. Montes and Camilo J. Vásquez
     3.1   Increasing competition and price competitiveness   46
     3.2   The impact of new information technologies on
           subcontracting processes   49
     3.3   Price competition versus relationship banking   51
     3.4   Conclusions   61

4   Emerging Methods of Payment   64
     Jack Revell
     4.1   Introduction   64
     4.2   Plastic cards   65

	4.3	Credit cards	66
	4.4	Chip cards and prepaid cards	67
	4.5	The Internet	69

5 Dimensions of Actions Distribution 71
Marcel R. Creemers

	5.1	Introduction	71
	5.2	Distribution concepts	72
	5.3	Types of actions	74
	5.4	Market-driven businesses	75
	5.5	Community building	75
	5.6	Dimensions of actions distribution	76
	5.7	Analysing distribution channels	78
	5.8	Actions distribution research	83
	5.9	Implications	85

6 Card Payments: Pricing and Competition 87
Ted Lindblom

	6.1	Introduction	87
	6.2	Current pricing of card payments	90
	6.3	Recent card pricing trends	94
	6.4	Theoretical guidelines	96
	6.5	Conclusions	100

7 The Unified European Banking Market and the Convergence of National Banking Sectors 106
Elisabetta Montanaro, Claudio Scala and Mario Tonveronachi

	7.1	Introduction	106
	7.2	Regulation, competition and convergence	108
	7.3	The recent experience	114
	7.4	Conclusions	124
		Methodological Appendix	125
		Appendix	130

8 Product Mix of the Spanish Banking Firms: Do Competition Clubs Exist? 139
Francisco Pérez and Emili Tortosa-Ausina

	8.1	Introduction	139
	8.2	Basic product mix indicators	141
	8.3	Product mix measures	142
	8.4	Do competition clubs exist?	148
	8.5	Where is the banking sector diversity?	154
	8.6	Concluding comments	157

9   **Institutional Investment Flows and the Regions of the**
     UK: a Case for a New Financial Infrastructure?   164
     Jonathan Williams
     9.1   Introduction and background   164
     9.2   Financial liberalisation and the space economy   166
     9.3   The financial system and regional development   168
     9.4   The spatial distribution of institutional
            investment in the UK   172
     9.5   Policy implications for Wales and the regions   181

10   **Characteristics of International Financial Centres**   193
     Joe Falzon
     10.1   Concepts and characteristics   194
     10.2   Historical development   197
     10.3   Communications and financial centres   198
     10.4   Conclusions   199

11   **Globalisation, Cross-Border Trade in Financial Services**
     and Offshore Banking: the Case of Ireland   201
     Philip Bourke and Ray Kinsella
     Introduction   201
     11.1   Background   202
     11.2   The IFSC   205
     Conclusion   211

12   **The Impact of CAR on Bank Capital Augmentation**
     in Spain   213
     Yener Altunbaş Santiago Carbo and Edward P.M. Gardener
     12.1   Introduction   213
     12.2   Background and model   215
     12.3   Statistical methodology   221
     12.4   Data and results   223
     12.5   Conclusions   227

13   **The Management of Foreign Exchange Exposures**
     and Interest Rate Exposures in a Number of UK and
     Swedish Firms between 1985 and 1996   232
     Göran Bergendahl
     13.1   Background   232
     13.2   Exposure management in business firms   235
     13.3   Experiences from treasury departments   252
     13.4   Conclusions   265
     Appendix   269

14   Fat Tails and the Effect on Optimal Asset Allocations   272
André Lucas and Pieter Klaassen
   14.1   Introduction   272
   14.2   The model   274
   14.3   Theoretical effects of fat tails   278
   14.4   An application to Dutch asset classes   280
   14.5   The effect of misspecification of fat tails   283
   14.6   Concluding remarks   287

Index   289

List of Tables

1.1	Staff reductions in the major clearers	4
1.2	Quoted major clearers – potential staff reductions and financial impact	5
1.3	British non-cash money transmission: 1980–2000+	6
2.1	Descriptive statistics of the outputs, inputs and time variable used in the model	26
2.2	Hypotheses test result	27
2.3	Decomposition of technical progress between 1988–95 (annual average)	27
2.4	Overall technical progress for European banks 1988–95	29
2.5	Decomposition of technical change according to bank size	31
2.A1	Number of banks and mean asset sizes according to years	32
2.A2	Number of banks according to specialisation and asset sizes	34
2.A3	Descriptive statistics of total assets	35
2.A4	Maximum likelihood parameter estimation of the cost frontier for European banks	36
2.A5	Scale economies for European banks 1988–95	38
2.A6	Mean X-inefficiency levels of banks in the EU 1988–95	40
6.1	Number of EFTPOS terminals in EU countries (1990–95)	88
6.2	Current pricing of payment cards to Swedish cardholders (summer 1997)	91
6.3	Current charges paid by Swedish retailers to bank/ network operators (spring 1997)	93
7.1	Variables of banking performance	115
7.2	Variables of banking structure	115
7.3	Country co-ordinates in terms of principal components	117
7.4	Principal components: percentages of total variability (variance–covariance matrix)	117
7.5	Explicative variables for C_1	118
7.6	Explicative variables for C_2	118
7.7	Qualitative values for C_1 and C_2	119
7.8	ER and corrected ER	123

7.A1   Performance variables (mean values 1989–92)   130
7.A2   Performance variables (mean values 1993–95)   130
7.A3   Structure variables (mean values 1989–92)   130
7.A4   Structure variables (mean values 1993–95)   131
7.A5   Explicative variables of the 1st principal component C_1
        (mean values 1989–92)   131
7.A6   Explicative variables of the 1st principal component C_1
        (mean values 1993–95)   131
7.A7   Explicative variables of the 2nd principal component
        C_1 (mean values 1989–92)   132
7.A8   Explicative variables of the 2nd principal component C_2
        (mean values 1993–95)   132
7.A9   Regression of the 1st principal component C_1
        versus its explicative variable (1989–92)   132
7.A10   Regression of the 1st principal component C_1
        versus its explicative variables (1993–95)   133
7.A11   Regression of the 2nd principal component C_2
        versus its explicative variables (1989–92)   133
7.A12   Regression of the 2nd principal component C_2
        versus its explicative variables (1993–95)   133
7.A13   Euclidean distances (1989–92)   134
7.A14   Euclidean distances (1993–95)   134
7.A15   Variance–covariance matrix (1989–92)   134
7.A16   Variance–covariance matrix (1993–95)   135
7.A17   Variance–covariance matrix (1989–95   136
8.1   Convergence in specialisation (relative dispersion):
        banking firms (1985 versus 1995)   142
8.2   Convergence in specialisation (relative dispersion):
        banking firms (1985–1995)   143
8.3   Convergence in specialisation: banking firms (1985–95) 147
8.4   Selected groups by product mix in the Spanish banking
        sector (1995)   150
8.5   Convergence in specialisation: banking firms (1985–95) 153
9.1   Household expenditure on select investment items,
        by standard region, 1995–96   173
9.2   Regional household expenditure on institutional
        investment, 1995–96   175
9.3   Number of pension funds with capital values: by
        region and size   179
9.4   Value of total pension fund assets: by region and
        size   180

11.1a	Stand alone activities in the IFSC: by sector and geographical distribution (December 1996)	208
11.1b	Agency activities in the IFSC: by sector and geographical distribution (December 1996)	208
11.1c	Captive insurance activities in the IFSC: by sector and geographical distribution (December 96)	209
12.1	Descriptive statistics of model variables in 1996	223
12.2	Distribution of banks according to KR_t variable	224
12.3	Panel regression results of capital augmentation on posited explanatory variables	225
13.1	Firms interviewed by sector in 1996	234
13.2	Aggregated transaction exposures	238
13.3	Interest rate exposures for a fictitious firm	244
13.4	Interest rate exposures and currency exchange exposures for a fictitious firm	245
13.5	Arguments for and against hedging	250
14.1	Optimal asset allocations	282
14.2	The effect of misspecification of v on the required shortfall return	286

List of Figures

1.1	Payment categories	10
5.1	Scoring distribution characteristics	78
5.2	Characteristics of a physical book shop	79
5.3	Characteristics of a virtual book shop	80
5.4	Characteristics of a physical branch	81
5.5	Characteristics of a virtual bank	82
7.1	Interest margin (yield on assets–cost of debt)	113
7.2	Bank spread	113
7.3	Typology of banking models of the selected European countries (1989–92)	116
7.4	Typology of banking models of the selected European countries (1993–95)	116
7.5	Mapping of the two principal components (1989–92)	119
7.6	Mapping of the two principal components (1993–95)	120
7.7	ER: deviations from countries averages	123
7.8	Corrected ER: deviations from countries averages	123
8.1	Convergence in specialisation: banks and savings banks (assets)	145
8.2	Convergence in specialisation: banks and savings banks (liabilities)	146
8.3	Convergence in specialisation, total balance sheet: banks and savings banks	154
8.4	Convergence in specialisation, total balance sheet (product mix groups)	156
8.5	Evolution of product mix groups inequality: assets	158
8.6	Evolution of product mix groups inequality: liabilities	159
8.7	Evolution of inequality decomposition: assets	160
8.8	Evolution of inequality decomposition: liabilities	160
11.1	Globalisation and emerging risk management needs	203
11.2	MNCs: risk management options	209
13.1	The transaction exposure of an individual sale	237
14.1	Student t distribution for various values of the degrees of freedom parameter v	277

14.2 Critical shortfall probability Ψ for the Student t
distribution with v degrees of freedom (benchmark
is the normal distribution)   279

14.3 True shortfall probability for several combinations
of v_m and v_t.   284

Preface

This volume was sponsored by Amsterdamse Academie and produced in partnership with the Institute of European Finance at the University of Wales, Bangor. The co-editors represent these two institutions.

The papers collected in this volume are largely from the 1997 annual seminar of the European Association of University Teachers of Banking and Finance (or the 'Wolpertinger Club'). This volume is the fourth in a series that brings together papers delivered by some of the leading European academic thinkers and researchers who study banking, finance and the development of financial systems.

The 14 chapters embrace some of the key issues that confront EU and global banking systems today. The volume covers the following broad areas:

- Overview of recent key trends and strategic drivers in global banking, together with their implications for the economic role of banks (Chapter 1).
- The next group of papers embraces several strategic issues that are shaping the modern banking firm and cover:
    - technical change and information technology (Chapters 2 and 3);
    - emerging methods of payment, electronic service distribution and pricing and competition in the plastic card market (Chapters 4, 5 and 6);
    - the single market, banking performance and competition (Chapters 7 and 8)
- Institutional investment flows and the UK regions (Chapter 9)
- Financial centres, cross-border trade in financial services and off-shore banking (Chapters 10 and 11)
- Capital adequacy regulation, risk and optimal asset allocations (Chapters 12, 13 and 14)

Taken together these chapters provide an overview and insight into some of the challenges that confront practitioners, policymakers and students of banking and finance.

Several key themes run through this collection of papers. Change and change management are two, overarching themes. Deregulation, intensifying competition and the increasing influence of technology on banking are particularly important strategic drivers of modern banking and they figure highly in many of these papers. The strategic and managerial challenges to banks are enormous and complex in this new environment. New approaches and techniques of regulation are also necessary.

What is clear from this volume is that EU and global banking are continuing to evolve and change in a sustained and fundamental manner. It also seems clear that this process of change, adaptation and realignment is unlikely to slow down in the immediate future. Under the influence of fundamental and pervasive changes, especially those associated with technology, banking is entering a new world. Turning back the clock is never going to be a feasible option in this new environment.

The 1997 annual seminar of the European Association of University Teachers of Banking and Finance was hosted by Amsterdamse Academie in Amsterdam. We take this opportunity to thank Amsterdamse Academie and their sponsors for hosting the seminar in 1997. This book is the product of the seminar.

This book was a co-operative effort between Amsterdamse Academie and the Institute of European Finance. As was the case with the first three volumes in this 'Wolpertinger series', the Institute of European Finance shouldered the managerial responsibility for this book project. In particular, Christine Owen directed and organised the proof-reading and liaison with the publishers; Emily Smith managed the chapter production, and related aspects like liaison and follow-up work with authors. We thank them for their considerable efforts and forbearance. At the same time, we thank authors for their contributions and co-operation. Finally, of course, we must thank the publishers for their positive support and help in getting this volume into production.

EDWARD P.M. GARDENER
PETER C. VERSLUIJS

Notes on the Contributors

Yener Altunbaş holds a B.Sc. (Economics) degree from the University of Hacettepe, Ankara and a Ph.D. from the University of Wales, Bangor. He has worked as an analyst and economist with Etibank Banking Inc. and as a Research Officer within the Institute of European Finance at the University of Wales, Bangor. Since 1998 Dr Altunbaş has been employed as a Research Fellow in the Business School at South Bank University, London. Author of many articles on the structure and efficiency of banking markets, his main fields of research interest include the study of European banks, efficiency, stock market analysis, electoral studies, regional economics and urban economics.

Göran Bergendahl has been Professor of Business Administration at Gothenburg University since 1971 and Dean of the School of Economics and Commercial Law at the same university since 1997. Before that he worked as an economist for the National Road Administration, Stockholm and the Swedish Association of the Farmers Cooperations, Malmö. He holds a doctorate degree in Business Administration from Stockholm University. He has edited several books and written monographs in the areas of transport economics, international financial management and bank management and has published numerous articles about agricultural economics, transportation economics, energy economics and financial management. His present research concerns the analysis of efficiency and productivity in the financial sector.

Philip Bourke is currently Irish Banks' Professor of Banking and Finance in the Graduate School of Business at University College, Dublin. He has held this appointment since 1989, prior to which he was Director, Australian Centre for Banking and Finance at the University of New South Wales in Sydney. His previous appointment was as Director of the Centre for the Study of Financial Markets in University College Dublin, an appointment that he combined with a position in the Department of Banking and Finance. He has also worked for Chase Manhattan Bank in Paris. He holds Bachelors and Masters degrees from University College Dublin, an MBA from Boston

College and a doctoral degree from the National University of Ireland. He has published extensively in the field of banking, finance and investment. His publications appear in international and domestic journals and in book form, and he has also presented conference papers in Europe, Asia and Australia.

Santiago Carbo holds a Licenciado (BA) in Economics (University of Valencia, Spain), an MA in Banking and Finance and a Ph.D. in Economics (University of Wales). He is currently Professor Titular of the Department of Applied Economics at the University of Granada (Spain) and Director of the Financial System Research of the Savings Banks Foundation for Economic and Social Research (Fundación de las Cajas de Ahorros Confederadas).

Marcel R. Creemers has been Information Systems Management Professor at the economic faculty of the Vrije Universiteit Amsterdam since 1995, and he is also an independent consultant in the field of corporate IT strategy. Between 1980 and 1995 he worked for the Netherlands based Rabobank as strategy adviser. He has studied in the fields of electronics (polytechnical, 1972), psychology (University of Nymegen, 1982) and his Ph.D. is in business science (University of Amsterdam, 1993). At the Vrije Universiteit he teaches IT strategy and organisation and researches electronic commerce. He is chairman of the Business Renewal department, a member of the faculty's research committee, chairman of the Business Science research group and head of the postdoctoral educational programme in IT and finance.

Joe Falzon holds a Ph.D. in Economics from Northwestern University, Evanston, Illinois. He was a lecturer in Economics at Roosevelt University, Chicago and a Visiting Assistant Professor in Economics at Northwestern University and the University of Cincinnati. Since 1988, he has served as a consultant to several ministries of the government of Malta and other financial and corporate institutions in Malta. He is the author of numerous economic papers and research projects and is currently the Head of the Department of Banking and Finance at the University of Malta.

Esteban Fernández is Professor of Business Administration and he has been Director of the University Institute of the Firm and Vice Rector at Oviedo University.

Edward P.M. Gardener is Professor of Banking and Finance and Director of the Institute of European Finance at the University of Wales, Bangor. He has held visiting professorial posts at Queen Mary and Westfield College and at the Universities of Malta, Gothenburg, the Catholic University of Eichstätt and the Swedish School of Economics. He obtained his Ph.D. from the University of Wales and has been awarded an honorary doctorate from the University of Gothenburg. Professor Gardener was the banking expert on the British Council Special Mission to Hungary on behalf of the HMG 'Know How Fund' for Eastern Europe (March, 1990). During 1997/98 he was a consultant to the World Bank. His current research spans banking strategies, efficiency regulation and strategies for offshore financial centres. He has published many books and articles and was co-author of the recent EC DG XV Study on *Credit Institutions and Banking* (1997).

Ray Kinsella is Professor of Banking and Financial Services at the University of Ulster and Visiting Professor of Banking and Insurance at the Graduate School of Business, University College Dublin, where he is Director for the Centre for Insurance Studies. He has worked with the Central Bank of Ireland and as an Economic Advisor to the Minister for Trade and Commerce. He has published extensively in banking, finance and insurance including *Internal Controls in Banking* (1996) and (with Professor McBrierty) *Ireland and the Knowledge Economy: the Emerging Techno-Academic Paradigm* (1999).

Pieter Klaassen is Vice President Credit Risk Modeling at the ABN-AMRO Bank N.V. in Amsterdam and researcher at the department of Finance and Financial Sector Management of the Vrije Universiteit.

Ted Lindblom is a specialist in pricing, particularly pricing in decreasing cost industries. Presently, his main research interests have included technology advances in the information field and their implications for market competition and pricing strategies. In the banking sector he has researched for many years on the pricing of payments services and market structural changes mainly in retail banking. He has authored and co-authored several articles and books regarding these fields. He is currently Professor and Director of Postgraduate Studies in Business Administration at the University of Gothenburg.

André Lucas is research fellow at the Department of Finance and Financial Sector Management of the Vrije Universiteit in Amsterdam, the Netherlands. He also holds the post of Research Fellow at the Tinbergen Institute.

Philip Molyneux is currently Professor in Banking and Finance and Director of the Institute of European Finance at the University of Wales, Bangor and he has also recently been appointed to Special Chair of Financial Services and Financial Conglomerates at Erasmus University, Rotterdam, the Netherlands. His main area of research is on the structure and efficiency of banking markets and he has published widely in this area. He has acted as a consultant to the New York Federal Reserve Bank and World Bank, and is currently a member of the UK's National Institute's Advisory Panel on the European Financial Markets Programme. Some of his recent books include: *Efficiency in European Banking* (1996), *Private Banking* (1996) *Banking in Germany* (1996), *Bancassurance* (1998) and *Financial Innovation* (1999).

Elisabetta Montanaro is Professor of Banking at the University of Siena, Department of Law and Economics. From 1982 to 1996 she was Director of the Postgraduate School of Banking of the same University. She is a member of the Société Universitaire Européenne de Recherches Fianciéres (SUERF), and has published seven books and many articles and papers on banking issues. Her main research interests are in the fields of banking strategies, insurance and risk management, evolution of financial systems and central banking.

José M. Montes is Assistant Professor of Business Administration and Vice Dean of the Faculty of Economics at Oviedo University. He has written extensively on the innovation process as well as topics in industrial organisation and business strategy.

Francisco Pérez is Professor of Economic Analysis at the University Valencia and Research Director of the IVIE in Spain. His specialised fields are financial economics – banking and public finance – and the analysis of economic growth and regional economics. He has published ten books and over 50 articles in specialist journals. He was an Eisenhower Fellow during 1998 in the USA.

Jack Revell is Professor Emeritus of the University of Wales, having retired from the Chair of Economics at the University College of North Wales in 1983 after fourteen years. He founded the Institute of European Finance at the College in 1973 and was its first Director until

1985; he was at the Department of Applied Economics in the University of Cambridge. He has been consultant to the Statistical Offices of the United Nations and the European Union, the OECD and several banks and banking associations. He has published many articles and books on aspects of banking systems, among which are *The Wealth of the Nation: the National Balance Sheet of the United Kingdom* (1967), *The British Financial System* (1973), *Solvency and Regulation of Banks* (1973), *Cost and Margins in Banking: an International Survey* (1980), *Banking and Electronic Fund Transfer* (1983), *Mergers and the Role of Large Banks* (1987), *The Future of Savings Banks* (1987), *Changes in West European Public Banks* (1991) and *The Changing Face of European Banks and Securities Markets* (1994).

Claudio Scala is Professor of Statistics at the University of Siena. He has published many articles, books and textbooks. His main fields of research interest include non-linear dynamical systems and the Winger transform.

Ray Shaw is a director of a management consultancy company in Birmingham that specialises in corporate organisation and development. During his early banking career he was a corporate banker with Westminster Bank. From 1974 to 1983 he was a Director of Loughborough University Banking Group, and then became a Director of TSB Group Management Training and Development until 1989. From 1989 to 1990 he was Deputy Director of Institute of Banking in Saudi Arabia.

Mario Tonveronachi is Professor of Monetary Economics at the University of Siena. His current research fields are central banking, financial systems, currency regimes and Keynesian theory.

Emili Tortosa-Ausina is Teaching Assistant in Economics at the Universitat Jaume I. His specialised fields are financial economics (banking and finance). He has published articles in Spanish economic reviews and participated in projects financed by Spanish banking firms. He studied at the Institut für Wirtschaftswissenschaften in the University of Vienna in 1995 during his participation in the Q.E.D. program.

Camilo J. Vásquez is Professor of Business Administration at Oviedo University.

Jonathan Williams is a lecturer in Banking and Finance at the University of Wales, Bangor. Holder of two University of Wales degrees, he is currently researching a Ph.D. in the area of bank efficiency and ownership characteristics. As an associate of the Institute of European Finance, he has contributed to a number of important studies in the field of banking, such as the EC 1997 Single Market Review on Credit Institutions and Banking, and studies relating to European savings banks and public banks. Author of a number of articles on banking, his main interests include the study of savings banks, efficiency, and regional and international banking.

Synopses of Contributions

1   The bank is dead, long live the bank

The chapter reviews the crucial pressures faced by banks world-wide as they are threatened by growing competition, changing technology and increased regulation. It is concluded that despite these pressures the fundamental functions of banks remain the same: maturity transformation, risk assessment and risk assumption. For the present the fundamental economic role of banks is unlikely to change.

2   Technical change in European banking

This chapter examines technical change in European banking by applying the Fourier Flexible functional form and stochastic cost frontier methodologies using 13 603 bank observations across 15 EU countries between 1988 and 1995. The results show that technical progress has had a similar influence across European banking markets, making a positive contribution to costs of around 3 per cent every year. Large banks appear to benefit more from technical change than their smaller competitors. The authors also break down technical progress into its three main components: pure, scale and (input) non-neutral effects. This shows that pure technical change is the main contributor to overall technical progress for small banks (assets size less than $1 billion), and larger banks appear to gain more from technical advances which alter the optimal input mix. Technical change also becomes increasingly scale biased as banks become larger. This implies that technological change increases the minimum efficient bank size for larger banks to a greater extent than for their smaller competitors. Given that technical change is non-neutral with respect to optimal bank size and input-mix, it is tentatively suggested that the formation of larger banks may be in the public interest.

3   Competitive advantage based on information technology in banking

The development and diffusion of information technologies (IT) and the intense competition of the 1980s have induced two kinds of organisational restructuring as a means of reducing costs: first, outsourcing of activities which are computer and telecommunications intensive and second, downsizing by heavily investing in IT and streamlining employment. This study analyses the influence of these organisational changes on the evolution of business processes and competitive strategies in banking.

4   Emerging methods of payment

This chapter contains a brief survey of changes in methods of payment from the mid-1960s to the present time. It concentrates on retail payments, in which there are two main paths of change: the development of the plastic card and the automation of regular payments. The plastic card started off as a means of identification and retains this function, but in cheque using countries it soon became a means of guaranteeing the payment of cheques. The next two steps were the addition of a magnetic stripe to enable the automatic withdrawal of cash from machines and the development of credit cards. The use of credit cards for payments by post or telephone led to a large drop in the numbers of cheques. The final development was the substitution of an integrated circuit for the magnetic stripe, enabling the development of 'electronic purses' and, with extra security features, payment on the Internet. A parallel development has been the creation of special circuits for payments, such as salaries, pensions and instalments on insurance policies and loans of various kinds. On the wholesale side, use was made of the inherent security of the giro method for high value payment circuits.

5   Dimensions of actions distribution

The growing digital economy requires rethinking of the distribution concept. The author concludes that digital distribution comes down to the availability of actors who perform virtual actions as part of a service. Three dimensions – access, availability and functionality – are proposed which together characterise the quality of the distribution, both in physical and in virtual situations. Ranking these dimensions shows the progress in electronic service distribution that has taken place throughout the last decade.

6   Card payments: pricing and competition

Attention is drawn to the increasing use of plastic cards as payment media and the remarkable rise in the number of such cards in circulation. A prerequisite for this development is the improved accessibility of speedy and cost-efficient card payment systems. However, these systems incur considerable capacity costs for operators, like banks, that have to be financed: the key questions are by whom and how? Should the costs be distributed to both retailers and card possessors or only to one of the two categories? Should the costs be covered by a combination of fixed annual fees and variable transactions fees or only by one type of fee? These questions are analysed from both practical and theoretical standpoints. The recent launch of new types of payment cards – retailer cards and co-branded cards – is given special attention. These cards may serve as a means to strengthen the competitiveness of the issuing retailers and to increase their sales through improved customer loyalty.

7 The unified European banking market and the convergence of national banking sectors

The project to unify the European banking systems into a single internal market presupposes the possibility of overcoming the differences in financial structure and banking performances among the European countries. This study argues that the existence of dynamic oligopolistic barriers renders the creation of a single, highly competitive market quite doubtful. On these premises, an empirical analysis, based on the principal components method, is used to compare national indicators of banking structure and performance before 1989–92 and after 1993–95, the European banking market unification. Contrary to widely held expectations, the recent experience of regulatory harmonisation in a context of liberalisation points to a lack of convergence in the structural models of banking and to a significant process of polarisation and divergence in the performance of the European banking sectors.

8 Product mix of the Spanish banking firms: do competition clubs exist?

The expansion and intensification of banking competition which has occurred in Spain during the last ten years has allowed commercial banks and savings banks to define their competitive strategies with more freedom. This study analyses the similarities and the differences in the product mix of these firms and their time evolution. In particular, it aims to identify the different kinds of firms and to analyse whether competition leads to the homogenisation (convergence) of product mixes between firms or groups of firms (clubs). The empirical success is higher when specialisation clubs are considered, finding increased heterogeneity within the banking system as a whole but also increased homogeneity within certain clusters of banks and savings banks.

9   Institutional investment flows and the regions of the UK: a case for a new financial infrastructure

Institutional investment flows have assumed greater significance in the UK as the financial system has evolved from a market-oriented phase into the present securitised phase. UK capital markets are now dominated by institutional investors while the financial system dominates over the real sector. In this setting there has been comparatively little consideration of the spatial distribution of institutional investment flows in the UK. The available empirical evidence suggests that institutional investments flow out of peripheral regions and are centralised and controlled in the national financial centre. This study aims to quantify such flows, in particular from the perspective of Wales, and to consider how a more regional-oriented financial infrastructure might redress some of the imbalances associated with the present, centralised financial system.

10   Characteristics of international financial centres

International financial centres have become increasingly more important in the world financial system because they have contributed to the explosive growth in the volume of international financial transactions witnessed in the 1980s and 1990s. They can be classified and distinguished in terms of historical growth, regional influence, number of international banks located and volume of international transactions generated. However, in spite of these apparent differences, there seem to be underlying common characteristics that can help explain the growth and development of these international financial centres. This short chapter traces the main underlying forces that are shaping and driving international financial centres.

11   Globalisation, cross-border trade in financial services and offshore banking: the case of Ireland

The International Financial Services Centre (IFSC) in the Dublin Docklands region has developed from a 'green-field' site in 1987 to a major global offshore financial centre, notably in reinsurance, fund management and asset financing. This chapter evaluates, as a case study with important policy lessons, the critical 'success factors' which have underpinned and supported this process. The rationale for cross-border banking is discussed: particular attention is focused on globalisation and emerging risk management needs of companies as a new and important factor in explaining offshore banking. Within this framework, the chapter discusses the contribution of the policy regime in Ireland, including a rigorous and flexible regulatory regime, taxation, a world class technology platform and human capital 'knowledge equity' as key success factors.

12 The impact of CAR on bank capital augmentation in Spain

Exploratory tests, using panel methods, are reported of a model that seeks to explain capital augmentation in the Spanish savings bank sector over the period 1987 to 1996. Various reasons are advanced to explain why this EU banking sector and time frame are a particularly interesting 'laboratory' of the potential impact of regulation on bank capital augmentation. Early US modelling work in this area is built on by *inter alia* including two previously omitted and key bank portfolio risks (liquidity and interest rate) and a new productive efficiency variable. The results indicate strong evidence of the impact of the new capital adequacy regulatory regime on bank capital augmentation. At the same time the model confirms the importance of bank profitability and productive efficiency in explaining capital augmentation.

13 The management of foreign exchange exposures and interest rate exposures in a number of UK and Swedish firms between 1985 and 1996

Business firms that operate in foreign countries are often heavily exposed to sudden changes in exchange rates and interest rates. This chapter gives an analysis of how 23 Swedish and UK firms handle such exposures and how they use financial market instruments to protect themselves from substantial financial losses. Furthermore, interviews conducted in 1996 are compared with interviews with the same firms conducted in 1985. In so doing, information is given on how these firms have changed their focus on financial risk over time. This chapter illuminates the work done in multinational firms in order to balance risk and return from financial transactions.

14 Fat tails and the effect on optimal asset allocations

In investment management problems one often uses scenarios to determine optimal strategies and to quantify the uncertainty associated with these strategies. Such scenarios are mostly based on the assumption of normality for variables like asset returns, inflation rates and interest rates. Financial economic time series often display leptokurtic behaviour, implying that the assumption of normality may be inappropriate. In this study we use a simple asset allocation problem with one shortfall constraint in order to uncover the main consequences of non-normal distributions on optimal asset allocations. It is found that the probability of shortfall plays a crucial role in determining the effect of fat tails on optimal asset allocations. Depending on this probability, the presence of fat tails may lead to either more aggressive or more prudent asset mixes. We also examine the effect of misspecification of the degree of leptokurtosis. Using distributions with an incorrect tail behaviour may lead to portfolios with a minimum return that is up to 418 basis points below the minimum return imposed in the model. In VAR (value-at-risk) calculations, this implies that the true VAR may deviate by more than 4 per cent (as a fraction of the invested notional) from what an incorrectly specified model suggests. This illustrates the importance of using scenario generators that exhibit the correct tail behaviour.

1

The Bank is Dead, Long Live the Bank

Ray Shaw

1.1 Introduction

This chapter examines the future role of banks and to what extent that future is threatened by growing competition, changing technology and regulations. The main thrust of this chapter will focus on new technology and the emergence of the Internet and complementary technologies. Some comment will also be made concerning regulatory issues.

The most radical changes have been occurring in the retail banking sector and, while the pace and direction of change seem to vary from country to country, banks everywhere are working vigorously to address new technological, regulatory and competitive realities. They are trying to determine the strategies and tactics needed to secure their franchises for the future.

1.2 Changing functions and processes

Many observers are prophesying the terminal decline of commercial banks and their long-standing deposit taking and loan functions. In the USA, for example, the commercial banks' share of total assets in financial institutions has fallen from over 70 per cent in 1900 to barely 30 per cent in 1995, and the banks' share of corporate debt has fallen from 19.6 per cent in 1979 to 14.5 per cent in 1994. So competition on both sides of the balance sheet has increased. On the liability side new technologies and deregulation have given customers a choice through the use of the telephone and the computer and access to mutual funds, some of which require the use of a bank branch.

On the asset side of the balance sheet the growth of money and bond markets and commercial paper has given companies alternative

(and often cheaper) ways of borrowing money. To counter these problems the banks are responding, albeit slowly, by rethinking the form in
which they deliver their functions. Traditionally also, the banks have
always had a lender of last resort facility provided by the central banks:
this facility is unlikely to be withdrawn and thus the banks can still
continue to carry out arguably their most important function which is
to *guarantee* money at short notice to customers.

The most important influence on the banks, however, has been the
information technology revolution. New databases and information
producing agencies, such as rating agencies, and new services have
made huge inroads into the advantage banks once had in being more
informed about their client base than anyone else. Faster data processing techniques have made the markets more liquid and efficient, providing opportunities particularly to well-known companies to raise
funds from many sources. Private customers have also benefited from
an increasing choice of service providers and automated cash machines
which have further foreshadowed degrees of deregulation as organisations have bypassed the regulatory system.

The process of deregulation has had two important effects. First,
deregulation removed or reduced the economic franchises, increasing
competition between banks and financial institutions thereby increasing risk in their balance sheets, rendering them seemingly less sound
than their large corporate customers. The second and more subtle but
no less important change arises from the ability of the banks to seek
new business in much wider fields of activity (for example, such as
loan purchases) and off-balance sheet transactions. These transactions
have fundamentally changed the nature of the risks in the balance
sheets, for example market risks which can be large and sudden. There
is, therefore, much more uncertainty about the probity of bank balance
sheets. Both of the above factors substantially increased the cost of
funds to banks, thus reducing their competitiveness.

The shift to the use of new technologies

The pace of technological change in electronics has been visible for all
to see and with hindsight in 1997 it is easy to forget that in 1994 most
people, including the technology community, knew little of 'the
Internet'. In February 1995, *Business Week* reported that 'there are
27,000 web-sites and this number is doubling every 53 days'. While
accurate figures for the growth rate of the Internet are highly specula-
tive, it is acknowledged that there are now well over 60 000 individual
networks linking millions of computers throughout the world.

Information can be accessed and transferred using common communications protocol thereby fulfilling at long last the promise of the computer industry of any computer being able to communicate with any other computer!

Impact on retail banks

While corporate bankers have made extensive use of electronic transmission services, the impact on retail banking, which is essentially about processing, storing and transmitting numbers, has been less rapid. Deloitte & Touche Consultancy Group (*The Future of Retail Banking: A Global Perspective*) reported in 1995 the extraordinary drop in the costs associated with the processing, storing and transmitting of data since 1987. Between 1987 and 1993 the real cost of processing in a PC dropped by no less than a factor of 100 and the cost of storing data has in the same period fallen twenty-fold. Why have these dramatic cost savings been slow to impact on the banks? There are several reasons for this apparent paradox. First, until relatively recently, competition in retail banking came mainly from other banks and, in the UK, building societies. More recently, however, companies such as Intel, Microsoft and Compaq have entered the market selling their technology and cutting costs as noted above. This has revolutionised the way in which services can be delivered and the new remote channels can largely replace the functionality of the retail bank.

These factors are now having an accelerating impact on the bankers who have in the main only added hi-tech peripherals to their large, outdated mainframes. In the UK, for example, the major clearing banks are currently implementing large-scale redundancy programmes as new technology is put in place.

1.3 Impact of technological change on costs for the UK clearing banks

Method of payment

The methods of making payments in the UK has shifted considerably during the 1990s with a strong trend towards automated settlement and away from paper transactions. This trend is expected to continue into the 21st century, with major gains being achieved in bank profitability as customers move from high cost transactions, such as cheques, to low cost methods of payment such as debit cards. (See Table 1.3) It is estimated (by Crédit Lyonnais/Laing) that almost half the 60 000 staff employed by the UK clearing banks is currently linked to money transmission services, with an annual cost of operating the system of approximately £4.5 billion. Since 1990 there has been an annual reduction in the use of cheques from 3.2 million items to less than 2.2 million. In the same period staff numbers fell by 120 000, indicating the high correlation between cheque numbers and staff costs. Laing's estimate that by the year 2000, a saving of £2 billion will have been achieved in staff costs on an assumed cost of approximately £25 000 per employee per annum (10 per cent of total costs) and that total staff numbers in UK banks will have fallen by some 30 per cent (78 000). The estimated increase in operating profit is 15 per cent per annum or 90 per cent in the five years to 2000. Table 1.1 shows the trends for UK clearers.

Cost savings – distribution between UK banks

Table 1.2 shows that the possible cost savings will differ from bank to bank. Clearly some will have greater capacity to reduce staff than others and there will also be differences in unit labour costs depending on geographical concentrations. There is, for example, approximately £4000 difference in per capita remuneration between English and

Table 1.1: Staff reductions in the major clearers

	Annual fall %		Potential numbers
Fall in	1990–94	1995	1995–2000
Barclays	−7	−1	20 995
Lloyds/TSB	−5	+1	22 077
Midland	−3	−5	7 961
NatWest	−6	−8	22 179
Bank of Scotland	−2	n/a	1 582
RBS	−2	−4	2 758
	Staff per branch, 1994		
Barclays	30		
Lloyds/TSB	22		
Midland	25		
NatWest	28		
Bank of Scotland	26		
RBS	27		

Source: Crédit Lyonnais/Laing, 13 March 1996 with their estimates for potential reductions.

Table 1.2: Quoted major clearers – potential staff reductions and financial impact

	Actual Annual change 1990–95 %	Actual Staff end 1995	Annual change 1995–2000 %	Staff end 2000	Estimates Staff reduction	Estimates Costs per head (£000s)	Total annual savings (£m)	(Savings as % of) Income 1996E	(Savings as % of) Operating profit 1996E	Memo item: cost income 1996E %
Barclays	–6	61 200	–6.5	43 758	17 442	27.7	483	6.3	17.7	64.5
Lloyds/TSB	–1	66 400*	–6.5	47 476	18 924	22.0	416	6.1	14.1	57.1
HSBC (Midland)	–2	43 400	–3.5	36 326	7 074	27.0	191	1.9	4.0	52.1
NatWest	–7	61 000	–6.5	43 615	17 385	26.9	468	6.4	18.5	65.2
Bank of Scotland	–2	11 300	–3.5	9 458	1 842	22.0	41	2.3	4.9	52.9
Royal Bank of Scotland	–2	19 500	–3.5	16 322	3 178	24.7	78	3.0	12.1	48.9
Total/Average	–5	262 800	–5.6	196 955	65 845	25.5	1 677	5.4	11.6	58.1

* pro-forma

Source: Crédit Lyonnais/Laing, 13 March 1996.

Table 1.3: British non-cash money transmission: 1980–2000+

	1980 (% of total)		1990 (% of total)		1995 (% of total)		2000E (% of total)		1990/80	Rate of change 1995/90 annualised %	2000/95
Paper	**n/a**	**n/a**	**4357**	**(54.1)**	**3582**	**(37.6)**	**2728**	**(24.0)**	**n/a**	**-4**	**-5**
Cheque Clearing	2124E	(55.0)	3122	(38.8)	2614	(27.4)	(2400)	(21.1)	+4	-3	-6
In-house Cheques	n/a	n/a	746	(9.3)	589	(6.0)	–	–	n/a	-5	-4
Credit Clearing	448E	(11.6)	489	(6.1)	399	(4.2)	328	(2.9)	–	-4	-4
Automated	**n/a**	**n/a**	**1741**	**(21.6)**	**2403**	**(25.2)**	**3323**	**(29.3)**	**n/a**	**+7**	**+7**
Standing Orders	169	(4.4)	242	(3.0)	216	(2.3)	193	(1.7)	+4	-2	-2
Direct Debits	173	(4.5)	846	(10.5)	1299	(13.6)	2000	(17.6)	+17	+9	+9
Customer Credits	96	(2.5)	514	(6.4)	753	(7.9)	1000	(8.8)	+18	+8	+6
Other	n/a	n/a	139	(1.7)	135	(1.4)	130	(1.1)	n/a	-1	-1
Plastic Cards	**n/a**	**n/a**	**1949**	**(24.2)**	**3544**	**(37.2)**	**5300**	**(46.7)**	**n/a**	**+13**	**+8**
Debit Cards	–	–	193	(2.4)	1004	(10.5)	2000	(17.6)	n/a	+39	+15
Credit Cards	163E	(4.2)	738	(9.2)	1018	(10.6)	1400	(12.3)	+16	+7	+7
ATMs	55	(1.4)	984	(12.2)	1441	(15.1)	(1900)	(16.7)	+32	+8	+5
Other Cash Withdrawal	n/a	n/a	34	(0.4)	81	(0.9)	–	–	n/a	+19	
Total Non-Cash	**3864**	**(100.0)**	**8047**	**(100.0)**	**9529**	**(100.0)**	**11351**	**(100.0)**	**+9**	**+3**	**+4**

Source: Association for Payment Clearing Services (APACS). Yearbook of Payment Statistics 1996; 1996 Payments Market Briefing, August 1996; and forecasts are substantially those of APACS.

Scottish banks. Other factors affecting staff reductions are the variations in product and customer bases which will impact on the ability of individual banks to cut costs. Table 1.2 shows that the largest estimated falls will be Barclays, Lloyds/TSB and NatWest, with nearly 20 000 staff reductions each. Barclays and NatWest also had the highest staff/branch ratios in 1994 (30) making them higher than the peer group average of 26 so there is pressure there to make a higher rate of reduction. In the case of Lloyds/TSB it is expected that the 'new' bank will be able to generate additional cost savings resulting from the merger as well as substantial income gains.

1.4   The architecture of future electronic banking

In this chapter a brief review has been made of why the new technologies are slow to be adopted by the banks. It is clear that the old monopolised ways of moving money are now under threat from companies such as Microsoft and recently liberalised telephone companies, television companies, Visa and MasterCard, and computer service companies such as EDS and AMS. A fundamental question which all banks must answer before they adopt any new technology, however, is to ask 'can it deliver something that cannot presently be delivered any other way and at lower cost?' If not, then it should not be used. Given such a philosophy what does the future hold?

Changes in the global landscape

The first and most obvious change to affect retail banks is that the new technology will not only drastically reduce branch numbers but will also lead to a shrinkage in the overall share of the market place. It is almost certain that the banks will face similar problems to the telecoms industry and the airline industry where a combination of technology and regulatory change led to significant restructuring. Like these industries the banks will be challenged by falling costs and pressure on prices so only the sharpest will survive. Indeed, it raises the question of how many of the existing market leaders will survive in such a hostile environment. Those banks which are slow to adapt will be taken over through managed regulatory mergers, rather than be allowed to fall by the wayside. The analogy with the telecoms industry is valid since the activities carried out previously by monopolistic providers in each country have been disaggregated into a large number of different players, each vying for competitive advantage not within the industry as a whole but within a number of sub-activities or collection of activities. The significance of such disaggregation is that a bank must win a large share of a strategically defensible activity or a collection of activities, not gain a small share of all activities.

All this raises the questions of how far and how fast? In other words how quickly is deregulation likely to progress. There is no doubt that the technology is available now for almost anyone to enter the banking market, as Direct Line Insurance has demonstrated. In the past the UK and the USA have led the deregulatory trend while Canada, continental Europe and Japan have been slower to embrace it. There seems little doubt that in those countries where deregulation occurs quickly, this will favour new entrants into the market over the banks.

There are already many very successful examples of new entrants into liberalised markets such as DirectLine Insurance (UK), Sofinco (France), Deutsche Telecom and Quelle (Germany), Countrywide Pasadena (USA), and the threat from these organisations and others in the pipeline is obvious.

New forms of distribution

The financial sector is undergoing a process of radical transformation as a result of increasing competition and changes in the purchasing habits of customers. There is also a shift in perception by customers of the products and services offered and the value they place on them. For example, customers are much more focused on the type of account and service that they want and how they use it. This trend has been targeted by building societies offering current or cheque accounts and various levels of access to funds, thereby increasing the pressure on banks.

In this environment the development of new distribution channels has become a key strategy in improving value added and satisfying customer requirements. As we noted earlier, the branch bank as we know it is currently under threat and, crucially, the banks must quickly redefine avenues of distribution. The former marketing philosophy of 'the right product must be available at the right time' has been replaced by 'any product must be available at any time, anywhere'.

The key factors in gaining competitive advantage are:

- Increasing revenue and value added by correctly combining customers, products and distribution
- Cost reduction to allow competitive pricing policies
- Quality and levels of service (that is, availability!) must satisfy customer demands

- Development of crucial processes and elimination of low value added activity.

The major challenge for banks in the new climate lies in the complexity and cost of shifting their long standing business culture and expertise to match potential new entrants to the market. Businesses are now (mostly) accustomed to interactive and on-line technology, such as ATMs. The expertise and technology is now available through convergence to combine telephones, television and PCs in the home and access services, and companies such as Microsoft will undoubtedly change the rules of the game for the customer.

1.5 Developing payment systems on the Internet

The essence of a payment system is that both payer and payee believe it to be efficient and secure. In the case of cross-border transactions there are also questions of liability which arise, especially through the Internet. To date, banks and other users have not agreed a liability framework for when things go wrong. One present difficulty for handling payments on the Internet is the need to make payment systems which will be cost-effective for both small and large payments.

Types of payment system

There are two main methods of making payments on the Internet: centrally accounted payments and electronic/cybercash payments. Centrally accounted payments are made from the normal bank current account or credit card account and payment is cleared through the clearing system. It is currently estimated that payment of electronic/cybercash systems will be between 1 and 5 cents per transaction compared with 30 cents to $1 for centrally accounted payments. Such a cost structure would indicate that these systems are likely to be used for different types and sizes of payments (see Figure 1.1).

The major card companies, such as Visa, MasterCard, Europey and their partners Microsoft, Netscope, SAIC, GTE, IBM and Verisign, are establishing new SET (secure electronic transaction) standards which will fundamentally affect how business is transacted on the Internet.

The seven standard specifications are:

1. To provide confidentiality of payment information and of the instructions transmitted with it
2. To provide authentication of the card holder

Figure 1.1: Payment categories

Payment system	Nano-payments 1¢–25¢	Micro-payments 25¢–$15	Mini-payments $15–$1,500	Macro-payments $1,500+
Cyber tokens/ coins	◄――――――――――►			
Stored-value cards	◄―――――――――――――――――►		
Credit cards		◄――――――――――――――――►	
Debit cards		◄―――――――――――――――――――――――►
Electronic cheques		◄――――――――――――――――――――――――――►

Source: J & W Associates.

3. To ensure integrity of all data transmitted
4. To provide authentication that a merchant can accept branded payment card transactions through its relationship with an acquiring financial institution
5. To ensure the use of the best security and system design practices to protect all parties to an electronic commercial transaction
6. To provide a protocol that neither depends on transport security mechanisms nor prevents their use
7. To encourage and assist interoperability across software and network providers.

Since the publication of the SET specifications in 1996, Diners Club, Amex and others have confirmed that they will support them. These moves should encourage consumers and businesses to use the system and to be confident in its integrity. First estimates indicate that SET will not be operational until 1998 as the participants pilot a number of trials worldwide. It is evident that once SET standards are fully operational the processing costs will be substantially reduced so injecting even more competition into the payment market.

Another important development is the growth of cyber wallets, issued firstly by Cyberbank and then followed by Microsystems, Javawallet and Verifore. These wallets are secure pieces of software stored on a customer's PC where details are recorded of the cards being used and the means to make SET-compliant payments on the Internet.

Electronic cash payments on the Internet

These are payments which transfer value for which no clearing or settlement is required and, as such, are cheaper to operate. There are two basic types of electronic cash payments on the Internet: electronic cash/software tokens and stored-value cards. Stored-value cards hold the value on the card and are used for coffee machines and parking meters. The card is placed in a reader attached to the PC and value is transferred from the card holder to the retailer's card and stored in the PC. Hewlett Packard and others are already producing PCs with integral smart card readers which will be available in 1998.

Mondex International, owned by MasterCard is the market leader in prepayment smart cards and believes that, in future, consumers will use the cards for everyday shopping[1] on the Internet. Digicash, a Dutch company and pioneer in the development of electronic software tokens, designed a system for low value payments, from 1 cent to $25, or the currency equivalent. The system works by the donor loading the software tokens from a bank or credit card account to a PC. These are then used to pay for goods and services by transaction. Digicash uniquely numbers each 'coin' to prevent fraud. The system has been piloted around the world, the latest trial being in Germany with 1000 customers of Deutsche Bank and 30 service providers.

The chief drawback to cyber wallets is that at present they can only be used exclusively on the Internet. However, a joint initiative of MasterCard and Visa has been established to adopt the key elements of SET standards (which only apply to magnetic strip cards) and merge them with point-of-sale smart card standards by end 1997. When these arrangements are in place it will extend consumer use of cards at retailers to electronic commerce in cyberspace.

Electronic cheque/ACH based payments

Notwithstanding their falling share of the payment system market, cheques still remain the most common form of local (as opposed to international) payment using automatic clearing house (ACH) or cheque clearings. This was confirmed recently by Rabobank, the Netherlands, when it established separate pages for each of its businesses on its web site and found that almost all enquiries and payments were local and not cross-border requests.

The Financial Services Technology Consortium (FSTC)[2] has developed a new electronic cheque which, in effect, gives the user an electronic chequebook on their PC. The system will be used by businesses and private customers utilizing the current interbank ACHs in the US. Basic standards for overall systems design for the electronic cheque have been agreed and it will use a signature card for both the payer's and payee's PC to ensure total security.

The important advantage of the electronic cheque for a merchant is the lower cost involved in each transaction. For the future, the banks as a whole must provide this basic service or other new competitors most certainly will. Of course, it will still be possible to send money transfer *instructions* on the Internet but such instructions do not constitute *making* a payment.

Future development

It is anticipated that all of the systems noted above will be operative in 1998, allowing business on the Internet to expand quickly. It is clear that the cyber wallet can hold cyber tokens, electronic cheques, debit and credit cards, and individuals and merchants will choose which medium of payment to use for various payments on the Internet. Equally, it is possible for most of the facilities in a cyber wallet to be put onto smart cards so enabling the user to make payments on the Internet at any time using a range of methods of payment.

1.6 Specialist corporate network services

The Intranet

The Intranet can be defined as a private network of trusted web services used by a single organisation for intraorganisational applications. In effect, the user can use a browser to access all the applications on a server so it is not necessary to install new software on any machines and it is not necessary to open different packages for different applications.

An Extranet extends the corporate information source beyond the company to known outside interested parties who are part of a closed user group.

At present most Intranet applications concentrate on publishing corporate information such as annual accounts and information, and banks are developing Internet applications targeted at corporate customers. London foreign exchange brokers Tullett & Tokyo have a subscription-based real-time rates and commentary service and Banque Paribas is providing research reports to its customers via the World Wide Web.

Bank of Boston is basing new corporate banking services on Internet/Intranet technology. The bank is co-operating with FICS Group, a Belgian financial group, to develop a system for corporate customers to replace its Boston Net Service. The first phase of the new service will provide information reporting transaction initiation, cheque facilities and some trade finance services.

Security issues

A major concern of Internet/Intranet/Extranet services is the integrity of the system and Bank of Boston will deliver its services over fixed lines on a private network using familiar passwords, IDs and strong encryption. Interestingly, the Royal Bank of Scotland is using levels of security similar to those that apply to corporate-to-bank electronic services for their Internet banking services used by customers who wish to access their bank accounts from their home PC.

There are two main concerns which arise when connecting to the Internet. First, who can gain access to a corporate LAN or system, and, second, is the transaction which is sent over the net secure? The first problem can be overcome by the use of 'firewall' software. The second problem, the security of the transaction, is less easy to remedy. Key questions arise in regard to authenticity (who is engaged in the transaction?), integrity (that the message received is the message sent), confidentiality (that no one else can read the message), and non-repudiation of origin and receipt (that neither sender nor recipient can deny the validity of the message).

These difficulties are largely being addressed by strong encryption technology to which the banks have had long standing, and privileged, access.

Effective policing

In addition to securing a transaction it is critical that organisations develop good operational policies which can be translated into action. A study was carried out by Compliance Methodology Consultants in co-operation with the Netherlands Ministry of Justice and the Erasmus University in Rotterdam to determine to what extent people will take account of policies once they are in place. They found that a key factor was knowledge and understanding of the regulations, how often checks were carried out to see that there had been compliance with rules and policies, the loyalty of target groups, and the sanctions and rewards involved. At present, UK regulators are less than welcoming towards the coming technical revolution and provision of financial services on the Internet. In fairness there is already a very broad spectrum of services appearing on the Internet which are subject to varying forms and degrees of regulation and law.

In 1995 the UK Securities and Investments Board (SIB) launched an enquiry into the problems of keeping track of a virtually limitless number of Net home pages, and expressed concern about the potential for fraudulent schemes to be advertised on the Internet and escape detection. In the field of financial services there is a genuine problem because if an advert can be accessed by someone in the UK, it is considered to have been issued in the UK. Under the Financial Services Act (FSA) the issuer must be authorised or, alternatively, the advertisement must be approved by the regulators. However, the SIB finds it imposs-ible to monitor advertisements that come from, say, the USA, or to force the withdrawal of adverts which do not comply with UK law. The ques-tion therefore arises as to whose role is it to regulate such activities.

Although the European Commission announced in 1996 that it would not (then) regulate any areas of 'virtual banking' services, the Commission's working groups of bankers, consumers and retailers of small and medium-sized businesses are formulating their own 'basic prin-ciples' towards solving the problem. The chief difficulty for all concerned, bankers, regulators, retailers and consumers, is the fast changing nature of the types of activities: it is analogous to trying to hit a moving target. As a result most bankers feel it is too early to regulate when it is unclear how best to develop appropriate controls. There are concerns, however, about money laundering (in 1996 there were five virtual banks operating cur-rency services without supervision) and also the need to adopt consumer protection and develop legal aspects of electronic purses and chip cards.

At the macro level, perhaps more alarmingly for the UK, the intro-duction of EMU could bring pressure on sterling through the adoption of electronic cash. The fear is that domestic money could be used only for taxation, as euro cash cards could replace domestic currencies, espe-cially on the Net.

Three possible regulatory routes

As we have seen, the Internet is already making rapid inroads into tra-ditional ways of doing things and many financial web sites are already in breach of the law in dozens of countries where they can be accessed. Clearly, a wide-ranging debate will be required to reach an acceptable solution.

There appear to be three possible approaches. One is to require an investment firm to be authorised in every country where investors can access its web site. However, it is not feasible to insist that a company is authorised in over 100 countries. This would cause chaos and bring the law into disrepute.

A second method, recently proposed by the US Securities and Exchange Commission (SEC) is that companies should be regulated at the point of entry into the USA. The 'point of entry' could be Internet service providers who transmit foreign web sites into the USA or it could be achieved through stockbrokers who act as local agents for foreign firms. Whether or not such entry points would be willing to take on such a responsibility, and have the resources to manage the process, is debatable.

The third possibility would be to presume that a potential 'foreign' investor 'travels' to the investment company's country (in this case the USA), when the deal is made. This would reverse the usual presumption that it is the investment firm which travels into another country when contacting the foreign investor. In this case the investment company need only be authorised in its own country.

The Internet web site of the investment company would, however, have to make it clear which country it was operating from. This latter approach would have the virtue of being simpler and at the same time recognize that investment markets are global and that a nationally based approach to regulation is no longer appropriate. It would also highlight the need for care by the private investor when contemplating overseas investment. There is, of course, a risk with international investment regulation, as with attempts at international banking regulation, that the system allows the lowest common denominator to operate. For example, in the past, small 'foreign' banks with little known 'pedigree' have opened branches in London and assumed the mantle of respectability by being seen to have a London base.

1.7   Will the banks survive?

The *Financial Times* (25 July 1997) noted the emergence of the first competitive attack on the commercial banks from outside the sector when Morgan Stanley, Dean Witter, Discover, announced that the group was to start a direct banking business over the Internet using the Discover credit card brand name. There is no doubt that this is the forerunner to many similar developments. Prior to this Discover announcement, innovations in electronic banking have only been launched by leading commercial banks such as Barclays, Citibank, Royal Bank of Scotland and Wells Fargo.

The pressure on the banks to innovate is, therefore, already with us and only the best will survive the technological revolution. Certainly the writer believes that only the 'world class' banks will survive and prosper for a number of significant reasons. First, notwithstanding the acceptance of cyber technology by an ever-increasing segment of consumers (the young especially), there remains an innate distrust of many of the players in the financial markets, in the UK at least, stemming from financial scandals such as BCCI and the over-enthusiastic selling of personal pensions by almost every large UK assurance company. Against this background, the banks universally have a reputation for integrity and are seen as the most trusted financial service provider.

Moreover, in real terms, at present the number of people prepared to use electronic media for their finance is small. The banks, albeit slowly, are beginning to capitalise on these advantages using their branches to give guidance and advice in trustworthy surroundings. By the time the bank customers feel comfortable with electronic gadgetry, the banks should have their own user-friendly systems in place. In the USA, the number of bank branches rose by 27 per cent between 1985 and 1994, indicating that personal relationships are still important.

Regulation, relationships and human capital

The above commentary points to the importance of the banks' ability to put together creative solutions for both their private customer as well as the large corporations. It was noted in the first part of this study that one of the unique features of banks is their guarantee function, that is to pay on demand and provide funding at short notice. Although this is an important asset for corporations, the real strength of the bank is its ability to put together innovative customised solutions to strategic problems. Such solutions are based on an intimate knowledge of the client and long-standing trust on both sides. It is, therefore, innovation, expertise and relationships which differentiate banks from their competitors.

Bank failures are usually political (as well as economic and social) dynamite and the importance of reputation is crucial. This was demonstrated in 1991 when Salomon Bros, the US investment bank, experienced a massive loss of credibility when its involvement in the Treasury auction came to light. It liquidated a third of its assets and suffered a loss of market capitalisation of $1.5 billion as customers deserted the bank. It also lost key staff, paid fines and saw a dramatic drop even in unrelated business.

The future of regulation

With the advent of real-time collateralised settlement systems, institutions can no longer put the system at risk. Thus the need to restrict access to the lender of last resort function only to those institutions which are supervised, diminishes. Even so, it seems likely that the very large banks will continue to be regulated because of the political implications of a major institution failing. Possibly the way forward will be to encourage self-regulation of banks by putting directors on notice that they will bear criminal responsibility for negligence or fraud. The Financial Services Act already does this in the UK. It has been suggested that regulators may use the market to monitor banks by requiring large banks regularly to issue derivatives and use the price of the derivative as a measure of the banks' standing in the market. The principal of such 'peer judgement' was propounded in the 1970s when George Votja of Citibank, when asked what is 'adequate' capital, said (in essence) 'Your capital needs to be at the level your competitors think it should be.' Unfortunately in the past every bank failure has been seen as a failure of regulation instead of as a cost of doing business, precipitating even more draconian regulation!

Perhaps the most fundamental issue of all is, does technology change the basic functions of banks? Traditionally, the key functions are maturity transformation, risk assessment and assumption. For the present it would seem not, in which case the problems for regulators remain the same, but much more complex!

Notes

1. A pilot study is being carried out in Swindon, UK, by Mondex.
2. Comprising major US banks including Bank of America, Citibank, Chase Manhattan and many industrial participants such as Amex, Equifax, and IBM.

References

Banker, The (1997), 'Caught in the net', *The Banker*, July

Bank Systems & Technology (1997), 'Visa, CommerceNet send secure data in Net tests', *Bank Systems & Technology*, **34** (4), April, p. 17

Bannister, D. (1996), 'A point of protocol: an introduction to financial information protocol', *Banking Technology*, November

Coopers & Lybrand Banker's Digest International (1996), 'New forms of distribution in the banking sector', March, pp. 12–14

Crédit Lyonnais/Laing (1966), 'Banking 2000 – Technology: changes in payment systems and productivity gains', *Crédit Lyonnais Laing*, March

Crédit Lyonnais Laing (1995), 'Technology development – crucial competitive edge', *Crédit Lyonnais Laing*, October

Deloitte Touche Consulting Group (1995), *Future of Retail Banking: a Global Perspective*

Financial Times (1997), 'Banks may face Internet challenge from outsider', *Financial Times*, 18 July

Gandy, A. (1997), 'Community link-up', *The Banker*, February, pp. 74–5

Groenfeldt, T. (1997), 'First Union testing electronic "wallet"', *Bank Systems & Technology*, **34** (4), p. 19

Internet Research (1996), 'Banking on the Internet', *Internet Research*, **6** (1), p. 31

Jay, M. (1996), 'Bank group warns of consumer crisis and money laundering', *Management Accounting*, **74** (8), p. 12

Jay, M. (1996), 'Implications of virtual banking', *Management Accounting*, July/August, p. 58

Kelly, S. (1996), 'Bank gain net interest: online banking', *Computer Weekly*, October, p. 46

Large, J. (1997), 'Direct purchasing on the Internet', *Corporate Finance*, March, pp. 39–41

Marketing (1997), 'RBS to pioneer online banking', *Marketing*, 30 January, p. 37

Muth, R.E. (1997), 'Becoming Internet access provider expands horizons for Apollo Trust', *Journal of Retail Banking Services*, Spring, pp. 11–16

Penrose, P. (1996), '9 day wonder: Internet in the UK', *Banking Technology*, **13** (2), p. 22

Queree, A. (1997) 'Private and public nets intermesh', *Corporate Finance*, March, pp. 36–7

Rajan, R. (1997), *The Bank is Dead, Long Live the Bank*, Financial Times Mastering Finance Series

Redman, R. (1997), 'Notoriety about Internet access presents image test for PC banking', *Bank Systems & Technology*, **34** (4), April, p. 8

Rose, H. (1997), *Key Role of Financial Middle Men*, Financial Times Mastering Finance Series

Seegers, F. (1996), 'Online banking: the future according to Citibank', *Bank Management*, July/August, pp. 42–4

Spicer, C. (1997), 'Advancing technology means new rules in playing the customer-service game', *Bank Systems & Technology*, **34** (4), April, p. 55

Talmor, S. (1997), 'Landscaper for commerce', *The Banker*, January, p. 69

Talmor, S. (1996), 'Tech notes', *The Banker*, April, pp. 94–5

Talmor, S. (1996), 'Tech notes', *The Banker*, July, pp. 100–1

Talmor, S. (1996), 'Tech notes', *The Banker*, October, pp. 110–11

Webb, A. (1997), 'Towards the plug "n" play bank', *Euromoney*, July, p. 122

2
Technical Change in European Banking

Yener Altunbaş and Philip Molyneux

Abstract

This chapter examines technical change in European banking by applying the Fourier Flexible functional form and stochastic cost frontier methodologies using 13 603 bank observations across 15 EU countries between 1988 and 1995. The results show that technical progress has had a similar influence across European banking markets, making a positive contribution to costs of around 3 per cent every year. Large banks appear to benefit more from technical change than their smaller competitors. We also break down technical progress into its three main components: pure, scale and (input) non-neutral effects. This shows that pure technical change is the main contributor to overall technical progress for small banks (assets size less than $1 billion) and larger banks appear to gain more from technical advances which alter the optimal input mix. Technical change also becomes increasingly scale biased as banks become larger. This implies that technological change increases the minimum efficient bank size for larger banks to a greater extent than for their smaller competitors. Given that technical change is non-neutral with respect to optimal bank size and input-mix, we tentatively suggest that the formation of larger banks may be in the public interest.

2.1 Introduction

Technological progress has been widely cited as one of the major strategic drivers in the EU banking industry (see Arthur Andersen 1993 and Cecchini 1988) yet only a handful of European studies has attempted to quantify its effect on the costs of providing financial services as well its impact on efficient bank size. Maudos *et al.* (1996)

provide a detailed analysis of the impact of technical progress in the Spanish savings bank sector between 1985 and 1994 and conclude that it reduced average costs by 0.64 per cent and operating costs by 1.93 per cent per annum (total costs were reduced by 0.68 per cent per annum). They also find that larger savings banks have benefited more from technical progress compared to their smaller counterparts. Lang and Welzel (1996) studied the influence of technical change in the German co-operative banking sector between 1987 and 1992 and found that it reduced total costs by 2.5 per cent per annum, with smaller banks experiencing larger cost reductions.

The positive impact of technical progress on bank costs found in the aforementioned European studies is also confirmed in the US literature. For example, Hunter and Timme (1991), using a sample of large US commercial banks for the period 1980–86, also concluded that techno-logical change lowered the real cost of bank production by about 1.0 per cent per year over the sample period. Larger banks also realized a greater percentage reduction in costs than smaller banks. They also found that technological change affected the cost-minimising product mix for all but the smallest banks in their sample. Humphrey (1993) also identifies the positive influence on bank costs resulting from tech-nical change in US banking following bank deregulation. (McKillop *et al.* (1996) also find that large Japanese banks have benefited from cost reductions through technical progress.)

The aim of this chapter is to extend the established literature by exam-ining the impact of technical change in 15 European banking systems between 1988 and 1995. Using the Fourier Flexible functional form and stochastic cost frontier methodologies we evaluate the impact of techni-cal change for different bank types (private, savings and co-operative banks) and bank sizes in each of the 15 different countries. Technical progress is also decomposed into three types: pure technical change; non-neutral technical progress (a measure of technological change associated with the change in the use of inputs because of variation in input prices); and scale-augmenting technical progress (a measure of technical change which identifies whether the cost-minimising firm size has altered).

2.2   Methodology

An improvement in technology, holding the inputs employed con-stant, results in more output. As such, technical progress can be defined as the shift in the average cost curve along a given ray induced by technical change. Thus, if technical progress is less than zero, holding constant the composition of production, technical progress results in an increase in the optimal production level.

The rate of technical progress may be inferred from changes in a firm's cost or production function over time. For instance, let the firm possess a cost function:

$$TC = f(Q_i, P_i, T_i) \tag{1}$$

where TC is total cost, Q_i is a vector of outputs, P_i is an input price vector and T_i is a parameter describing features of the firm's technology. A time trend variable, T, serves as a proxy for disembodied technical change. The time-trend is a 'catchall' variable that captures the effects of technological factors, such as learning by doing and organisational changes allowing for the more efficient use of existing inputs, together with the effects of other factors, such as changing regulations and shifts in peak and off-peak demands. The latter effects do constitute technical progress, but the time trend is unable to disentangle these effects (Koop and Smith, 1982). However, caution should be exercised when interpreting the coefficient of this variable as the rate of disembodied technical progress (see Hunter and Timme 1991 and Nelson 1984).

Technological progress can be measured on the cost side of the production process. For a firm at internal equilibrium, given input prices and other state of nature constraints, technological progress would allow the firm to produce the same level of output at a lower level of expenditure. In other words, technical progress permits the firm to produce a given output, Q, at lower levels of total cost over time, holding input prices constant. The rate of technical progress, T_c, can be expressed as:

$$T_c = \frac{\partial lnTC}{\partial T} \tag{2}$$

If T_c is less than zero, then the same output vector Q can be produced at lower cost as a result of technological progress.

The estimation of T_c requires the specification of specific total cost equation. For our purposes we estimate a stochastic cost frontier using the Fourier Flexible (FF) functional form shown as:

$$lnTC = \alpha_0 + \sum_{i=1}^{3} \alpha_i lnQ_i + \sum_{i=1}^{3} \beta_i lnP_i + t_1 T +$$

$$\frac{1}{2}\left[\sum_{i=1}^{3}\sum_{j=1}^{3} \delta_{ij} lnQ_i lnQ_j + \sum_{i=1}^{3}\sum_{j=1}^{3} \gamma_{ij} lnP_i lnP_j + t_{11}T^2\right] +$$

$$\sum_{i=1}^{3}\sum_{j=1}^{3} \rho_{ij} lnP_i lnQ_j + \sum_{i=1}^{3} \psi_{it} lnP_i T + \sum_{i=1}^{3} \theta_{it} lnQ_j T +$$

$$\sum_{i=1}^{3} [a_i \cos(z_i) + b_i \sin(z_i)] + \sum_{i=1}^{3}\sum_{j=1}^{3} [a_{ij} \cos(z_i + z_j) + b_{ij} \sin(z_i + z_j)] +$$

$$\sum_{i=1}^{3}\sum_{j=1}^{3}\sum_{k \geq j, k \neq i} [a_{ijk} \cos(z_i + z_j + z_k) + b_{ijk} \sin(z_i + z_j + z_k)] + \varepsilon \qquad (3)$$

where
$lnTC$ = the natural logarithm of total costs (operating and financial cost);
lnQ_i = the natural logarithm of bank outputs (with one added to avoid problems with taking the log of zero);
lnP_i = the natural logarithm of ith input prices (that is wage rate, interest rate and physical capital price);
T = time trend;
Z_i = the adjusted values of the log output lnQ_i such that they span the interval $[0, 2\pi]$;
α, β, δ, γ, θ, Ψ, ρ, a, t and b are coefficients to be estimated.

The definition of outputs used follows along the lines of the traditional intermediation approach as suggested by Sealey and Lindley (1977), where the inputs, labour, physical capital and deposits are used to produce earning assets. Two of our outputs, total loans and total securities, are earning assets and we also include total off-balance sheet items (measured in nominal terms) as a third output. Although the latter are technically not earning assets, this type of business constitutes an increasing source of income for all types of banks (including co-operative banks where it is mainly in the form of guarantees and letters of credit) and, therefore, should be included when modelling banks' cost characteristics otherwise total output would tend to be understated (Jagtiani and Khanthavit 1996). (See Appendix 2.A1 for descriptive statistics on input and output data.)

Following Berger *et al.* (1994), this note applies Fourier terms only for the outputs, leaving the input price effects to be defined entirely by the translog terms. The primary aim is to maintain the limited number of Fourier terms for describing the scale and inefficiency measures associated with differences in bank size. Moreover, the usual input price homogeneity restrictions can be imposed on logarithmic price terms, whereas they cannot be easily imposed on the trigonometric terms.[1]

In addition, the scaled log-output quantities, z_i, are calculated as $z_i = \mu_i (lnQ_i + w_Q)$; lnQ_i are unscaled log-output quantities; μ_i and w_Q are scaled factors. It should be noted that it is important to scale the data to limit the periodic sine and cosine trigonometric functions within one period of length 2π before applying the FF methodology (see Gallant, 1981). The μ_i's are chosen to make the largest observations for each scaled log-output variable close to 2π; w_Q's are restricted to assume the smallest values close to zero. In this study, we restricted the z_i to span between 0.001 and 6 to reduce approximation problems near the endpoints as discussed by Gallant (1981) and applied by Mitchell and Onvural (1996).[2]

Since the duality theorem requires that the cost function must be linearly homogeneous in input prices, the following restrictions have to be imposed on the parameters of the cost function in equation (4):

$$\sum_{i=1}^{3} \beta_i = 1 \sum_{i=1}^{3} \gamma_{ij} = 0 \quad \text{for all } j; \tag{4}$$

$$\sum_{i=1}^{3} \rho_{ij} = 0 \quad \text{for all } j;$$

Furthermore, the second order parameters of the cost function in equation (4) must be symmetric so:

$$\delta_{ij} = \delta_{ji} \quad \text{for all } j; \tag{5}$$

$$\gamma_{ij} = \gamma_{ji} \quad \text{for all } j;$$

The cost frontiers are estimated using the random effects panel data approach (as in Lang and Welzel 1996).[3]

Following Lang and Welzel (1996) and McKillop *et al.* (1996), the rate of technical progress may be inferred from changes in a firm's cost function over time. A time trend variable, T, serves as a proxy for dis-embodied technical change. The time trend is a 'catch-all' variable that captures the effects of technological factors: that is learning by doing and organisational changes allowing for the more efficient use of exist-ing inputs, together with the effects of other factors, such as changing environmental regulations (see Baltagi and Griffin 1988; Nelson 1984).

Technical progress allows the firm to produce a given output, Q, at lower levels of total cost over time, holding input prices and regulatory effects constant. In order to estimate the impact of technical change we calculate the variation in the average cost due to a given change in technology. This can be measured by the partial derivative of the estimated cost function with respect to the time trend (T) and can be shown as follows:

$$T_c = \frac{\partial \ln TC}{\partial T} = t_1 + t_{11}T + \sum_{i=1}^{3} \psi_i \ln P_i + \sum_{i=1}^{3} \theta_i \ln Q_i \tag{6}$$

Given equation (6), the estimated rate of technical progress can be broken down into three components:
(1) pure technical progress shown as:

$$t_1 + t_{11}T \tag{7}$$

(2) non-neutral technical progress (a measure of technological progress associated with the change in the use of inputs because of altered input prices):

$$\sum_{i=1}^{3} \psi_i \ln P_i \tag{8}$$

and (3) scale-augmenting technical progress (a measure of technical change which identifies whether the cost-minimising firm size has altered):

$$\sum_{i=1}^{3} \theta_i \ln Q_i \tag{9}$$

While the focus of this study is on technical progress, scale efficiency and X-inefficiency measures are also estimated (and reported in the Appendix) using the stochastic cost frontier approach. This approach labels a bank as inefficient if its costs are higher than those predicted for an efficient bank producing the same input/output combination and the difference cannot be explained by statistical noise. The cost frontier is obtained by estimating a cost function with a composite error term, the sum of a two-sided error representing random fluctuations in cost and a one-sided positive error term representing inefficiency.

Ferrier and Lovell (1990) have shown that inefficiency measures for individual firms can be estimated using the stochastic frontier approach as introduced by Aigner *et al.* (1977), Battese and Corra (1977), and Meeusen and van den Broeck (1977). Following Aigner *et al.* (1977), we assume that the error of the cost function is:

$$\varepsilon = u + v \tag{10}$$

where u and v are independently distributed. u is usually assumed to be distributed as half-normal, that is a one-sided positive disturbance capturing the effects of inefficiency, and v is assumed to be distributed as two-sided normal with zero mean and variance σ^2, capturing the effects of the statistical noise.

Observation-specific estimates of the inefficiencies, u, can be calculated by using the distribution of the inefficiency term conditional on the estimate of the composed error term, as proposed by Jondrow *et al.* (1982). The mean of this conditional distribution for the half-normal model is shown as:

$$E(u_i \mid \varepsilon_i) = \frac{\sigma\lambda}{1+\lambda^2}\left[\frac{f(\varepsilon_i\lambda/\sigma)}{1-F(\varepsilon_i\lambda/\sigma)} + \left(\frac{\varepsilon_i\lambda}{\sigma}\right)\right] \tag{11}$$

where $F(.)$ and $f(.)$ are the standard normal distribution and the standard normal density function, respectively. $E(u\varepsilon)$ is an unbiased but inconsistent estimator of u_i, since regardless of N, the variance of the estimator remains non-zero (see Greene, 1993, pp. 80–2). Jondrow *et al.* (1982) have shown that the ratio of the variability (standard deviation, σ) for u and v can be used to measure a bank's relative inefficiency, where $\lambda = \sigma_u/\sigma_v$, is a measure of the amount of variation stemming from inefficiency relative to noise for the sample. Estimates of this model can be computed by maximising the likelihood function directly (see Olson *et al.* 1980). Previous studies modelling international bank inefficiencies, such as Allen and Rai (1996), and those which examine USA banks, such as Kaparakis *et al.* (1994), and Mester (1996), all use the half-normal specification to test for inefficiency differences between banking institutions.[4]

Within sample, scale economies are calculated as in Mester (1996) and are evaluated at the mean output and input price levels for the respective size quartiles. A measure of economies of scale (*SE*) is given by the following cost elasticity by differentiating the cost function in equation (3) with respect to output. This gives us:

$$SE = \sum_{i=1}^{3} \frac{\partial \ln TC}{\partial \ln Q_i} = \sum_{i=1}^{3} \alpha_i + \sum_{i=1}^{3}\sum_{j=1}^{3} \delta_{ij} \ln Q_j + \sum_{i=1}^{3}\sum_{j=1}^{3} \rho_{ij} \ln P_i + \sum_{i=1}^{3} \Theta_{ir} T \qquad (12)$$

If $SE < 1$ then increasing returns to scale, implying economies of scale;
If $SE = 1$ then constant returns to scale;
If $SE > 1$ then decreasing returns to scale, implying diseconomies of scale.

2.3   Data and results

This study uses banks' balance sheet and income statement data for a sample of European banks between 1988 and 1995, obtained from the London-based International Bank Credit Analysis Ltd's 'Bank Scope' database. Table 2.1 reports the definition, mean and standard deviation of the input and output variables used in the cost frontier estimations and the descriptive statistics, along with the parameter estimates shown in the appendix.[5]

Table 2.1: Descriptive statistics of the outputs, inputs and time variable used in the model

Variables	Description	Mean	Standard deviation
TC	total cost (US$ m)	677	2 489
P_1	price of labour (US$ m) (total personnel expenses/total asset)	0.0145	0.0121
P_2	price of funds (%) (total interest expenses/total funds)	0.0665	0.0408
P_3	price of physical capital (%) (total depreciation and other capital expenses/total fixed assets)	0.2252	0.1661
Q_1	The dollar value of total aggregate loans (US$ m)	4 036	14 691
Q_2	The dollar value of total aggregate securities (US$ m)	2 997	11 630
Q_3	The dollar value of the off-balance sheet activities (nominal values) (US$ m)	1 312	7 914
T	Time Trend between 1988 to 1995		

Table 2.2 reports diagnostic statistics confirming that the FF form is the appropriate functional firm (with the translog specification being rejected under the null hypothesis). The Chi-squared tests also reveal that it has a statistically significant influence on changing the optimal input mix and minimum efficient bank size.

Table 2.2: Hypotheses test result[6]

Restriction	Degrees of freedom	Loglikelihood function	Chi-square value	Critical value (5%)	Decision
FF Form	None	647.70			
Translog	32	592.40	110.60	43.77	Reject H_0
Neutral	3	615.46	64.47	7.82	Reject H_0
No-technical progress	8	579.84	135.73	15.51	Reject H_0

Table 2.3 shows that for the whole sample overall technical progress has reduced total costs by 3.2 per cent every year between 1988 and 1995. Pure technical change accounted for 0.95 per cent of the cost fall while non-neutral technical change (brought about by technical advances which resulted in changes in input usage) helped reduce costs by 1.29 per cent. In addition, Table 2.3 also shows that technical progress has increased the efficient bank size as the scale-augmenting

Table 2.3: Decomposition of technical progress between 1988–95 (annual average)

EU countries	Pure effect	Non-neutral	Scale augmenting	Overall
Austria	−0.0097	−0.0127	−0.0045	−0.0269
Belgium	−0.0096	−0.0174	−0.0082	−0.0353
Denmark	−0.0095	−0.0087	−0.0085	−0.0267
Finland	−0.0103	−0.0203	−0.0129	−0.0435
France	−0.0098	−0.0139	−0.0114	−0.0351
Germany	−0.0090	−0.0107	−0.0100	−0.0297
Greece	−0.0096	−0.0150	−0.0088	−0.0333
Ireland	−0.0079	−0.0126	−0.0096	−0.0302
Italy	−0.0101	−0.0112	−0.0106	−0.0319
Luxembourg	−0.0097	−0.0224	−0.0053	−0.0373
Netherlands	−0.0085	−0.0175	−0.0106	−0.0366
Portugal	−0.0095	−0.0165	−0.0085	−0.0346
Spain	−0.0105	−0.0116	−0.0091	−0.0311
Sweden	−0.0097	−0.0252	−0.0139	−0.0489
UK	−0.0093	−0.0147	−0.0093	−0.0333
All	−0.0095	−0.0129	−0.0097	−0.0321

measure is negative (– 0.97 per cent) for the whole sample and in each country.

Panel A in Table 2.4 shows that the impact of technical progress on bank costs has generally declined over the period under study in virtually every European banking system. The banking systems of Finland and Sweden appear to have benefited most from technical advances, with the Austrian, Danish and German banks obtaining the smallest cost savings from technical progress. Having said this, however, in most cases the impact of technical change does appear to be rather similar across different banking systems.

Panel B in Table 2.4 shows that over the sample period the impact of technical progress on banks' costs declined, although it is also noticeable that larger banks experienced more technological change than smaller banks. The scale economy and X-inefficiency results shown in Appendix Tables 2.A5 and 2.A6 show that scale economies are widespread across all European banking systems and different sizes of banks, typically around 5 per cent; X-inefficiencies average around 25 per cent. This suggests that scale-augmented technical change may be important for all sizes of banks. This, in fact, is not confirmed in Table 2.5 which shows the decomposition of technical progress according to bank size.

Table 2.5 shows that pure technical change is the main contributor to overall technical progress for small banks with assets size under $1 billion, although larger banks appear to gain more from technical advances which alter the input mix. It is also interesting to note that technical change becomes increasingly scale biased as banks get bigger. This implies that technological change affects efficient bank size to a greater extent for larger banks.

2.4 Conclusions

Between 1988 and 1995 technological change made a positive contribution to reducing European banks' costs, on average, somewhere in the region of 3 per cent every year. The impact of technical change also appears to be similar across different banking systems. However, our results suggest that the impact of technical progress on bank costs has generally declined over the period.

Larger banks systematically derive greater cost savings from technological advances. The decomposition of technical change also shows that pure technical change is the main contributor to overall technical progress for small banks (assets size under $1 billion) and larger banks

Table 2.4: Overall technical progress for European banks 1988–95

PANEL A EU Countries	1988	1989	1990	1991	1992	1993	1994	1995	1988–95
Austria	-0.0339	-0.0341	-0.0324	-0.0307	-0.0278	-0.0248	-0.0236	-0.0231	-0.0269
Belgium	-0.0405	-0.0415	-0.0419	-0.0397	-0.0381	-0.0334	-0.0312	-0.0317	-0.0353
Denmark	-0.0349	-0.0335	-0.0343	-0.0333	-0.0297	-0.0264	-0.0215	-0.0214	-0.0267
Finland	-0.0506	-0.0506	-0.0505	-0.0474	-0.0463	-0.0411	-0.0341	-0.0352	-0.0435
France	-0.0384	-0.0388	-0.0396	-0.0385	-0.0362	-0.0341	-0.0318	-0.0321	-0.0351
Germany	-0.0384	-0.0384	-0.0385	-0.0376	-0.0326	-0.0282	-0.0275	-0.0272	-0.0297
Greece	-0.0419	-0.0417	-0.0410	-0.0343	-0.0332	-0.0315	-0.0319	-0.0292	-0.0333
Ireland	–	–	–	–	-0.0359	-0.0321	-0.0286	-0.0295	-0.0302
Italy	-0.0372	-0.0353	-0.0356	-0.0360	-0.0340	-0.0291	-0.0282	-0.0285	-0.0319
Luxembourg	-0.0480	-0.0485	-0.0471	-0.0441	-0.0394	-0.0331	-0.0312	-0.0329	-0.0373
Netherlands	–	–	-0.0769	-0.0783	-0.0397	-0.0360	-0.0348	-0.0350	-0.0366
Portugal	-0.0393	-0.0373	-0.0386	-0.0376	-0.0353	-0.0343	-0.0328	-0.0315	-0.0346
Spain	-0.0335	-0.0340	-0.0339	-0.0331	-0.0319	-0.0302	-0.0272	-0.0273	-0.0311
Sweden	-0.0521	-0.0485	-0.0543	-0.0528	-0.0521	-0.0490	-0.0454	-0.0412	-0.0489
UK	-0.0434	-0.0436	-0.0433	-0.0412	-0.0356	-0.0310	-0.0290	-0.0297	-0.0333
All	-0.0382	-0.0381	-0.0387	-0.0377	-0.0346	-0.0302	-0.0286	-0.0287	-0.0321

Table 2.4: Overall technical progress for European banks 1988–95 (*continued*)

PANEL B EU Countries	Asset Sizes (US$ m)							
	1–499	500–999	1000–2999	3000–4999	5000–9999	10 000–49 999	50 000+	All
Austria	-0.0214	-0.0273	-0.0299	-0.0315	-0.0304	-0.0347	-0.0261	-0.0269
Belgium	-0.0275	-0.0371	-0.0404	-0.0398	-0.0426	-0.0404	-0.0406	-0.0353
Denmark	-0.0227	-0.0263	-0.0292	-0.0369	-0.0339	-0.0392	-0.0491	-0.0267
Finland	-0.0308	-0.0365	-0.0455	-0.0453	-0.0535	-0.0459	-0.0371	-0.0435
France	-0.0284	-0.0331	-0.0356	-0.0371	-0.0411	-0.0440	-0.0463	-0.0351
Germany	-0.0246	-0.0279	-0.0306	-0.0346	-0.0401	-0.0488	-0.0495	-0.0297
Greece	-0.0291	-0.0362	-0.0331	-0.0356	-0.0391	-0.0378	–	-0.0333
Ireland	-0.0280	-0.0285	-0.0293	-0.0339	-0.0298	-0.0324	–	-0.0302
Italy	-0.0246	-0.0288	-0.0317	-0.0364	-0.0421	-0.0407	-0.0406	-0.0319
Luxembourg	-0.0263	-0.0351	-0.0417	-0.0439	-0.0479	-0.0465	–	-0.0373
Netherlands	-0.0247	-0.0333	-0.0370	-0.0419	-0.0472	-0.0516	-0.0445	-0.0366
Portugal	-0.0352	-0.0354	-0.0341	-0.0327	-0.0323	-0.0378	–	-0.0346
Spain	-0.0257	-0.0299	-0.0310	-0.0324	-0.0336	-0.0408	-0.0383	-0.0311
Sweden	-0.0326	-0.0436	-0.0527	-0.0563	-0.0374	-0.0573	-0.0496	-0.0489
UK	-0.0265	-0.0334	-0.0344	-0.0356	-0.0352	-0.0402	-0.0434	-0.0333
All	-0.0255	-0.0301	-0.0331	-0.0362	-0.0396	-0.0443	-0.0448	-0.0321

Table 2.5: Decomposition of technical change according to bank size

Assets size ($m)	Pure effect	Non-neutral	Scale augmenting	Overall
0–99	–0.0157	–0.0007	–0.0006	–0.0156
100–199	–0.0158	–0.0012	–0.0015	–0.0185
200–299	–0.0156	–0.0015	–0.0017	–0.0189
300–399	–0.0157	–0.0020	–0.0019	–0.0195
400–599	–0.0158	–0.0026	–0.0027	–0.0211
600–799	–0.0159	–0.0035	–0.0031	–0.0224
800–1000	–0.0158	–0.0037	–0.0034	–0.0229
1000–1999	–0.0003	–0.0217	–0.0092	–0.0312
2000–2999	–0.0003	–0.0213	–0.0100	–0.0316
3000–4999	–0.0004	–0.0217	–0.0105	–0.0326
5000–9999	–0.0004	–0.0226	–0.0116	–0.0347
10 000–24 999	–0.0006	–0.0248	–0.0127	–0.0380
25 000–49 999	–0.0006	–0.0242	–0.0146	–0.0394
50 000+	–0.0006	–0.0219	–0.0168	–0.0393

appear to gain more from technical advances which alter the optimal input mix. It is also interesting to note that technical change becomes increasingly scale biased as banks get bigger. This implies that technological change increases the minimum efficient bank size for larger banks to a greater extent than for their smaller competitors. Given that technical change is non-neutral with respect to optimal bank size and input mix, we tentatively suggest that the formation of larger banks may be in the public interest.

APPENDIX

Table 2.A1: Number of banks and mean asset sizes according to years

EU countries	1988	1989	1990	1991	1992	1993	1994	1995	All
Austria	19	22	24	27	40	47	65	64	308
Belgium	25	29	29	32	51	82	83	79	410
Denmark	19	29	31	35	62	87	99	92	454
Finland	7	8	9	11	11	15	14	9	84
France	137	161	174	193	383	453	431	349	2 281
Germany	144	164	180	232	565	1 442	1 384	1 035	5 146
Greece	5	5	6	9	15	21	23	16	100
Ireland	–	–	–	–	3	10	15	19	47
Italy	124	132	141	148	174	294	296	196	1 505
Luxembourg	31	37	68	75	96	171	145	119	742
Netherlands	–	–	1	1	43	57	56	54	212
Portugal	8	8	14	16	35	37	35	38	191
Spain	105	104	123	134	137	141	157	141	1 042
Sweden	4	5	10	16	21	21	23	16	116
UK	35	40	47	53	176	214	215	185	965
All	663	744	857	982	1 812	3 092	3 041	2 412	13 603

EU countries	1988	1989	1990	1991	1992	1993	1994	1995	All
Austria	2 645	2 701	2 835	2 686	2 040	2 821	4 511	6 629	3 837
Belgium	7 879	7 842	9 404	8 147	10 136	6 361	8 189	9 960	8 446
Denmark	6 402	5 938	6 768	7 136	3 656	4 259	4 442	5 210	4 999
Finland	11 597	12 330	13 003	13 357	10 419	7 306	11 335	20 162	12 002
France	12 262	13 969	16 587	16 750	9 410	8 171	9 874	13 294	11 508
Germany	10 919	11 583	14 000	12 087	5 873	2 880	3 736	5 597	5 292
Greece	1 361	1 589	2 193	1 591	2 274	3 497	4 598	6 248	3 555

Table 2.A1: Number of banks and mean asset sizes according to years (*continued*)

EU countries	1988	1989	1990	1991	1992	1993	1994	1995	All
Ireland	–	–	–	–	18 969	6 765	5 409	5 615	6 646
Italy	5 995	8 027	10 133	11 940	9 196	6 204	6 860	9 729	8 213
Luxembourg	3 477	3 795	4 133	3 776	3 749	2 160	3 120	4 327	3 381
Netherlands	–	–	47 718	47 252	15 504	15 044	17 751	21 933	17 913
Portugal	1 374	1 771	1 434	3 011	4 617	4 419	5 606	7 046	4 620
Spain	4 123	5 285	6 424	7 275	6 688	6 234	6 483	8 278	6 457
Sweden	21 319	20 914	26 613	25 500	18 889	16 304	16 401	23 463	20 307
UK	26 954	26 017	29 098	26 138	9 815	9 461	9 806	12 068	13 295
All	9 099	10 247	12 005	11 909	7 606	5 042	6 038	8 358	7 611

Table 2.A2: Number of banks according to specialisation and asset sizes

EU countries	1–499	500–999	1000–2999	3000–4999	5000–9999	10 000–49 999	50 000 +	All
Austria	108	59	66	35	13	23	4	308
Belgium	147	70	95	19	19	32	28	410
Denmark	302	35	27	26	22	23	19	454
Finland	6	16	16	2	9	33	2	84
France	644	333	531	264	184	207	118	2 281
Germany	2 151	981	1 095	279	238	287	115	5 146
Greece	42	17	12	7	14	8	–	100
Ireland	2	7	23	5	2	8	–	47
Italy	348	272	451	106	121	131	76	1 505
Luxembourg	219	133	176	58	82	74	–	742
Netherlands	59	28	49	19	15	25	17	212
Portugal	46	25	49	19	28	24	–	191
Spain	247	129	312	122	113	81	38	1 042
Sweden	19	9	14	12	8	34	20	116
UK	319	84	173	89	104	131	65	965
All	4 659	2 198	3 089	1 062	972	1 121	502	13 603

Table 2.A3: Descriptive statistics of total assets

EU countries	N	Mean	Median	Standard deviation	Min	Max
Austria	308	3 837	848	9 064	14	68 115
Belgium	410	8 446	933	22 310	11	161 082
Denmark	454	4 999	276	13 877	9	71 886
Finland	84	12 002	6 300	14 148	61	63 938
France	2 281	11 508	1 401	40 759	2	387 131
Germany	5 146	5 292	675	22 814	29	461 184
Greece	100	3 555	647	7 552	88	46 597
Ireland	47	6 646	2 086	10 542	325	37 809
Italy	1 505	8 213	1 333	21 960	16	178 133
Luxembourg	742	3 381	1 104	5 304	3	32 164
Netherlands	212	17 913	1 781	51 845	59	340 642
Portugal	191	4 620	1 657	7 404	71	46 168
Spain	1 042	6 457	1 718	15 781	19	135 060
Sweden	116	20 307	7 715	24 044	111	81 523
UK	965	13 295	1 643	35 845	1	260 062
All	13 603	7 611	982	26 924	1	461 184

Table 2.A4: Maximum likelihood parameter estimation of the cost frontier for European banks *(continued)*

Variable	Parameter	Coefficient	Standard error	T-value
Constant	α_0	−0.0686	0.0138	−4.971
lnQ1	α_1	0.5289	0.0048	111.120
lnQ2	α_2	0.3950	0.0047	84.071
lnQ3	α_3	0.0181	0.0042	4.324
lnP1	β_1	0.1524	0.0069	22.007
lnP2	β_2	0.7804	0.0095	82.381
lnQ1 lnQ1/2	δ_{11}	0.0110	0.0009	11.862
lnQ1 lnQ2	δ_{12}	−0.0113	0.0004	−29.269
lnQ1 lnQ3	δ_{13}	0.0014	0.0004	3.863
lnQ2 lnQ2/2	δ_{22}	0.0102	0.0009	11.525
lnQ2 lnQ3	δ_{23}	−0.0020	0.0004	−5.250
lnQ3 lnQ3/2	δ_{33}	0.0055	0.0010	5.451
lnP1 lnP1/2	γ_{11}	0.0151	0.0019	7.746
lnP1 lnP2	γ_{12}	−0.0164	0.0074	−2.217
lnP2 lnP2/2	γ_{22}	0.0161	0.0067	2.396
lnP1 lnQ1	ρ_{11}	−0.0055	0.0008	−6.559
lnP1 lnQ2	ρ_{12}	−0.0240	0.0010	−23.170
lnP1 lnQ3	ρ_{13}	0.0019	0.0008	2.522
lnP2 lnQ1	ρ_{21}	0.0376	0.0013	29.493
lnP2 lnQ2	ρ_{22}	0.0107	0.0013	8.046
lnP2 lnQ3	ρ_{23}	0.0013	0.0012	1.055
cos (z1)	a_1	−0.0162	0.0037	−4.437
sin (z1)	b_1	−0.0122	0.0041	−2.940
cos (z2)	a_2	−0.0047	0.0035	−1.354
sin (z2)	b_2	0.0217	0.0040	5.455
cos (z3)	a_3	0.0204	0.0036	5.609
sin (z3)	b_3	−0.0006	0.0040	−0.150
cos (z1 + z1)	a_{11}	0.0008	0.0037	0.216
sin (z1 + z1)	b_{11}	−0.0042	0.0035	−1.193
cos (z1 + z2)	a_{12}	0.0075	0.0042	1.783
sin (z + z2)	b_{12}	−0.0076	0.0040	−1.910
cos (z1 + z3)	a_{13}	−0.0002	0.0039	−0.052
sin (z1 + z3)	b_{13}	0.0153	0.0038	3.984
cos (z2 + z2)	a_{22}	−0.0015	0.0033	−0.448
sin (z2 + z2)	b_{22}	0.0047	0.0034	1.376
cos (z2 + z3)	a_{23}	−0.0091	0.0038	−2.379
sin (z2 + z3)	b_{23}	−0.0156	0.0037	−4.263
cos (z3 + z3)	a_{33}	0.0026	0.0032	0.804
sin (z3 + z3)	b_{33}	0.0017	0.0036	0.478
cos (z + z1 + z2)	a_{112}	0.0129	0.0034	3.825
sin (z1 + z1 + z2)	b_{112}	−0.0121	0.0034	−3.556
cos (z1 + z1 + z3)	a_{113}	0.0026	0.0036	0.724
sin (z1 + z1 + z3)	b_{113}	−0.0050	0.0035	−1.425
cos (z1 + z2 + z2)	a_{122}	−0.0053	0.0033	−1.602

Table 2.A4: Maximum likelihood parameter estimation of the cost frontier for European banks *(continued)*

Variable	Parameter	Coefficient	Standard error	T-value
sin (z1 + z2 + z2)	b_{122}	0.0059	0.0034	1.731
cos (z1 + z2 + z3)	a_{123}	0.0170	0.0040	4.202
sin (z1 + z2 + z3)	b_{123}	0.0122	0.0043	2.842
cos (z1 + z3 + z3)	a_{133}	−0.0111	0.0035	−3.184
sin (z1 + z3 + z3)	b_{133}	0.0068	0.0038	1.807
cos (z2 + z2 + z3)	a_{223}	−0.0144	0.0035	−4.156
sin (z2 + z2 + z3)	b_{223}	0.0023	0.0036	0.642
cos (z2 + z3 + z3)	a_{233}	−0.0026	0.0035	−0.753
sin (z2 + z3 + z3)	b_{233}	−0.0126	0.0037	−3.412
T	τ	−0.0157	0.0047	−3.376
T*T	τ_{11}	0.0011	0.0004	2.460
lnQ1T	$\psi_{1\tau}$	−0.0031	0.0005	−6.376
lnQ2T	$\psi_{2\tau}$	0.0024	0.0006	4.238
lnQ3T	$\psi_{3\tau}$	−0.0012	0.0004	−2.834
lnP1T	$\theta_{1\tau}$	0.0077	0.0010	7.674
lnP2T	$\theta_{2\tau}$	−0.0079	0.0014	−5.838
	σ^2_u/σ^2_v	8.1452	0.1484	54.884
	σ^2_v	0.1150	0.0163	7.064
lnP3	β_3	0.0672		
lnP1lnP3	χ_{13}	0.0013		
lnP2lnP3	χ_{23}	0.0003		
lnP3lnP3	χ_{33}	−0.0016		
lnP3lnQ1	ρ_{31}	−0.0321		
lnP3lnQ2	ρ_{32}	0.0133		
lnP3lnQ3	ρ_{33}	−0.0032		
lnP3T	$\theta_{3\tau}$	0.0002		
Loglikelihood function		647.6994		
Variance components:				
	$\sigma^2_v =$	0.0141		
	$\sigma^2_u =$	0.1150		

Table 2.A5: Scale economies for European banks 1988–95

EU countries	1988	1989	1990	1991	1992	1993	1994	1995
Austria	0.9295	0.9298	0.9299	0.9302	0.9307	0.9305	0.9302	0.9292
Belgium	0.9414	0.9413	0.9443	0.9418	0.9490	0.9534	0.9555	0.9563
Denmark	0.9488	0.9486	0.9500	0.9511	0.9485	0.9473	0.9478	0.9486
Finland	0.9595	0.9606	0.9574	0.9552	0.9553	0.9479	0.9514	0.9597
France	0.9541	0.9551	0.9557	0.9567	0.9548	0.9557	0.9565	0.9581
Germany	0.9504	0.9499	0.9503	0.9494	0.9477	0.9475	0.9501	0.9513
Greece	0.9494	0.9501	0.9539	0.9499	0.9489	0.9500	0.9514	0.9510
Ireland	–	–	–	–	0.9496	0.9441	0.9408	0.9409
Italy	0.9581	0.9488	0.9539	0.9588	0.9552	0.9446	0.9507	0.9519
Luxembourg	0.9503	0.9503	0.9488	0.9483	0.9465	0.9436	0.9457	0.9463
Netherlands	–	–	0.9544	0.9691	0.9495	0.9479	0.9496	0.9511
Portugal	0.9412	0.9416	0.9402	0.9414	0.9425	0.9450	0.9471	0.9461
Spain	0.9454	0.9479	0.9470	0.9467	0.9476	0.9477	0.9482	0.9484
Sweden	0.9540	0.9515	0.9489	0.9454	0.9503	0.9488	0.9464	0.9455
UK	0.9419	0.9389	0.9373	0.9388	0.9451	0.9458	0.9460	0.9457
All	0.9504	0.9491	0.9498	0.9504	0.9493	0.9480	0.9500	0.9508

Table 2.A5: Scale economies for European banks 1988–95 *(continued)*

EU countries	Asset Sizes (US$ m)							
	1–499	500–999	1000–2999	3000–4999	5000–9999	10 000–49 999	50 000 +	All
Austria	0.9320	0.9307	0.9303	0.9292	0.9268	0.9220	0.9217	0.9300
Belgium	0.9471	0.9484	0.9523	0.9561	0.9571	0.9503	0.9622	0.9507
Denmark	0.9479	0.9528	0.9507	0.9469	0.9451	0.9546	0.9445	0.9484
Finland	0.9326	0.9469	0.9461	0.9435	0.9602	0.9655	0.9679	0.9549
France	0.9506	0.9531	0.9571	0.9582	0.9601	0.9620	0.9673	0.9560
Germany	0.9466	0.9490	0.9507	0.9526	0.9515	0.9550	0.9637	0.9493
Greece	0.9475	0.9536	0.9538	0.9595	0.9433	0.9595	–	0.9505
Ireland	0.9336	0.9333	0.9419	0.9342	0.9362	0.9591	–	0.9421
Italy	0.9448	0.9498	0.9524	0.9534	0.9577	0.9592	0.9618	0.9517
Luxembourg	0.9393	0.9435	0.9493	0.9491	0.9518	0.9575	–	0.9464
Netherlands	0.9409	0.9407	0.9484	0.9580	0.9578	0.9599	0.9667	0.9496
Portugal	0.9387	0.9408	0.9396	0.9429	0.9500	0.9617	–	0.9442
Spain	0.9423	0.9463	0.9474	0.9502	0.9504	0.9534	0.9548	0.9474
Sweden	0.9455	0.9486	0.9438	0.9464	0.9322	0.9471	0.9616	0.9480
UK	0.9410	0.9438	0.9432	0.9439	0.9526	0.9423	0.9580	0.9445
All	0.9457	0.9483	0.9505	0.9518	0.9534	0.9549	0.9617	0.9496

Table 2.A6: Mean X-inefficiency levels of banks in the EU 1988–95

EU Countries	1988	1989	1990	1991	1992	1993	1994	1995
Austria	0.136	0.148	0.198	0.186	0.206	0.219	0.372	0.230
Belgium	0.198	0.201	0.216	0.224	0.195	0.206	0.202	0.241
Denmark	0.201	0.192	0.215	0.258	0.259	0.271	0.261	0.304
Finland	0.228	0.223	0.197	0.256	0.268	0.482	0.414	0.336
France	0.271	0.314	0.325	0.367	0.251	0.258	0.292	0.278
Germany	0.163	0.165	0.177	0.175	0.159	0.162	0.171	0.177
Greece	0.146	0.174	0.172	0.159	0.161	0.172	0.180	0.196
Ireland	–	–	–	–	0.085	0.088	0.084	0.080
Italy	0.286	0.270	0.274	0.280	0.301	0.394	0.426	0.389
Luxembourg	0.153	0.210	0.258	0.228	0.245	0.267	0.291	0.316
Netherlands	–	–	0.340	0.473	0.193	0.232	0.225	0.223
Portugal	0.164	0.204	0.164	0.192	0.208	0.241	0.217	0.179
Spain	0.388	0.337	0.369	0.386	0.365	0.391	0.471	0.420
Sweden	0.169	0.129	0.197	0.307	0.336	0.347	0.388	0.382
UK	0.229	0.229	0.235	0.275	0.312	0.323	0.321	0.291
All	0.249	0.248	0.264	0.275	0.237	0.235	0.257	0.249

Table 2.A6: Mean X-inefficiency levels of banks in the EU 1988–95 (*continued*)

EU countries	Asset Sizes (US$ m)							
	1–499	500–999	1000–2999	3000–4999	5000–9999	10 000–49 999	50 000 +	All
Austria	0.300	0.218	0.182	0.202	0.195	0.207	0.352	0.237
Belgium	0.231	0.258	0.194	0.172	0.213	0.160	0.139	0.212
Denmark	0.247	0.312	0.371	0.271	0.267	0.286	0.184	0.261
Finland	0.809	0.235	0.384	0.143	0.200	0.281	0.426	0.321
France	0.293	0.333	0.275	0.288	0.269	0.240	0.252	0.285
Germany	0.157	0.161	0.164	0.171	0.215	0.244	0.202	0.168
Greece	0.152	0.182	0.172	0.106	0.288	0.134	–	0.174
Ireland	0.042	0.062	0.083	0.093	0.103	0.101	–	0.083
Italy	0.687	0.326	0.237	0.241	0.228	0.153	0.183	0.347
Luxembourg	0.250	0.268	0.272	0.284	0.282	0.248	–	0.264
Netherlands	0.187	0.201	0.226	0.218	0.203	0.252	0.337	0.221
Portugal	0.164	0.200	0.200	0.296	0.228	0.191	–	0.204
Spain	0.758	0.371	0.283	0.260	0.235	0.244	0.258	0.394
Sweden	0.199	0.237	0.447	0.600	0.434	0.320	0.192	0.324
UK	0.312	0.307	0.278	0.319	0.271	0.279	0.356	0.300
All	0.275	0.241	0.225	0.246	0.244	0.235	0.237	0.249

Notes

1. Mitchell and Onvural (1996; p. 181) did not impose restrictions on the trigonometric input price coefficients for computational reasons. Gallant (1982), however, has shown that this should not prevent an estimated FF cost equation from closely approximating the true cost function.

2. Berger and Humphrey (1997) restricted z_i to span [0.1, 0.9]. However, the use of this interval provided inconsistent results in the present study. While Mitchell and Onvural (1996) adopted a second trigonometric order in their study, we preferred to use a third trigonometric order following Berger and Humphrey (1997). According to Gallant (1982), increasing the number of trigonometric orders, relative to sample size, reduces approximation errors. Eastwood and Gallant (1991) show that the FF cost function produces consistent and asymptotically normal parameter estimates when the number of parameters estimated is set to the number of effective observations raised to the two-thirds power. However, Gallant (1981) advocates that even a limited number of trigonometric orders is sufficient to obtain global approximations. The choice of the range used by different researchers is, however, subjective and relative to the size of data set analysed.

3. We use the panel data approach because technical efficiency is better studied and modelled with panels (see Baltagi and Griffin, 1988; Cornwell *et al.*, 1990; Kumbhakar, 1993). The random effects model is preferred over the fixed effects model because the latter is considered to be the more appropriate specification if we are focusing on a specific set of N firms. Moreover, and if N is large, a fixed effects model would also lead to a substantial loss of degrees of freedom (see Baltagi, 1995).

4. See Bauer (1990) for an excellent review of the frontier literature and how different stochastic assumptions can be made. Cebenoyan *et al.* (1993), for example, use the truncated normal model. Mester (1996), in common with many (non-banking) studies uses the half-normal distribution. Stevenson (1980) and Greene (1990) have used the normal-gamma model. Altunbaş and Molyneux (1994) find that efficiency estimates are relatively insensitive to different distributional assumptions when testing the half-normal, truncated normal, normal-exponential and gamma efficiency distributions, as all distributions yield similar inefficiency levels for the German banking market.

5. Various structural tests were undertaken to test for data poolability and heteroscedasticity and these confirmed the applicability of the panel data approach. These results are available upon request from the authors.

6. A variety of hypotheses regarding the nature of technical progress may be investigated using an analog of the likelihood ratio test. The test statistic, depending on differences in the weighted mean squared errors, is distributed asymptotically as chi-square with degrees of freedom equal to the number of restrictions. The statistical significance of technological progress may be measured by employing a likelihood ratio test. Defining L_R and L_U as the maximum likelihood values of the restricted and unrestricted model, respectively, note that the term $-2\ln(L_R/L_U)$ has a chi-square distribution with degrees of freedom equal to the number of independently imposed

restrictions. The following restriction would be applicable for the likelihood ratio test, assuming equation (3) is the unrestricted model.

References

Aigner, D., C. Lovell and P. Schmidt (1977), 'Formulation and estimation of stochastic frontier production models', *Journal of Econometrics*, 6, pp. 21–37

Allen, L. and A. Rai (1996), 'Operational efficiency in banking: an international comparison', *Journal of Banking and Finance*, 20(4), pp. 655–72

Altunbaş, Y. and P. Molyneux (1994), *Sensitivity of Stochastic Frontier Estimation to Distributional Assumptions: the Case of the German Banks*, Institute of European Finance Paper (preliminary version, unpublished in 1994)

Andersen, A. (1993), *European Banking and Capital Markets: a Strategic Forecast*, Research Report, London: The Economist Intelligence Unit

Baltagi, B.H. (1995), *Econometric Analysis of Panel Data*, Chichester, UK: John Wiley

Baltagi, B.H. and J.M. Griffin (1988), 'A general index of technical change', *Journal of Political Economy*, 96(1), pp. 20–41

Battese, G.E. and G.S. Corra (1977), 'Estimation of a production frontier model: with application to the pastoral zone of Eastern Australia', *Australian Journal of Agricultural Economics*, 21(3), pp. 169–79

Bauer, P. (1990), 'Recent developments in the econometric estimations of frontiers', *Journal of Econometrics*, 46, pp. 39–56

Berger, A.N. and D.B. Humphrey (1997), 'Efficiency of financial institutions: international survey and directions for future research', *European Journal of Operational Research*, 98, pp. 175–212

Berger, A.N., J.H. Leusner and J.J. Mingo (1994), *The Efficiency of Bank Branches*, Working Paper, Wharton Financial Institutions Centre, Philadelphia

Cebenoyan, A.S., E.S. Cooperman, C.A. Register and S.C. Hudgins (1993), 'The relative efficiency of stock versus mutual S&Ls: a stochastic cost frontier approach', *Journal of Financial Services Research*, 7, pp. 151–70

Cecchini, P. (1988), *The European Challenge in 1992: the Benefits of a Single Market*, Aldershot: Gower

Chalfant, J.A. and A.R. Gallant (1985), 'Estimating substitution elasticities with the Fourier cost function', *Journal of Econometrics*, 28, pp. 205–22

Cornwell, C., P. Schmidt and R.C. Sickles (1990), 'Production frontiers with cross-sectional and time-series variation in efficiency levels', *Journal of Econometrics*, 46, pp. 185–200

Eastwood, B.J. and A.R. Gallant (1991), 'Adaptive rules for seminonparametric estimators that achieve asymptotic normality', *Economic Theory*, 7, pp. 307–40

Elbadawi, I., A.R. Gallant and G. Souza (1983), 'An elasticity can be estimated consistently without a priori knowledge of functional form', *Econometrica*, 51, pp. 1731–53

Ferrier, G.D. and C.A.K. Lovell (1990), 'Measuring cost efficiency in banking: econometric and linear programming evidence' *Journal of Econometrics*, 46, pp. 229–45

Gallant, A.R. (1981), 'On the bias in Flexible Functional forms and essentially unbiased form: the Fourier Flexible form', *Journal of Econometrics*, 15, pp. 211–45

Gallant, A.R. (1982), 'Unbiased determination of production technologies', *Journal of Econometrics*, **20**, pp. 285–324

Gallant, A.R. and G. Souza (1991), 'On the asymptotic normality of Fourier Flexible form estimates', *Journal of Econometrics*, **50**, pp. 329–53

Greene, W.M. (1990), 'A gamma-distributed stochastic frontier model', *Journal of Econometrics*, **46**, pp. 141–63

Greene, W.M. (1993), 'The econometric approach to efficiency analysis', in H.O. Fried, C.A. Lovell and P. Schmidt (eds), *The Measurement of Productive Efficiency: Techniques and Applications*, Oxford: Oxford University Press

Humphrey, D.B. (1993), 'Cost and technical change: effects from bank deregulation', *Journal of Productivity Analysis*, **4**, pp. 9–34

Hunter, W.C. and S.G. Timme (1991), 'Technological change in large US commercial banks', *Journal of Business*, **64**, pp. 339–62

Jagtiani, J. and A. Khanthavit (1996), 'Scale and scope economies at large banks: including off-balance sheet products and regulatory effects (1984–1991)', *Journal of Banking and Finance*, **20** (7), pp. 1271–87

Jondrow, J., C.A. Lovell, I.S. Materov and P. Schmidt (1982), 'On estimation of technical inefficiency in the stochastic frontier production function model', *Journal of Econometrics*, **19**, pp. 233–8

Kaparakis, E.I., S.M. Miller and A.G. Noulas (1994), 'Short-run cost inefficiencies of commercial banks', *Journal of Money, Credit and Banking*, **26** (4), pp. 875–93

Koop, R. and V.K. Smith (1982), 'An evaluation of alternative indexes of technological change', unpublished Working Paper, University of North Carolina, Chapel Hill

Kumbhakar, S.C. (1993), 'Production risk, technical efficiency and panel data', *Economics Letters*, **41**, pp. 11–26

Lang, G. and P. Welzel (1996), 'Efficiency and technical progress in banking: empirical results for a panel of German cooperative banks', *Journal of Banking and Finance*, **20**, pp. 1003–23

Maudos, J., J.M. Pastor and J. Quesada (1996), 'Technical progress in Spanish banking: 1985–1994', University of Valencia and IVIE Discussion Paper, WP-EC 96–06

McKillop, D.G., J.C. Glass and Y. Morikawa (1996), 'The composite cost function and efficiency in giant Japanese banks', *Journal of Banking and Finance*, **20**, pp. 1651–71

Meeusen, W. and J. van den Broeck (1977), 'Efficiency estimation from Cobb–Douglas production functions with composed error, *International Economic Review*, **18**, pp. 435–44

Mester, L.J. (1996), 'A study of bank efficiency taking into account risk-preferences', *Journal of Banking and Finance*, **20**, pp. 1025–45

Mitchell, K. and N.M. Onvural (1996), 'Economies of scale and scope at large commercial banks: evidence from the Fourier Flexible functional form', *Journal of Money, Credit and Banking*, **28** (2), pp. 178–99

Nelson, R.A. (1984), 'Regulation, capital vintage, and technical change in the electric utility industry', *Review of Economics and Statistics*, **66**, February, pp. 59–69

Olson, R.E., P. Schmidt and D.M. Waldman (1980), 'A Monte Carlo study of estimators of stochastic frontier production functions', *Journal of Econometrics*, **13**, pp. 67–82

Sealey, C. and J.T. Lindley (1977), 'Inputs, outputs and a theory of production and cost at depository financial institution', *Journal of Finance*, **32**, pp. 1251–66

Stevenson, R.E. (1980), 'Likelihood functions for generalised stochastic frontier estimation', *Journal of Econometrics*, **13**, pp. 57–66

Tolstov, G.P. (1962), *Fourier Series*, London: Prentice-Hall

3
Competitive Advantage Based on Information Technology in Banking

Esteban Fernández, José M. Montes and Camilo J. Vásquez

Abstract

The development and diffusion of information technologies (IT) and the intense competition of the 1980s have induced two kinds of organisational restructuring as a means of reducing costs: (1) outsourcing of activities which are computer and telecommunications intensive and (2) downsizing by heavily investing in IT and streamlining employment. This study analyses the influence of these organisational changes on the evolution of business processes and competitive strategies in banking.

3.1 Increasing competition and price competitiveness

The intense competition of recent years in national and international markets is generating significant restructuring in firms. Managers are looking for more efficient organisations, with lower fixed costs and greater flexibility in the face of changing market conditions. The banking sector is also affected by these processes and the subsequent challenges. Where appropriate, the reorganisation processes are a reaction to the fact that banks have lost their leadership position in their traditional markets, and particularly to the impact of technological innovation.

In the last decade, market conditions in banking have undergone deep changes. On the demand side, customer preferences differ greatly from the traditional bank products (loans and savings). On the supply side, the globalisation of financial markets is accompanied by their governmental deregulation. Both factors imply an increase in the number of competitors, followed by reductions in costs and narrowing of profit margins. Thereby, banks are faced with strong competition from non-banking companies, which also accentuates the competition between the banks themselves. In the retail banking sector, the savings market share is lost, savers preferring mutual funds, money market funds, pension funds, insurance products and so on. Market position is also lost in other segments (credit cards) in favour of specialised suppliers. In the wholesale segment, the securitisation and financial disintermediation processes imply that bank loans lose share in credit operations. The companies, originally the large ones and now, to an increasing extent, the medium-sized and small ones, focus less on the banking system and search for new financing sources directly or concede higher importance to internal funds.

As a whole, the macrotendencies marking the evolution of financial markets entail the continuous erosion of the bank's market share, in retail operations as well as in wholesale ones. Although the general tendencies are common to all financial systems, the behaviour and final outcomes are not the same in all of them. So, whereas the loss of market share has been relatively important in the USA, in other countries (for example, Germany) banks maintain stable market positions. These varying results can usually be explained according to the differences in government regulation,[1] the degree of competition in the different financial systems, and the different attitude (more or less conservative) of consumers in different countries when facing the mentioned changes. Nevertheless, the competitive policies and strategies followed by banks in response to these tendencies enjoy great importance in this sense (Keltner 1995).

Under the pressure of intense competition, banks have reacted in several ways. Some of them, with the aim of rapidly improving profits, have increased the income obtained from fee based business activities or have ventured into high-risk segments, such as securities derivatives. Others have tried to benefit from all the opportunities offered by the application of new ITs for aggressive price competition and to introduce product and process innovations that imply great changes in the services offered to customers. In this sense, we can distinguish two clear types of policies.

On the one hand, following a general tendency in the economy, greater specialisation is to be found in those areas of business or activities in a position of competitive advantage. The firm excludes other activities which are complementary to that core competence where there is no improvement in the results offered by other suppliers or competitors who will be external supply sources (outsourcing). In banking, and in reference to applying new ITs, outsourcing basically concerns those processes or products which are new technology intensive, requiring great investments, and which are subcontracted in order to benefit from the economies of scale obtained by specialised suppliers. The economical rationale underlying these processes, as well as the risks of outsourcing, are studied in Section 3.2.

On the other hand, and also with the aim of reducing costs, some banks have undertaken important restructuring processes using technology as a labour substitute. They have invested heavily in new IT and carried out considerable job reduction and substantial changes in the human resources policies (downsizing). The possibilities offered by new ITs, for example telephone banking, play a key role in the introduction of these changes. The underlying economic logic and associated risks are studied in Section 3.3.

Both processes, outsourcing and downsizing, respond to a fundamental change in the competitive strategy which implies a greater emphasis on acquiring new customers rather than on maintaining current customer loyalty. In this strategy, cost together with convenience become the main competitive priorities and the main attraction for new customers through periodic adjustments in interest rates and commissions discounts, accompanied by intense advertising campaigns with various promotions.

Price competition is particularly clear in the segment of retail banking (savings, consumer loans) and to a lesser extent in the market for medium and large companies. This type of competition tries to avoid risk and seeks profits in short-term transactions rather than maintaining stable long-term relationships. The granting of loans follows a clearly pro-cyclical behaviour: in times of prosperity, when there is excess capital, credits are given more easily and at low interest rates. In times of crisis, credit is rationalised and interest rates rise significantly. The decision to concede a loan is based on analysing the financial situation of the customer or the available collateral. Other questions such as the company management competence or business plan receive less attention. In a crisis situation, the bank does not help the firm but rather takes it into receivership and claims the collateral.

If price competition is generalised and intensified, and it is argued that this may have happened in the North American banking sector (see Keltner 1995), pressure is increased to be efficient in all business processes. This search for greater efficiency underlies the processes of outsourcing and downsizing. To attain this efficiency other sources of competitive advantage in banking may be sacrificed. This applies, in the case of the bank, introducing its own innovations based on apply-ing new ITs or attaching an advantage to customer loyalty based on relationship banking.

3.2 The impact of new information technologies on subcontracting processes[2]

Following the hypothesis proposed by Adam Smith ('the division of labour is limited by the extent of the market'), the processes of out-sourcing could be explained as a consequence of increased market size. When the market grows, firms tend to specialise to a greater extent and subcontract those activities in which they are not especially competi-tive to highly specialised independent suppliers (Stigler 1968).

In the infant phases of an industry, demand may be insufficient for a great number of specialised firms to be able to coexist in the different phases of the production process simply because there is no market for them all. In this case, the companies in the industry themselves carry out all the activities necessary to produce the final product and get it to the consumer. There is a tendency towards subcontracting activities to inde-pendent suppliers when the final product market becomes larger. Firms tend to subcontract those activities presenting important scope dis-economies with their core activities (Stigler 1968). This avoids the com-plexity and costs associated with co-ordinating activities and production processes within a firm which are complementary but quite dissimilar.

The continuous growth in the market of services provided by firms specialised in applying new ITs makes it possible to attain important economies of scale in data processing and software application which, in accordance with the previous arguments, should lead to the subcon-tracting of computer and telecommunication intense activities. This is partly what is happening in banks. New companies with their own computer equipment, databases and software have specialised in pro-viding financial services and managing various transactions. In the sector jargon, this type of firm is called Value Added Network Services (Totonis and Spitler 1990) and essentially provides a service on the basis of lines leased from a telecommunications operator or a common carrier. Value is added to the mere capacity of data transmission by means of processing such data and converting them into useful infor-mation for problem-solving or decision-taking with the aid of the firms' own highly specialised software and hardware.

The economic logic underlying these subcontracting processes is rel-atively similar in most cases. In banking, some functions and processes are characterised by a high degree of standardisation (back office operations, cash management, securities transactions, credit cards) that facilitates their later automation (Minnerop and Stoll, 1986; Penrose, 1990; Revell, 1983; Schmerken, 1990). The high fixed costs associated with the investments to be made in the purchase of equipment and developing the software necessary to automate the various processes generate important economies of scale, difficult to attain in the case of small banks;[3] this is why subcontracting is preferred. In other cases the bank does not have specialised personnel capable of developing internally the software required and so subcontracts software development and its later application. So long as the banking sector continues to subcontract services to these specialised suppliers, banks will gradually become specialists in managing information services provided by highly specialised companies via telecommunications networks.

Langlois (1988) and Von Weizsäcker (1991) argue that in some cases the market may grow and companies may still remain highly integrated. According to these authors, this situation is likely to arise when market growth takes place in a context characterised by important technological change. In other words, there is no need to subcontract those activities where market growth is accompanied by substantial innovations. Several reasons support this argument.

1. In periods of rapid technological change with important product or process innovations, it may be difficult to convince the independent suppliers to make the specific investments necessary to manufacture the components or intermediate products, or to provide the specialised service required by such innovations (Williamson 1986).
2. In periods of rapid technological change it is important to shorten the reaction time when facing changes in market conditions and to secure sufficient organisational flexibility. Rigidity is greater and reaction times longer when it is necessary to negotiate with each supplier every time the introduction of changes in the products or processes is necessary.
3. When a company introduces some kind of innovation to its products or processes it will try to avoid diffusion to competitors through their suppliers and so companies only subcontract those activities that do not entail risks in this sense (Teece 1986). It is supposed that there are good reasons for believing that confidential information can be controlled at a lower cost within a firm's boundaries than in a contractual relationship with an independent firm (Wieland 1993).

In short, when a firm subcontracts processes in a context of market growth and technological change, with the aim of reducing costs in internal organisation and taking advantage of the economies of scale obtained by external suppliers, there is the risk that on the one hand such suppliers may not make investments which are co-specialised with innovations and on the other hand, the firm may lose organisational flexibility and become incapable of protecting its innovation rents from imitations. These risks should also be taken into account when analysing the subcontracting processes in banking. Thus, banks should assess the interest in retaining those operations requiring the banks' own databases, since passing on confidential information which could be very interesting for competitors would be avoided.

Technological uncertainty and the pace of change are so high that the introduction of innovations based on applying new ITs constitutes an important source of rents. The technological leaders in certain services or products are those sustaining the most important market shares in the future. Therefore, it would be best to retain those operations (custody of security portfolios, cash-management systems, home-banking operations, complex software to grant and monitor loans) for which banks have developed highly specialised software internally. These constitute a significant innovation since they are not available in the marketplace and are capable of generating important innovation rents. As the different solutions or software become standard in the industry, the potential of sustaining these innovation rents is lowered; at the same time it is more important to lower costs by benefiting from the economies of scale attained by suppliers.

3.3 Price competition versus relationship banking

The fast growing development of new ITs has opened the gateway to new banking forms. Telephone banking generates important growth opportunities without substantially increasing costs by substituting human contact transactions for electronic means. Telebanking offers bank services by substituting for services offered at the branches with a high degree of technology which allows customers to establish a commercial relationship from their offices or homes. This can radically change the customer–bank relationship and affect the importance of the branch network. Branches lose importance since a great number of customers make all their bank operations without having to visit the branch office.

The products of technological banking are already being widely offered to customers. This is one of the most developed markets. Most predictions concerning banking foresee that in five years time the volume of operations made by telebanking systems will be double, especially if a solution is found for the main problem, which is the implicit risk of fraud and the need to establish mechanisms giving customers the same security as when carrying out an operation at a branch.

Downsizing by applying new ITs in an industry characterised by numerous routine transactions and tons of paperwork necessarily supposes higher productivity and efficiency as well as an improvement in the services that can be offered to customers. However, this should not mean that the bank distances itself from customers, losing a great part of the advantages to be reaped from the development of a stable relationship.

Aggressive price competition and the cost-reduction policies have contributed to eroding some of the traditional sources of competitive advantage in the banking sector. Price competition breaks with customer loyalty. When this is accompanied by intense advertising campaigns, customer information asymmetry is reduced and customers become more price-sensitive. This means that customers finally discover that other entities or financial instruments are cheaper and respond to their needs better. Moreover, the customers attracted by low prices are precisely the most sensitive to this variable and the first to change entity when they are offered better conditions.

Cost reductions could be insufficient to overcome competition from other firms. Competition is also surmounted by giving the customers better value for money. In this sense, in the search for price competitiveness one of the most distinctive and traditional features of banking is lost: relationship banking. There is the risk of sacrificing the quality of service offered with the aim of improving costs, when it is precisely the possibility of providing a superior quality and personalised service, together with the offer of financial advice on a wide range of products, that gives the bank its competitive advantage over other financial entities.

The close contact between the bank and customers is not machine-based but is rather based on human capital resources where training and ability become key competitive factors. Some banks have opted to invest heavily in the training of their human capital and the creation of organisational capabilities necessary to follow competitive strategies based on the development of relationship banking. In this case, banks are looking for higher profitability and growth through maintaining a stable customer base, offering customers a high quality of services and a wide range of products and financial services (in many cases in co-operation with other entities), the composition of which is constantly modified and updated to adapt to a continuously changing environment.

Empirical evidence suggests that the greater strength of the German banking system when facing the negative effects of the macrotendencies described in the previous sections could respond to the prevalence of this second type of competition as opposed to the current aggressive price competition in the USA financial markets. In order to explain the causes of these different outcomes, it is necessary to study in depth the relative benefits provided by relationship banking. These benefits are mainly derived from the permanent contact with a stable nucleus of customers. Relationship banking has two distinguishing features: the relationship between the parties (customer and bank) is mutually beneficial and the relationship is long-term.

The archetype model of Haus Bank constitutes perhaps the most traditional approach to the concept of relationship banking. In this case, the bank becomes the main supplier of financial services for the company, attaining a significant percentage of the loans and savings. Long-term contractual relationships are maintained and generate significant lowering of transaction costs. The bank is also represented on the Board of Directors of the company and may also own a significant part of its shares.[4]

Maintaining long-term relationships between banks and companies causes the former to play a reorganising role when the company goes through periods of crisis, contributing with additional funds, lengthening the terms for debt repayment and renegotiating this with other creditors, or even restructuring the organisation and the board of directors, among other measures. In practice, it means that the bank has an active presence in resource assignment in the company beyond the mere control of its economic outcomes. The bank's control reduces the conflict between creditors and shareholders, enabling the transfer of control, and it also influences the probability of the company's takeover. As an outcome of the continuity of the relationship, the bank obtains information about investment opportunities and management competence.

The Haus Bank in particular has a double advantage: first, it reduces the conflicting interests between shareholders and managers, controlling the latter, and aligning their interests with the strategic objectives of the company, and, second, it reduces the conflict between share-holders and creditors, facilitating the transfer of the control over the firm towards the latter in, for example, bankruptcy situations. Therefore, it is an organisational structure which is particularly efficient in contexts where these conflicts could be important, as happens in the case of investments in intangible resources. These are investments where it is difficult to assess risks and profits and which require an effective ownership transfer mechanism in case of crisis.

Investments in intangible resources are slow to mature and so their creation requires long-term financing funds. Retaining profits to finance these investments could be relatively complicated in a context in which more intense competition tends to reduce profits. Another possibility is to have recourse to long-term debt. The problem then resides in the fact that, by increasing investment in intangible resources, the value of the debt decreases and the possibilities of guaranteeing such a debt are lower.

In accordance with Myers (1977), the value of the company could be broken down into the sum of the value of its tangible resources (that does not usually depend on the discretionary decisions of managers) and the value of the so-called real options such as the opportunity of introducing a new product basing it on technology (current or under development) and on the reputation of the company. The value of these real options is practically null, since they rely on the continuity of the company and discretionary decisions about future investments. In a state of, or approaching, insolvency, the shareholders could decide not to invest as this would fundamentally benefit the creditors, so there is no advantage to be taken from these real options. On the other hand, if the level of the debt were greater than the liquidation value of the tangible assets, it would be better for the creditors to sell the company off. Nevertheless, this liquidation could be unnecessary and inefficient since it destroys the value of future investment options based on some of the company's intangible resources.

When the company debt is shared out between multiple creditors it is difficult for these investors to assume the responsibility for the reorganisation because each of them has a small part of the total debt, while the co-ordination of all the creditors is difficult. Something similar happens when the bank debt is shared out between a high number of banks. When the debt which is not covered by the liquidation value of the tangible assets is concentrated on a single creditor (in this case, the Haus Bank), this bank has powerful incentives to reorganise the company, being the main beneficiary of such a reorganisation.

The bank makes use of its experience and knowledge obtained during previous participation in similar processes and also risks its reputation, an asset of great importance, to guarantee participation in future reorganisation processes. In the German or Japanese case (perhaps the most frequent examples in the literature), the capacity shown by the banks to take on the functions of financing investments in intangibles and the reorganisation of the companies in crisis, avoiding the loss of value associated with the destruction of these intangibles, could be a key factor in explaining the competitive advantage acquired by these countries in the international context.

The Haus Bank is not the only form of relationship banking, there being multiple strategies and policies (Bergendahl and Lindblom 1996), the common objective of which is to reduce customer turnover (Keltner 1995). It is assumed that the closer the relationship between the bank and its customers, the lower the turnover will be and the higher the bank's potential profitability from the services it provides, simply because the marginal cost of retaining a customer is lower than the cost of attracting a new one (Fornell 1992). It is, therefore, a matter of retaining customers rather than acquiring new ones, avoiding the cost entailed in acquiring customers whose loyalty is questionable. If customer turnover is high, it is necessary to incur elevated costs in order to attract new ones, while maintaining a level of acceptable risk. Among these costs we include the promotional efforts and investments in marketing necessary to attract the interest of new customers, as well as the costs involved in information and the evaluation of customers' financial situations, especially if we bear in mind that, due to the scarce knowledge we have about them, they imply higher risks than current customers. By reducing customer turnover these costs are avoided. Besides, a lower turnover not only means lower costs but it also implies a high degree of repeating financial operations and secures a stable and, to a certain extent, predictable cash-flow behaviour as well as a more in-depth knowledge about customers.

There are plenty of policies encouraging the promotion of customer contact and long-term relationships (Bergendahl and Lindbolm 1996), the application of which reduces customer turnover. One possibility is to apply a pricing policy which stimulates the renewal of services, especially those of a short-term nature, by offering loyal customers better conditions, such as price bundling (Guiltinan 1989). For example, a discount could be offered in a service if the customer has previously used other services or contracted other products (mixed leader bundling), or else a set of services and products could be offered at a cost which is lower than the sum of the individual cost of these products and services (mixed joint bundling).

To a certain extent the discount obtained in the cost of contracting products or additional services transfers part of the economies of scope which are generated in this type of relationship to the customers. Price competition seeks, above all, economies of scale. The bank concentrates on certain segments and on providing some services, following a policy of aggressive price competition in order to attract new customers and acquire a higher market share. On the other hand, relationship banking is characterised by the search for economies of scope. These economies arise so long as the marginal cost of extending a new product to a current customer is lower than the cost of extending it to a new customer (Reichheld and Sasser 1990).

When a customer concentrates all or a great part of his financial operations in a bank, conditions are set for widening the scope of this relationship. The bank can become a kind of financial adviser for the customer. As employees familiarise themselves with customer problems and specific needs it is possible to find a mix of customised products and financial services so that customers can take advantage of all the synergies which may be generated by conveniently combining these. This facilitates the sale of new products and financial services with relatively low control costs and reduced risks due to prior knowledge of the customer. On the other hand, customer loyalty is also reinforced since it is more likely that a customer will leave the bank if he receives only one type of service than if he has several products and services contracted.

Another suitable base on which to build permanent relationships with customers is to establish lasting links by means of long-term contracts, such as mortgages, life assurances and pension plans. To this end, improved conditions could be offered in these long-term contracts, balancing out such loss with more costly conditions for customers in short-term transactions. In this case, it is supposed that the customer does not look for the bank offering lower commissions in such transactions but opts to make these transactions in the same entity where he has contracted or hopes to contract other long-term products with the aim of either avoiding the search costs or benefiting from these more favourable conditions in the long-term relationship.

Customer turnover is also reduced by increasing the switching costs of customers (for example, increasing the costs incurred due to unilateral and premature breach of contract), so that customers continue their relationship with the bank despite being dissatisfied with it

(Bergendahl and Lindbolm 1996). It could be even more beneficial to reduce turnover by incrementing customer satisfaction and so increase their desire to maintain the relationship with the bank through attaining high levels of service quality. There is loyalty to the extent that customers are satisfied with the services received (Reichheld 1993). This satisfaction contributes to lowering price elasticity at the same time as it generates a reputation effect, which is highly beneficial since it attracts new customers, especially those expecting good service in a long-term context, with lower costs for the bank since there is no need for using price promotions and marketing which are necessary to attract other types of customers.

The degree of customer satisfaction (or rather the perceived quality) is conditioned by many factors, one of which could be the variety of products and services offered, fundamentally because the needs of each customer are specific and different. Therefore, when the customer is a medium-sized company we should add to the typical needs of savings and loans other more specific ones such as investment advice, business projects, cash management, electronic banking products or management of international transactions. It is possible to offer services providing particularly useful information for those customers lacking in sufficient resources to generate this internally: complex financial analysis, study of market tendencies, sector information and specific information on the state of the customer's relationship with the bank.

The quality of service offered increases with the degree of customer contact. This proximity or contact increases when each customer, according to size and importance, is assigned to an employee or a management team that deals personally with his account and relationships with the bank. Thereby, the customer does not have to deal with several people depending on the operation or problem to be solved. Close customer contact is also the best way of getting information about customers and their business, information which can be of great interest for the bank, especially that which can only be obtained in an informal relationship based on a personal and continuous contact.

The knowledge generated by the customer–bank contact enables the rapid resolving of specific pressing problems by means of procedures which are not formally set down in the organisational norms and routines. In many cases this capacity for solving particular problems decisively influences the usual perception of the quality of the service. In cases of price competition, the greater part of the working day is devoted to acquiring new customers, trying to snatch them away from other banks with the promise of better interest rates. In relationship banking, the middle managers spend most of their time and attention cultivating their current customers. Acquiring new customers is a task dealt with exclusively by senior managers, although in many cases contact with new customers is made through other people informally rather than by telephone. Current satisfied customers tend to reward the benefits of a close relationship with the bank with high loyalty.

Service quality evaluated through the previous parameters depends directly on the policies of human resources that have been applied (Keltner 1995). In this case, there are great differences between the strategy followed by the banks aiming to be price competitive and those trying to develop relationship banking on the basis of high quality services. As part of the strategy of cost reduction, the introduction of new ITs has decisively influenced the policies of human resources, substituting labour for capital. In order to reduce personnel costs and redirect funds towards investment in technology acquisition, full-time jobs are replaced by a part-time labour force. As a consequence, wages are lower and so are the total number of hours paid after streamlining employment in line with demand fluctuation. Similarly, in a context of intense price competition, training is conceived more as a cost factor than as an investment. Therefore, personnel costs are also lowered after reducing the investments in training and skill formation. Those jobs demanding relatively qualified personnel are covered by means of external recruitment, assuming that internal training and promotion would be more costly.

The final result of these policies is that millions are invested in technologically up-dating offices and branches so that the personnel finally providing the services (and so forming the bank's image in the eyes of customers) can become minimally competent. In relationship banking, new ITs are going to play a subordinate and supporting role; they are not going to become the key to the company's competitive advantage. Among the different suppliers of financial services, banks are the only ones with an extensive distribution network which allows them to maintain a close relationship with customers, benefiting at the same time from the economies of scope obtained by offering a wide range of products and financial services and from several synergies that can be obtained by combining these products according to the specific needs of each customer. This constitutes one of the sources of competitive advantage in relationship banking. It is necessary to maintain an extensive network of small offices and branches in towns of diverse size in order to get to the final customer.

Customer contact is made by the employees, whose training and ability become a determinant factor in the quality of customer relationships. In this sense, it is essential to reduce employee turnover since a high degree of turnover hinders the necessary interaction between customers and the branch personnel. The emphasis placed on part-time employment and on external recruitment as part of the strategies of competition in costs increases employee turnover and reduces their level of commitment and loyalty to the bank. Part-time employees will always be on the lookout for a more stable job outside the bank, while the externally recruited qualified personnel tend to leave should they be offered better employment conditions in another entity. Employee turnover is reduced by the bank developing its internal labour market and committing itself to developing the abilities and organisational resources needed. The guarantees of permanent employment and internal promotion offered by the bank are a very important element for reducing employee turnover. If all the banks follow similar policies there are fewer possibilities of finding a similar post in other banks, which also lowers the degree of personnel turnover.

Making important investments in training is another important aspect in the development of relationship banking. These investments are necessary for workers in different branches to obtain an extensive knowledge of the many products and financial services offered by the entity and so be able to advise customers on several problems and products. It is expected that the range of products the customer demands increases with time, so that the employee is in the ideal position to search for the product mix that best satisfies customer needs. But to achieve this, he needs adequate training and wide product knowledge. Job rotation during the training process and continuous training enable personnel to attain an in-depth knowledge on the different products and services offered by the bank, as well as the problems that may arise in each case and the people whom they should contact to resolve issues.

The design of the incentives systems should also be in line with the objective of quality. Incentives systems in relationship banking have a rather collective character, for example, payment of profits. There are several reasons why these collective incentives systems are adopted. Individual incentives only benefit certain workers, especially those directly involved in selling products and financial services, and not those intervening in later management simply because their contribution, which is no less valuable, is more difficult to measure. On the other hand, individual incentives could lead to competition between the branch offices of a given bank in order to get new customers, not paying attention to current ones. It is also argued that collective incentives systems create a bureaucratic mentality in the workers which does not encourage individual creativity: the employees correctly manage walk-in customers but they have few incentives to look for new business opportunities.

Attaining a high degree of information about the specific circumstances of each customer is one of the characteristics of relationship banking. The usual information regarding age, occupation and the contracted products is considered insufficient. More information on the following matters is needed: customer investments, other sources of financing used, and information concerning matters of a personal nature (marital status, number and age of children, inheritances). In the case of small firms, such as professionals and the retail segment, private and business matters continuously overlap, so that, in order to identify the combination of more adequate financial products to solve their specific problems, more information is required about the particular situation and business of each customer. This type of information is only obtained on the basis of a close relationship established between the employees and the customer. Given the confidential character of this information, its transmission within a branch logically requires informal procedures. In order to maintain this contact and relationship with the customer, the substitution of one worker for another means that the new employee should work for some time alongside his predecessor to gain access to this specific information and at the same time to familiarise himself with the specific problems of customers.

Last, the processes of downsizing as a means of acquiring greater flexibility and competitiveness in costs present very well-known advantages through improvements in communication and in the decision-making processes and removing inconveniences that have not been considered in many cases. Downsizing breaks with a complex and subtle network of informal relationships between individuals and human teams supporting the whole organisational structure and the working routines within the firm (Timms and Finn 1996).[5]

Any organisation, besides having a purely technical component, implies an important social factor, of an informal type, based on personal relationships and the knowledge of the actual organisation, the accumulation and consolidation of which takes time. Problem-solving in a team produces shared experiences and a strong feeling of collective commitment which is used as a basis to solve future problems. All members use their knowledge of the organisation and their own reputation, influence and personal relationships to 'sell' their ideas and projects, and get the support of top management and the resources necessary to carry them out. Downsizing breaks with the former network of existing relationships and the high level of employee turnover hinders the creation of a new network, contributing very little to the creation and consolidation of the organisational capabilities necessary to develop relationship banking.

3.4 Conclusions

The development and diffusion of ITs are causing substantial changes in the way banking products are provided and distributed to customers. New IT and telecommunications networks allow the decentralised use of computing and software. The growth of the IT services market means that it is possible to exploit economies of scale in data processing and in the application of software. This growth induces banks to spin-off those activities which present diseconomies of scope with their core competencies (especially those which are computer and telecommunications intensive) and to subcontract them to independent specialised service firms. This is already happening. However, in some areas substantial innovation rents can be generated by installing sophisticated and highly specialised software. These investments are a potential source of competitive advantage which must be protected.

Some banks have invested heavily in IT and have taken on a temporary, part-time labour force as a means of reducing costs. These banks have moved away from many of their traditional sources of competitive advantage based on relationship banking. Price and convenience are considered as the major sources of competitive appeal. However, a bank can also give customers greater value by offering higher levels of financial advice and quality of service. It must also respond to changing needs with innovative products and employ new ITs without losing customer contact as a means of generating market information and 'bundling effects'. Banks can reap the benefits of relationship banking if they commit themselves to creating strong internal labour markets and reducing employee turnover.

Notes

1. Specially those rules governing the changes in the firm's property structure and the concentration of bank's industrial risk. For instance, with the notable exception of 'section 20 provisions', commercial banks in the USA are not allowed to own shares of non-financial firms on their own account

at all. Ownership of non-financial firms by banks is unrestricted in Germany and limited to 5 per cent in the Netherlands (Roe 1990).

2. This section relies heavily on Wieland (1993). See also Chorafas and Steinmann (1988) and Steiner and Texeira (1990).

3. The consulting firm Booz, Allen and Hamilton considers that the economies of scale associated with cheque transactions are not obtained until they reach a monthly volume of about 25 million cheques; in the USA only the largest banks reach such volumes (Wieland, 1993).

4. In Germany, in particular, Deutsche Bank, Commerzbank and Dresdner Bank own large blocks of industrial and trading firms over which they have the right to gather proxy votes from small investors or from other banks (Kester 1992). In addition, the bargaining power of German banks may be high as a result of the large number of their supervisory board places (Schneider-Lenné 1994).

5. Similar arguments have also been used in order to explain the effects of downsizing on productivity. It is said that the processes of downsizing improve the productivity of the company. However, there is not a clear causal connection between downsizing and the improvement of productivity. Jensen (1988) argues that downsizing lightens the company by reducing excess personnel and salaries thus permitting resources to be used in a more productive way.

References

Baldwin, C. (1991), 'What is the future of banking: a debate', *Harvard Business Review*, July–August, pp. 145–6

Barlow, R. (1990), 'Building customer satisfaction, market share and profitability: findings from Sweden', *The Bankers Magazine*, May/June

Bergendahl, G. and T. Lindblom (1996), *The Future of Relationship Banking*, paper presented at the European Association of University Teachers of Banking and Finance, 1996 Annual Seminar, 4–8 September, Malta

Chorafas, D. and H. Steinmann (1988), *Implementing Networks In Banking and Financial Services*, Basingstoke: Macmillan (– now Palgrave)

Fornell, C. (1992), 'A national customer satisfaction barometer: the Swedish experience', *Journal of Marketing*, January, 56(1), pp. 6–21

Guiltinan, J.P. (1989), 'The price bundling of services: a normative framework', in J.E.G. Bateson, *Managing Service Marketing*, Chicago: The Dryden Press

Jensen, M.C. (1988), 'Takeovers: their causes and consequences', *Journal of Economic Perspectives*, 2, pp. 21–48

Keltner, B. (1995), 'Relationship banking and competitive advantage: evidence from the US and Germany', *California Management Review*, 7(4), Summer, pp. 45–72

Kester, W.C. (1992), 'Governance, contracting and investment horizons: a look at Japan and Germany', *Journal of Applied Corporate Finance*, 5, pp. 83–98

Langlois, R. (1988), 'Economic change and the boundaries of the firm', *Journal of Institutional and Theoretical Economics*, 144, pp. 636–57

Minnerop, H.F. and H.R. Stoll (1986), 'Technological change in the back-office: implications for structure and regulations of the securities industry', in

A. Saunders and L. White (eds), *Technology and the Regulation of the Financial Markets*, Lexington, Mass.: Lexington Books, pp. 31–46

Myers, S. (1977), 'Determinants of corporate borrowing', *Journal of Financial Economics*, **5**, pp. 147–75

Penrose, P. (1990), 'The back-office takes a bow', *Banking Technology*, July/August, pp. 24–7

Reichheld, F.F. (1993), 'Loyalty-based management', *Harvard Business Review*, March–April, pp. 64–73

Reichheld, F.F. and E.W. Sasser (1990), 'Zero defections: quality comes to services', *Harvard Business Review*, September–October, pp. 105–11

Revell, J. (1983), *Banking and electronic funds transfers*, Paris: OECD

Roe, M.J. (1990), 'Political and legal restraints on ownership and control of public companies', *Journal of Financial Economics*, **27**, pp. 7–41

Schleifer, A. and L.H. Summers (1988), 'Breach of trust in hostile takeovers', in A.J. Auerbach (ed.), *Corporate Takeovers: Causes and Consequences*, Chicago: University of Chicago Press

Schmerken, I. (1990), 'Wall Street back offices: the 1990s avant-garde', *Wall Street Computer Review*, February, pp. 44–64

Schneider-Lenné, E. (1994), 'The role of German capital markets and the universal banks, supervisory boards, and interlocking directorships', in N. Dimsdale and M. Prevezer (eds), *Capital Markets and Corporate Governance*, New York: Oxford University Press

Steiner, T. and D. Texeira (1990), *Technology In Banking*, Homewood, Ill: Dow-Jones

Stigler, G.J. (1968), *The Organisation of Industry*, Chicago: University of Chicago Press

Teece, D.J. (1986), 'Profiting from technological innovation: implications for integration, collaboration, licensing and public policy', *Research Policy*, **15**, pp. 285–305

Timms, B. and R. Finn (1996), 'Banking on a wise investment in human resources', *People Management*, **2**(4), pp. 32–5

Totonis, H. and R. Spitler (1990), 'Operating services: new lines of business', *Bank Management*, August, pp. 16–24

Von Weizsäcker, C.C. (1991), 'Antitrust and the division of labour', *Journal of Institutional and Theoretical Economics*, **147**, pp. 99–113

Wieland, B.W. (1993), 'Economic change and industry structure: the example of banking', *Journal of Institutional and Theoretical Economics*, **149**(4), pp. 670–89

Williamson, O.E. (1986), *Economic Organisation*, Brighton: Whitesheaf

4
Emerging Methods of Payment
Jack Revell

4.1 Introduction

For the purposes of this study I must establish a starting point from which the new methods of payment emerged – the position in the middle of the 1960s perhaps, although it would not have made much difference if I had chosen the 1970s. For the present audience, coming from nearly all the countries of Western Europe, I must present a general picture and not dwell on the considerable differences in payment systems between all the countries. At that time computers were used only for maintaining the running records of the payment accounts kept with banks, savings banks and postal giros, but the payment instructions used for transfers between accounts were all paper instruments. Countries differed mainly in the proportions of giro transfers, which start with the debtor's account being debited, and cheque transfers, in which the creditor's account is credited before the debtor's account is debited. Because giro transfers are not very convenient for normal shopping, notes and coin are more frequently used for small value transactions in giro countries than in cheque using countries, where cheques are often written for amounts as low as, say, four or five ECUs.

Questions concerning the safety of various forms of payment will arise later and it is, therefore, useful to make a general point about the difference between cheques and giro transfers in this respect. Creditors can safely accept cheques in payment of purchases or debts only if the debtor's creditworthiness can be established at the time, and this can be done in two ways. The first, which applied far more in the 1960s than it does today, is from a lengthy personal knowledge of the debtor, and the second is if the cheque is backed by a bank guarantee (in

France a legal guarantee of all small value cheques). This is why banks issued cheque guarantee cards to those of their customers who were deemed creditworthy when cheques became much more widely used. The giro system has no such disadvantage and there is no risk. There is a parallel with the latest real-time gross settlement (RTGS) circuits for high value payments. Giro transfers are gross settlements, even if they do not take place in real time.

What happened after the mid-1960s was fairly common to all Western European countries, although the time at which the changes were made and the exact form of the changes continued to differ. The main changes can be summarised briefly as follows:

- the extensive use of plastic cards for various purposes
- the application of automation to special payment circuits for regular, fairly small value payments for salaries, loan repayments, insurance premiums and subscriptions and, eventually, for very high value payments

These changes had one thing in common: they provided substitutes for paper instruments like cheques and (less so) giro transfers, and also to a varying extent for notes and coin. If we follow plastic cards through the various forms that they took, we shall arrive on the threshold of the modern era, with its new, emerging methods of payment.

4.2 Plastic cards

Plastic cards are about the only standardised items in the payment systems of different countries, standardised that is as to size and shape. They started as a means of identification of the holder as somebody entitled to benefit from a particular service. The first such service, in the USA at least, was the credit card, but in some other countries they were first used as cheque guarantee cards. Soon after they were furnished with a magnetic stripe on the back to give details of the holder's account and a security number or PIN (personal identification number). They could then be used to withdraw banknotes from cash dispensers or automated teller machines (ATMs).

Perhaps the most important characteristic of plastic cards is that they are very versatile and adaptable: in the UK, the MasterCard credit card has an advertising slogan of 'my flexible friend'. It is not surprising, therefore, that both the guarantee cards and credit cards often perform exactly the same functions, the only difference between them being the delay before the cardholder's account is debited. For example, either a credit card or a guarantee card (called a debit card in this function) can be used for electronic shopping (EFTPOS), and the delay, or float, in the UK is about four or five days for a debit card and anything up to about 50 days for a credit card, the period for the latter depending on the timing of purchases.

4.3   Credit cards

Towards the end of the 1980s several important changes occurred in the UK credit card system; some of them were common throughout Western Europe and some of them later extended to the debit cards used in EFTPOS. The first was that it became possible to pay for purchases by credit card at a distance by quoting the holder's card number through the post or over the telephone, the technical term for this is 'card not present', and it became a very convenient way of ordering and paying for theatre seats, transport tickets, books, and even charges for Wolpertinger Club seminars! In the UK this was particularly important because the credit card became even more of a substitute for cheques and one, moreover, that avoided all the foreign exchange hassle when buying goods and services from abroad. This new function undoubtedly played a large part in the surge in card use in this period. It was a new method of payment in the areas mentioned.

It was also in the late 1980s that new methods of organising the processing of credit card vouchers and, later, the debit card transactions of EFTPOS came into effect in the UK. Up to that stage there were only two 'merchant acquirers', as they were called: Barclays Bank for Visa cards and a consortium of the other major banks for MasterCard. Their function was to collect the transaction vouchers from traders, which they passed on to the issuing banks, and arrange for the payment of the traders and the banks. At the end of the 1980s the MasterCard consortium broke up, leaving each of the member banks to act as merchant acquirers. New banks entered the market for merchant acquisition and a price war broke out, reducing profit margins. All sorts of banks now compete fiercely to act as merchant acquirer for individual traders.

At first sight this seems an entirely laudable bringing of competition to a stagnant market, but I am not so sure. It is in such processing services as this that most of the economies of scale in banking are to be found, and the new system has fewer realized economies of scale than the former one. I think it will not be long before this particular form of processing goes the same way as two other processing services in the financial system, correspondent banking and global custody. Banks with small operations in the field are selling these services to a few banks, not necessarily large in total assets but prepared to achieve economies of scale by specialising in this and similar processing services.

If that stage is reached in merchant acquisition there is little to object to, but in my opinion it has already caused considerable damage to the overall shape of the payment system. There are two examples, the first of which was the attitude of the UK banks to setting up an EFTPOS system. In the middle of the 1980s the banks invested many millions of pounds on a scheme to link the terminals in shops and supermarkets to the transactors' bank accounts by the packet-switched public data network. It would have been a real-time gross settlement system several years before that phrase became common. My immediate point is that the banks stopped the scheme because it had no place in it for merchant acquisition. It is one thing to praise merchant acquisition as competitive, but when it becomes the reason for stifling before birth a completely secure system, which would eventually have gone beyond the debit cards of electronic shopping to credit cards and to practically all other retail payments that were not already covered by automated networks, and which would still have allowed banks to compete as before on the conditions attached to each customer's account, this is a far less praiseworthy action. I do not know whether any other European countries have a system of merchant acquisition like that of the UK.

4.4 Chip cards and prepaid cards

The second example is to be found in the realm of chip cards and prepaid cards. There are many terms used. Chip cards are referred to as 'integrated circuit cards' by central banks, but journalists prefer 'smart cards'. They were pioneered largely in France in the early 1980s but banks in most other countries were not willing to pay the extra cost involved in embodying an integrated circuit (or chip) in cards hitherto using magnetic stripes for operation. What tipped the balance in the UK was a tremendous increase in fraud losses on plastic cards in 1990 and a belated realization that the chip would have spare space for incorporating other value-added services. They are likely to be added to credit cards in the near future.

Apart from the additional security that microchips bring to plastic cards, they have one other attribute, that of being able to store quite a large amount of information, including money balances. It is this ability that makes them suitable for use as prepaid (or prepayment) cards, also known as electronic purses, which could eventually reduce the use of notes and coin for small value payments to a great extent and also substitute somewhat for the use of giro transfers and cheques. It is the substitution for notes and coin that is the more interesting of these possibilities because their production and distribution are very costly parts of the payment system. The key to a large substitution of prepaid cards for notes and coin is that the cards should be easy to use in interpersonal transactions, including the purchase of items like newspapers, bars of chocolate or even small packets of pipe tobacco from street vendors, market stalls and small shops without the need for change being given.

Two alternative systems have been proposed. The first is Mondex, which can be recharged at specially adapted telephones or ATMs and can be used for telephone transactions with people who also have the adapted telephone. Since it is a giro-like system, in that the purchaser is offering undoubted money and not a piece of paper, there is no need for anybody to worry about the creditworthiness of the payer and the system can be opened to individuals without their having the qualifications for holding a credit card. Mondex is a complete substitute for notes and coin: it is completely anonymous, and neither purchases nor receipts have to be accounted for to anybody, except theoretically to the tax authorities on occasion.

The other contender for the title of electronic purse is the one put forward by the international credit card organisations, Visa and MasterCard, and consists of having a microchip in the card to store money acquired from an ATM. This will enable cardholders to go some way towards reducing their demand for notes and coin for small value purchases but, because it has no place for interpersonal transactions, it will not extend the facility beyond those already deemed creditworthy enough to have a credit card. Its impact on the use of notes and coin will be much less than that of Mondex. The credit card associations emphasize the point that their scheme will be fully accountable, which will endear it to the tax authorities, but the public will not be impressed because Mondex will operate just like notes and coins and by being completely non-accountable. I would back the mass system that Mondex promises against the accountable credit card system, even though I know that Mondex will allow certain people to continue to evade some taxes.

An article in the professional press gave a hint on the way that the argument will go. According to the 1994 ruling of the European

Monetary Institute, prepaid cards are acceptable only if they are issued by banks, which must count the money with which prepaid cards are charged as deposits. Both schemes fulfil that requirement but the article pointed out an essential difference between the two schemes: the card associations' scheme allows the continuance of merchant acquisition, whereas Mondex has no place for it. I fear that the majority of banks will line up with the credit card (and debit card) scheme for that reason, especially as less investment will be required because they are on the point of introducing microchips on their cards for security reasons. It will be a shame if merchant acquisition is once again allowed to thwart a scheme that would greatly improve the efficiency of the payment system.

4.5   The Internet

The Internet has attracted the attention of economists during the past few years in a way that few other information technology systems have. Some have written on the possibilities for selling all sorts of goods and services, some about the way in which it could transform electronic data interchange (EDI) for commercial interchange between all sorts of companies, suppliers, manufacturers and retailers, and yet others about ways in which it could turn home banking into something much more popular than at present. Behind all these and other commercial uses for the Internet lies the question of payment for the goods and services purchased. This has excited some economists to speculate whether any of the possible forms of Internet money will be entirely different from existing forms of money and will make the present methods of operating monetary policy impossible or much more difficult.

There are several methods either in existence or envisaged for the near future. One criterion against which all will be judged is that of security, protection against hackers either intervening in the transaction or obtaining information that could be used in fraudulent transactions. In the USA hackers are now so well organised that they have recently formed their own trade association. The first system uses existing methods to contact your bank and ask it to make a bank transfer or by writing a cheque and posting it to the seller; the disadvantage is that the transaction has to be split into two parts, the first part on the Internet and a subsequent part for paying off the Internet trader, but there are no new risks. A variant on this is to use a trusted third party (TTP), which need not be a bank. Both the buyer and the TTP have to be registered with the seller on the Internet, and the TTP's function is to act as broker and to contact your bank with instructions to make the payment. This seems to me to be only a more complicated method of contacting your bank.

One obvious method is to use credit cards, either the normal kind or the prepaid (electronic purse) variety, using the 'card not present' operation. Since this involves giving a credit card number in clear, it enables a hacker to collect the numbers and to use them fraudulently. The only answer is encryption of the numbers, and the credit card associations claim to have provided complete security. This is somewhat doubtful because the USA security organisations (the 'spooks') still refuse to allow what is called 'strong encryption' to be exported since that would hinder their efforts to penetrate messages used by the drug trade and money launderers.

The last method of payment is the use of electronic money, of which there are at least two forms, the better known of which is Digicash, issued by an organisation in Amsterdam. The money consists of unique numbers in digital, binary form. I do not know what link there is with a bank, but the second form, the American Cybercash, arranges for a bank to hold the funds in an escrow account. Cybercash seems to realize that the intervention of a bank is essential for acceptance by the public of these forms of electronic money.

I have used the term 'electronic money' but it is worth pausing to consider whether these Internet instruments are truly money. I think they are really tokens usable only in restricted circumstances, of which there are plenty of examples. The one point they have in common is that they must be acquired and paid for by normal money before they can be used, and this brings electronic money, and indeed electronic purses, into line with traveller's cheques, books of tickets for buses, trams and metro, and plastic cards for telephone calls or bridge and motorway tolls. In other words, they are not revolutionary and they will not cause more trouble for those carrying out monetary policy than the famous non-bank financial intermediaries of the 1960s and 1970s which provided close substitutes for money by allowing their savings deposits to be withdrawn on demand for the Saturday shopping.

5
Dimensions of Actions Distribution

Marcel R. Creemers

Abstract

Most business scientists define (financial) services as intangible products. If this is so, how then can one distribute services? The concept of service distribution is borrowed from the mass goods industry, but service suppliers have had problems applying the concept in their environment. The services industry needs a new approach to distribution, through which it can escape from the tangible/intangible discussion.

In this chapter, a concept of actions (instead of goods) distribution is proposed. Service products are actions mainly and the question is how actions are to be distributed. This can only be done by making actors (employees, computers) available to the customers. Three dimensions of actions distribution can be distinguished: access, availability and functionality. Scores on these three dimensions characterise service distribution channels and make them comparable.

5.1   Introduction

The Internet appears to create many new business opportunities for sellers of all kinds of goods and services. Many firms are expanding their distribution channel mix with electronic commerce facilities. There is practically no bank left without an Internet site full of information and, although simple, transaction opportunities for their customers. We have seen manufacturers, such as Cisco, enhancing their service by offering computerised product configuration help to potential buyers. We have seen new entrants too, but they have not been equally successful. So far, Amazon bookshop is an example of a very successful entry but others, such as the Security First Network Bank

71

(SFNB), just do not seem to get through. According to the *Economist* (1997), online business is likely to score when it adds extra value compared to the physical counterparts of the products, but what this added value might be and how it can be delivered is still unclear. To answer these questions, we must develop a different perspective on distribution, a well-known concept that has been successful for several decades but is becoming obsolete in the digital era.

5.2   Distribution concepts

It is not the first time in history that the distribution concept is being redefined. It has always been a moving target. In the Middle Ages most economies were dominated by agricultural activity. In those days, distribution of many goods was organised in networks of annual fairs in villages and cities. The calendars of these fairs were based on the time that merchants would need to travel from one place to another (Braudel 1979). Until the close of the eighteenth century, craft production was dominant and in this type of productive organisation, distribution was no more than the delivery of the single goods, simply because the output was unique and customer specific. But since then we have seen a gradual introduction of mass production in various economic sectors, starting with simple goods such as textiles and ending with the 'hi-tech', such as cars. When Henry Ford succeeded in the mass production of cars in 1913, mass distribution became important in the automotive industry too (Womack *et al.* 1990). This distribution concept is highly related to mass manufacturing of goods. Once goods are produced in one place, they must be split up and transported to many other places in order to enable the transfer and delivery to buyers. Since the Second World War we have seen a gradual shift towards mass customisation in manufacturing, which in essence is a trend towards client specific production. This trend has changed the distribution concept again because goods that are produced according to specific customer wishes lose their interchangeability with other goods, which makes distribution much more complex (Creemers 1993; Hoekstra and Romme 1992). Nevertheless, both in mass and modern manufacturing the core meaning of distribution is *making produced goods available to the customers.*

During the course of the 20th century and beyond the services industry has become dominant over both agriculture and manufacturing in most Western economies. The rise of this service economy has coincided with a shift from a craft to a mass (retail) orientation in the services industry as well. That is why it has become very common to use the term distribution as a label for the service delivery system, but this is definitely a distribution concept other than the one we use in manufacturing.

Services do not produce goods but must be viewed as (sequences of) actions (Creemers 1993) or 'a deed, a performance, an effort' (Berry 1980). But how does one distribute actions, performances or even a deed? Crucial in the performance of actions are those who perform. We call them actors, who/which can be people or machines, for example computers (Creemers 1993). And it is only through these actors that a supplier can distribute actions. This brings us to a definition of service distribution, which is somewhat parallel to goods distribution: *making actors available to the customers.*

Now it seems that we have two different definitions of distribution that apply in two different economic sectors, but this would not do justice to recent developments in the market. Due to tougher competition, manufacturers, retailers and wholesalers try to distinguish themselves by offering more complementary service components, such as helping customers with design, configuration, product choices, ordering, implementation, maintenance and the like. Today we see successful firms, such as Cisco, Dell Computers and Amazon bookshop adding more and more service elements to their physical products by making their computers available to customers through the Internet. Computer manufacturer Cisco, as an example, successfully introduced free of charge computerised help to its customers for configuring its products (*Information Week* 1997). These firms use the Internet as a distribution channel to make their actors available, even before anything has yet been sold. Transaction costs economists call this pre-stage of the transaction *ex ante* (Williamson 1985).

Amazon radically changed the art of selling books by introducing free (and also *ex ante*) computerised search facilities to support the customers' decision-making processes. This is what Champy *et al.* (1996) calls re-engineering the customer process, by which he means 'the steps that a person goes through to acquire and to use a product or service that fulfils a fundamental need'. The computers increase the added value for the customer and give the supplier a competitive advantage compared to manufacturers and sellers who do not make their actors available but restrict themselves to the traditional distribution concept of making goods available. This trend in modern distribution is what I refer to as the actions approach of distribution. Likewise, I prefer the term 'actions distribution' instead of 'service distribution'.

Actions distribution is important for both services and modern manufacturing. Electronic commerce makes actions distribution very important in the near future: it is a new distribution concept.

5.3   Types of actions

All actions are not alike. Lovelock (1991 p. 26) makes a distinction between tangible and intangible actions. Tangible actions are physical in the sense that they require the presence of the customer (for example, a hair cut or a taxi drive) or his/her possessions (for example, cleaning an office or garden services). Many actions are intangible, or rather *virtual*, in the sense that they can be performed at arm's length (such as payment processing or stock ordering) and that they can be initiated, controlled and terminated through telephone and telecommunication connections.

Many services consist of both physical and virtual actions, and in many situations we even do not distinguish between them. In a traditional bank branch, for example, we see numerous different actions being performed by various actors. The branch has long been the single physical place for the performance of financial service actions, both for physical actions and those that could be performed virtually. However, the last decade has shown a gradual process of unbundling between physical and virtual actions, and in co-development or the introduction of dedicated actors and means of actions distribution. Today we see ATMs performing physical actions such as cash dispensing and PC banking facilities for virtual actions.

This process of unbundling has often been justified as a cost-cutting operation but, perhaps as a side effect, it has opened the way to a further enhancement of customer value. Just like in the Amazon, Dell and Cisco cases, some banks have learned that they can add new virtual actions to their financial actions repertoire. Wells Fargo successfully experimented with sending personal automatic signals in the case of a negative account balance, combined with a solution proposal. UK banks and building societies offer a wide range of *ex ante* virtual actions related to mortgages, not just common calculations and product advice, but checklists for determining the quality of a house or for selecting a suitable living environment, explanations of mortgage related jargon, and the like. This is only the beginning of a change process in the financial industry, where we will see an Amazon like redefinition of retail banking in future.

This redefinition is not a matter of replacing physical actions with virtual actions, as the problematic development of five computerised loan origination systems (Hess and Kemerer 1994) has shown (see below), but rather a matter of enhancing customer value by adding *ex ante* virtual actions to physical ones. The physical actions are still needed and their quality has to be maintained. SFNB, the first bank to exist solely on the Internet, has shown that virtual actions alone are not enough to have a solid start on the web: the number of customers is relatively low (7000 in all 50 United States); total deposits are low ($20.1 m); the product offer is relatively simple. (All figures are as of November 1996, provided by SFNB's web pages.) For more complicated services, such as loans, and for physical actions, such as ATMs, traveller's cheques and safe boxes, SFNB has opened a dedicated city office.

5.4   Market-driven businesses

Making actors available to customers is only partly to do with the existing product or service itself. It has been mentioned above that modern manufacturers help customers make their *ex ante* decisions. They do so under the marketing assumption that satisfied customers are more likely to buy and that good customer relations are valuable over time (customer retention).

According to Day (1994 p. 49), market sensing and customer linking are important organisational capabilities. The market sensing capability determines 'how well the organisation is equipped to continuously sense changes in its market and to anticipate the responses to marketing actions'. The customer linking capability comprises 'the skills, abilities, and processes needed to achieve collaborative customer relationships so individual customer needs are quickly apparent to all functions and well-defined procedures are in place for responding to them'.

Making actors available to customers in the *ex ante* stage of transactions provides organisations with valuable information on how customers compare and decide, which is important as input for marketing processes.

5.5   Community building

Moreover, these available actors can be helpful in building virtual communities, a recent Internet development. Virtual communities are 'forming around groups of consumers with a common interest. The technology of the Internet gives these people an unprecedented means of interacting with each other, and with providers of goods and services, to achieve their goals.' (Champy *et al.* 1996)

A well-known virtual community is Parent Soup, in which parents communicate, discuss and give each other advice on a variety of family related topics (Parent Soup 1997). Manufacturers of relevant goods (toys, baby products, books, software) are invited to participate in the discussions and supply the community members with appropriate research. Parent Soup sets up 'bridge sites' (closely linked companion web sites) for participating manufacturers (such as a site for the children's cough syrup Triaminic), containing parenting information, including child safety tips. One of the preconditions for participating in a virtual community is that the organisation's actors (employees, computers) are highly available on the Internet, communicating with customers in the *ex ante* stage of transactions.

5.6 Dimensions of actions distribution

To get physical actions performed, either the customer has to go to an office or a machine, or the supplier has to visit the customer (or his or her possessions). For the performance of a virtual action, some electronic connection must be established between the supplier and the customer, or between their computers. In all cases availability of the supplier's actors is involved. Availability as such is not what customers are looking for. It is only a precondition to make an actor perform the right actions. At the same time, availability has no value if the customer cannot utilise appropriate means of access. Putting this together, there are three key issues in actions distribution: access, availability and functionality.

Access
A service without access to the performing actors is not viable. Access, however, is not a very strict concept since it depends on time and place. A customer at home in the evening will not have access to employees in offices that close at 5 p.m., but he will have access to computers through the Internet. On the other hand, while shopping downtown, entering a (physical) bookshop in the street may be easier or more attractive than accessing a virtual bookstore on the Internet. In general, however:

- access is *high* when a customer can contact a supplier's actor immediately and without having to leave the working or living area. This is the case when the actors work in a dense branch network (for a retail bank, less than 20 000 potential customers per branch) or are accessible through electronic means such as telephone (call centre, GSM) or datacommunication (electronic data interchange, Internet, PC applications)

- access is *medium* when a customer has to leave his working or living area to contact a supplier's actor. This is the case when a supplier has few branches (for a retail bank, between 20 000 and 200 000 potential customers per branch) or is accessible by telephone only during working hours
- access is *low* when the actors work in only one or a few branches (for a retail bank, more than 200 000 potential customers per branch) or are accessible only through mail (mail order firm).

Availability

Although access is the first precondition of actions distribution, it does not say a thing about what access brings to the customer. Even the Internet and dense office network may have congestions and queues, appropriate actors may be absent, or computers may be down. All this is a matter of availability of actors, which depends on the supplier's resource and business process management. Looking from a business process design perspective, there are three forms of availability:

- availability is *high* in interactive business processes where actors are immediately available to customers throughout the entire service process. A well-staffed helpdesk, a fire department, and a fault tolerant on-line computer are examples of actors with high availability scores
- availability is *medium* in transaction oriented processes where actors are also available to customers throughout the entire service process, though not immediately and not constantly. Many professionals (management consultants, programmers, dentists) are actors with medium availability scores
- availability is *low* when actors perform their actions according to the supplier's time scheme, without being influenced by the customer. This low availability is the case in many governmental services and in simple actions such as cheque handling.

Functionality

And then, when actors are accessible and available, what can they do for the customer? The actor's functionality and degrees of freedom to respond to customer wishes are important here. Functionality can be low or high, due to the capabilities of the actor it/him/herself. On the other hand, functionality is sometimes limited due to policy, regulations and legislation. In other words, suppliers do not, or cannot, always offer full functionality to customers. Examples are local government officials (who obey regulations and legislation), selling personnel in fast food restaurants (part of the formula), or a driver in public transport compared to a taxi driver (due to the transport system).

● functionality is *high* when an actor has a broad function repertoire and is free to choose service actions that add optimal customer value
● functionality is *medium* when the actor's repertoire is limited due to policy, regulations or legislation, or due to technological restrictions
● functionality is *low* when the actor can only perform one type of action (for example, bank ATMs).

5.7   Analysing distribution channels

With these three dimensions we can now analyse and compare existing distribution channels and, eventually, find opportunities for improvement. The scores on the dimensions of each channel can be represented by a graph, such as in Figure 5.1.

Figure 5.1: Scoring distribution characteristics

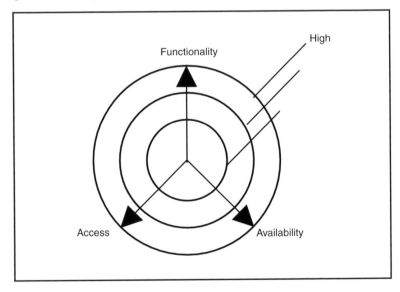

In Section 5.8, the three dimensions will be tested by comparing various distribution channels: a physical and virtual book shop, retail banking branch and banking on the Internet.

Book shops

If we characterise distribution in a physical book shop with employees, in a shopping centre of a middle-sized city, according to the three distribution dimensions, then we are likely to find the following scores:

- *access is low*: the employees work in the book shop, which may be part of a large chain of shops (like Barnes and Noble, but even with 1000 outlets in the US, access is low)
- *availability is low*: the number of employees visible in book shops is generally low and they often are busy with administrative and logistic work. So, they have relatively little time left for answering customer questions about alternative authors, titles and content. Of course these employees may be very willing to talk to individual customers, but if they do, they are not available to other customers
- *functionality is high*: employees potentially have a broad function repertoire with which they can serve customers. They sometimes can discuss content, search for alternative titles and authors in various computer systems, and even serve a cup of coffee.

Figure 5.2: Characteristics of a physical book shop

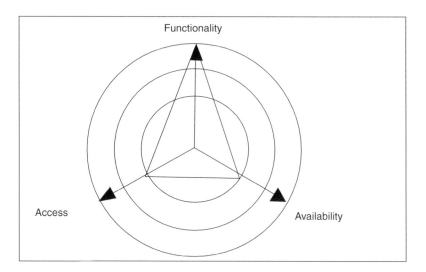

If we compare the distribution characteristics of this physical book shop with those of a virtual book shop on the Internet, like Amazon.com, we find considerable differences:

- *access is high*: the Internet provides high access (24 hours a day, 7 days a week) to the virtual book store computers
- *availability is high*: virtual book shops make their computers available to help customers to make a multitude of choices. Availability of these computers is high
- *functionality is low or medium*: computers have limited functions and, moreover, they can only work properly when they are provided with a correct and complete set of instructions from the customer.

This analysis makes clear that physical book shops have been designed primarily to make books available rather than the shop actors, whereas the virtual book shop is designed primarily to make the shop actors available and not so much the books themselves. This is why we may say that Amazon has changed the art of selling books by placing the books in the background and building its leading distribution channel for *ex ante* virtual actions. The same holds for Cisco in the computer and communications industry.

Figure 5.3: Characteristics of a virtual book shop

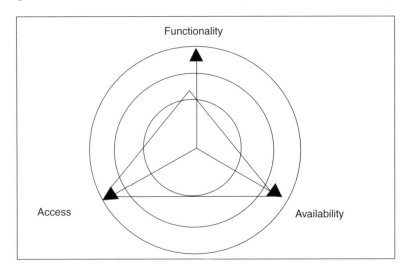

Retail financial services

In the area of retail financial services we can compare a traditional bank branch with a virtual bank too. Any type of actors may be selected for this comparison, but since we are most interested in *ex ante* actions, we will focus on employees and systems with advisory functions. This brings the following scores for employees in the branch:

- *access is medium or high*: most retail banks have dense branch networks in their working area. In most of these branches we find financial advisers
- *availability is low or medium*: the employees in the branch are not immediately available to customers. They may be busy with another customer inside or outside the bank branch. Making appointments for financial advice is very common
- *functionality is high*: as soon as a qualified employee is available, the functionality of this employee is high.

A virtual bank, such as SFNB, using computers on the web, is likely to have the following scores:

- *access is high*: the Internet provides high access (24 hours a day, 7 days a week)

Figure 5.4: Characteristics of a physical branch

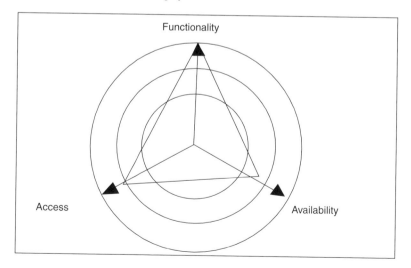

- *availability is high*: virtual banks have highly available computers
- *functionality is low*: computers have limited functionality.

From this comparison, we can learn that the differences between physical and virtual banks are somewhat smaller than those of book shops. Of course, bank branches have never been designed to make goods available to customers: they have always been channels of actions distribution. However, there are differences.

The physical branches' weakest point is the availability of the actors and this may be why many retail banks are today experimenting with electronic and telephone banking through call centres (KPMG 1997). These new electronic means are likely to increase both accessibility and availability. However, only telephone banking may leave functionality untouched, depending on how the call centre is staffed, whereas electronic means, such as the Internet and PC banking, bring only low or medium functionality.

The virtual bank's weakest point is functionality and this may be why they just do not succeed in financial services, no matter how high their access and availability may be. Financial services require higher functionality than book shops, because the customer's decisions are more complex. There are only two ways to solve this: provide the customer

Figure 5.5: Characteristics of a virtual bank

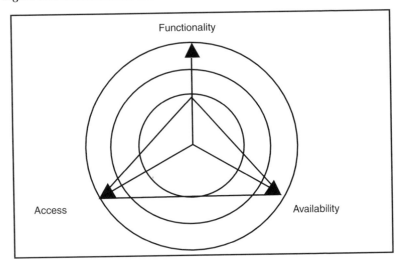

with software that supports the customer's decisions (for example, Microsoft's Money or Intuit's Quicken); introduce a call centre to which online customers are automatically linked when they need high quality advice. Such a call centre does not improve accessibility or availability, but it does increase functionality, provided that it is well staffed.

It is not the intention of the analysis above to propose that only the highest distribution scores are the best. Some types of services and manufacturing may very well match with low scores on one or more dimensions. The point is that, due to customer demands or due to increasing competition, improvements may be necessary. Actual scores may even be too high. Frequent flyers of several airline companies have been offered a software package with which they can search for convenient connections and flight numbers, and even book flights according to their wishes. With these facilities, the airline companies intended to bypass intermediaries, such as travel agencies, but not every customer could handle the complexity of this task properly. Flying as a customer is very different from searching and booking. Many of those customers have stopped using the software. In terms of distribution dimensions, the airline companies have offered high access, high availability (desk top), and *too* high functionality.

Therefore, the term rightsizing distribution channels is introduced here. Rightsizing a distribution channel means changing the channel characteristics of access, availability and functionality in order to bring the distribution quality to the desired level.

5.8 Actions distribution research

To determine the value of the actions distribution concept in research, a study will be reviewed and reinterpreted in terms of actions distribution dimensions. Hess and Kemerer (1994) investigated the life cycle of five electronic mortgage systems (CLOs) that were introduced as potential electronic market systems (multiple suppliers, transparently competing on the same electronic network) in the USA in the 1980s:

- First Boston Shelternet;
- PRC Advanced Systems Inc.'s LoanExpress;
- Rennie Mae, developed by a realtor's association;
- Prudential's CLOS;
- Citicorp's Mortgage Power Plus.

These systems had in common that they were installed in many estate agents' (realtors') offices, enabling both agent and customer to select and secure a mortgage.

The researchers hypothesised that customers, in this case borrowers, will be driven by their desire for lower interest and closing costs to favour electronic markets over electronic hierarchies (a single supplier system). The authors stress the importance of time and money savings, and not that of *ex ante* or virtual actions. The results show that none of the systems has been able to develop into an electronic market system, although they reduced the time and effort on the part of prospective borrowers to select and secure a loan.

Peculiarly, it appeared that the most successful system, the one with the highest loan volume, was a hierarchical system solely used by Citicorp. The authors had to conclude that the results give very little support for their hypothesis. However, when the mortgage systems and procedure descriptions are reinterpreted in the perspective of action distribution, it appears that the newly introduced actors (the mortgage systems) performed only few *ex ante* actions and did not improve the current distribution characteristics.

Both First Boston's Shelternet and Citicorp's Mortgage Power Plus performed some *ex ante* actions to support the customer's choice. The other systems were not much more than automated (rate and cost) listing services. Moreover, the introduction of the systems did not improve the current distribution characteristics. In the new situation:

- *access* was low or medium, since all entry points were located at a limited number of existing agent's offices. Some of the systems printed application forms, which had to be posted for further processing. In some cases customers even had to visit more than one office. Out of the five systems, the Citicorp system had the best access scores
- *availability* was high, but for only a limited number of actions, such as selecting the loan. In some systems large parts of the processing was still paper based and batchwise. Out of the five systems, the Citicorp system had the best availability scores
- *functionality* was low: the systems did not outperform the agent's nor the banker's quality. Both the First Boston and the Citicorp systems had the best functionality scores.

From the actions distribution perspective, the most successful implementation was Citicorp's Mortgage Power Plus with both some *ex ante* actions and the best distribution scores. This system appeared to generate the highest loan volume.

5.9   Implications

Comparing the problems of the five mortgage systems with the successes of the Amazon bookshop, Cisco and Dell computers, leads us to the hypothesis that electronic markets can only succeed through added customer value in terms of *ex ante* virtual actions and actions distribution improvements. On the other hand, it must be clear that offering *ex ante* support is much more difficult in financial services than in consumer goods. So, consumer goods markets profit more from communication technology than do more complex financial markets. This has been suggested by the *Economist* (1997) and has so far not been challenged by SFNB, which sells loans only in its single (physical) city office. The actions distribution approach postulates that this is due to difficulties in finding:

- either electronic actors who combine suitable functionality with their high access and high availability
- or human actors who are highly accessible and available.

Given these difficulties, it would be advisable for financial service suppliers to look for opportunities to participate in financial virtual communities, and to co-develop functionality with community members.

References

Berry, L. (1980), 'Services marketing is different', *Business*, May–June

Braudel, F. (1979), *Beschaving, Ecomonie en kapitalisme (15de–18de eeuw)*, deel 2: Het Spel van de Handel. Translated from French: *Civilisation matérielle, Economie et Capitalisme XVe–XVIIIe siècle*. Tome 2: Les Jeux de l' échange

Champy, J., J.B. Buday and N. Nohria (1996), 'The rise of the electronic community', *Information Week*, July (and available on the Internet: http://www.cscindex.com)

Creemers, M.R. (1993), *Transaction Engineering, Process Design and Information Technology Beyond Interchangeability*, doctoral thesis, University of Amsterdam

Day, G.S. (1994), 'The capabilities of market-driven organisations', *Journal of Marketing*, 58 (October), pp. 37–52

Economist (1997), 'A survey of electronic commerce', *Economist*, 10 May

Hess, M., and C.F. Kemerer (1994), 'Computerised loan origination systems: an industry case study of the electronic markets hypothesis', *MIS Quarterly*, September, pp. 251–75

Hoekstra, S. and J. Romme (1992), *Integral Logistic Structures, Developing Customer-oriented Goods Flow*, London: McGraw-Hill

Information Week (1997), 'Electronic commerce strictly business', 22 March

KPMG, *Distribution in Retail Banking, A Change of Style*, 1997

Lovelock, C.H. (1991), *Services Marketing*, 2nd edn, New Jersey: Prentice-Hall

Parent Soup, http://www.parentsoup.com, 5 August 1997
SFNB's web site, http://www.sfnb.com, November 1996
Williamson, O.E. (1985), *The Economic Institutions of Capitalism*, New York: The
   Free Press
Womack, J.P., D.T. Daniels and D. Rose (1990), *The Machine that Changed the
   World*, New York: Macmillan

6
Card Payments: Pricing and Competition*

*Ted Lindblom***

6.1 Introduction

As in most other countries in the EU, the relative importance of plastic cards as payment media has grown substantially over the past ten years in Sweden. At the end of the 1980s only about one in twenty cashless transactions was card based. During the 1990s this figure more than doubled and today payment cards are used in more than one in ten transactions.[1]

To a certain extent the relative growth of card payments may be explained by a gradual reduction in the use of cheques. However, card payments are also becoming a major substitute for the use of ready money. This is especially true for the retail sector, where almost every single retailer, regardless of its size, location or type of business, is now accepting payment cards as a means of payment. Even supermarket chains are accepting them. According to an investigation by Karp (1997) about as many as one out of five retail payments are card based in Sweden.

There are several reasons for the increasing use of payment cards for ordinary purchases in retail stores. One obvious reason is the remarkable rate of expansion of the number of EFTPOS (electronic funds transfer at the point of sale) terminals. Between 1990 and 1994 the number of terminals operated by banks more than quadrupled, from 6090 to 25 536. Even more astounding, the number of terminals more than doubled between 1994 and 1995. As is shown in Table 6.1, the development in Sweden (together with that in the Netherlands) is rather exceptional in comparison to the development in the other EU countries.[2]

Although EFTPOS terminals are not necessary for the processing of card payments, they do definitely make them more convenient to the

Table 6.1: Number of EFTPOS terminals in EU countries (1990–95)

Country	1990		1991		1992		1993		1994		1995
Austria	678	(54.9%)	1 050	(42.5%)	1 496	(22.4%)	1 831	(31.6%)	2 410	(40.3%)	3 382
Belgium	23 616	(12.5%)	26 578	(22.3%)	32 495	(32.0%)	42 903	(16.5%)	49 983	(11.8%)	55 883
Denmark[a]	15 804	(22.1%)	19 289	(16.2%)	22 411	(-2.8%)	21 778	(10.5%)	24 066	(8.9%)	26 214
Finland	26 500	(26.4%)	33 500	(16.4%)	39 000	(7.7%)	42 000	(14.3%)	48 000	(2.1%)	49 000
France[a,c]	n.a.		510 000	(2.0%)	520 000	(1.9%)	530 000	(1.9%)	540 000	(0.6%)	543 000
Germany[b]	23 152	(49.8%)	34 673	(49.4%)	51 806	(-46.0%)	28 000	(123.2%)	62 500	(12.1%)	70 048
Greece	n.a.		1 500	(66.7%)	2 500	(0.0%)	2 500	(351.8%)	11 296	(0.2%)	11 316
Ireland	0		0		0		0		0		0
Italy	22 185	(106.0%)	45 711	(36.2%)	62 251	(24.0%)	77 206	(34.8%)	104 051	(47.8%)	153 752
Luxembourg	n.a.		n.a.		n.a.		3 340	(9.7%)	3 663	(-8.2%)	3 340
Netherlands	2 223	(81.6%)	4 038	(183.3%)	11 440	(114.6%)	24 549	(93.8%)	47 588	(54.2%)	73 376
Portugal	n.a		n.a.		n.a.		n.a.		25 318	(16.0%)	29 364
Spain[a]	311 900	(-31.3%)	217 533	(20.4%)	261 949	(23.6%)	323 889	(23.6%)	400 184	(15.1%)	460 560
Sweden	6 090	(46.4%)	8 916	(60.1%)	14 276	(86.5%)	26 630	(-4.1%)	25 536	(113.8%)	54 589
UK[a]	110 000	(72.7%)	190 000	(15.8%)	220 000	(22.7%)	270 000	(29.6%)	350 000	(44.3%)	505 000

Notes:

1. n.a. – not available.
2. The percentage columns show the increase (or sometimes the decrease) in the number of EFTPOS terminals between two years, for example 1990–91, the number of terminals in Austria increased by 54.9 per cent = 1050/678.

a. number of machines.
b. from 1993 and onwards, 'electronic cash' and 'point of sale procedures' only. Non-bank systems are also included up to 1993.
c. estimated figures.

Source: Based on data from EMI (1996, incl. addendum) '*Payment Systems in the European Union*', Table 6.

customers as well as to the retailers. For one thing, paper based payments normally take longer to process and they are also somewhat riskier, especially for retailers and card issuers. It is harder to control that a customer does not exceed his/her balance or credit limit and that the card is valid. In an EFTPOS system such controls may be done on-line and, thus, access instantaneously to actual data.

Another reason for the more frequent use of payment cards around the world is that the number of cards in circulation has risen considerably: in Sweden the most common payment cards, that is, debit and credit cards, were almost four times as high at the end of 1994 as at the end of 1990.[3] In that respect Sweden does not differ from other European countries. However, unlike the development in many other countries, the increased number of payment cards in Sweden is assignable to debit cards only.[4] In fact the number of traditional credit cards in circulation has actually decreased over the period in question.[5]

The ordinary debit card is linked to a specific bank account of the possessor and in Sweden it is, therefore, referred to as a bank card.[6] Generally, the bank card combines different kinds of payment services. The possessor or cardholder may, for instance, use it for ordinary ATM withdrawals and point of sale payments (preferably electronic but also paper based). Furthermore, a majority of the bank cards may be used in foreign countries as well. Three out of four bank cards are linked to large international payment card (financial) organisations, like MasterCard and Visa.[7] Thus, the multifunctional nature of bank cards and their global usefulness may be regarded as vital explanations for the rapid growth in the number of possessors.

Along with the bank cards other new types of payment cards are emerging, too. These new cards are primarily issued by retailers, either by themselves (retailer cards) or together with a financial organisation (co-branded cards).[8,9] Both cards have in common that they may be either debit, credit or combined debit and credit cards. In that sense neither of them is different from the above mentioned bank cards. However, in contrast to a bank card or a traditional credit card, like American Express, MasterCard or Visa, the retailer card is to be viewed as a selective payment card. It is normally restricted to purchases only in the outlets of the retailer. The co-branded card is not the same and is more like other general debit and/or credit cards. Even though it features the name of the retailer, together with its financial collaborator, it may be used elsewhere as well. Hardly surprisingly, the cardholder often receives special benefits, like rebates and bonuses, when using it in the retailer's stores.[10] Similar benefits are also offered to possessors of retailer cards.[11] By this means, these new payment cards may serve to increase customer loyalty and to capture market shares,[12] resulting in the cards being not only attractive to consumers but to retailers as well.[13]

A further reason and an underlying driving force for the fast-growing interest in card payments is, of course, the rapid technology development that has taken place, especially in the information field. Due to the rapid progress in technology, payments made by cards have not only become more cost effective but also safer than payments in cash or by cheques.[14] However, card payments are not free of cost for either retailers or cardholders. The costs of the huge infrastructure investments in EFTPOS systems, as well as their maintenance and operational costs, have to be financed. The key questions are by whom and how? Should the costs be distributed to both retailers and cardholders or only to one of the two categories? Should the costs be covered by a combination of fixed annual fees and variable transaction fees or only by one type of fee?

In the following sections of this study these questions will be discussed in detail more. The aim of the chapter is to analyse the pricing of card payments from both practical and theoretical standpoints. This means that cost structures as well as competitive advantages will be taken into consideration.

6.2   Current pricing of card payments

With reference to the findings in Karp (1997) and to the preliminary results of our own recent study of the pricing of card payments, it is evident that the current pricing in Sweden can differ substantially between the existing payment cards.[15] Typically, cardholders are being charged an annual fee of about SEK 250 (ECU 30). However, as is shown in Table 6.2, some cardholders are being charged as much as SEK 1050 a year, while others are not paying any annual fee at all. Usually it is the retailer cards that are free of charge. Regarding cards with a credit or overdraft facility, a percentage charge may either be added to the annual fee or replace it. In most cases this fee is about 2 per cent of the agreed credit limit (see Table 6.2).

Table 6.2 also shows that an invoicing fee is levied on many payment cards. This fee can be as high as SEK 25 per invoice. Normally, the invoicing fee is charged only when the cardholder utilizes a credit or overdraft facility. This was the case for every retailer card and for about 50 per cent of the other payment cards that levy an invoicing fee.

Table 6.2: Current pricing of payment cards to Swedish cardholders (Summer 1997)

Type of payment card	Annual fee (SEK)				Invoicing fee (SEK)				Interest rate, credits(%)[b]				Bonus system	
	(n)	Average[a]	Max.	Min.	Average[a]	(n)	Max.	Min.	Average[a]	(n)	Max.	Min.	Yes(n)	No(n)
Bank cards	(8)	241[c]	295	150	9	(1)	9	0	14.3	(7)	21.0	11.0	(7)	(1)
Traditional debit/credit cards	(19)	424[d]	1050	0[f]	12	(9)	15	0	22.3	(10)	34.0	11.8	(14)	(5)
Retailer cards	(17)	60	60	0[g]	11	(12)[h]	25	0	22.4	(5)	32.0	18.9	(14)	(3)
Co-branded cards	(13)	240[e]	525	90	14	(4)	17	0	24.1	(9)	28.0	19.8	(13)	(–)

Notes:

a. All average figures are based only on those payment cards that are charging the particular fee or interest.

b. Effective interest rates.

c. For two of the bank cards, a percentage fee of 2 per cent of the overdraft facility is added to the annual fee (not included).

d. For four of the traditional debit/credit cards a percentage fee of 2–2.5 per cent of the credit limit is charged instead of an annual fee (not included).

e. For four of the co-branded cards, a percentage fee of 1.5–2 per cent is either added to the annual fee (2 cards) or replaces the annual fee (2 cards) (not included).

f. Four of the traditional debit/credit cards are free of (annual) charges.

g. Fifteen of the retailer cards are free of (annual) charges, that is only two retailer cards charge an annual fee.

h. The invoicing fee is charged only when the credit facility is utilized.

Furthermore, it is shown that most issuers of payment cards, (and all co-branded ones) are applying a reward programme, which may include anything from bonuses and rebates to travel insurance. Finally, it may be noticed that bank cards differ from other payment cards in that their lending interest rate on credits or overdraft facilities are approximately 10 per cent lower than that on other payment cards.

Today, the occurrence of transaction fees is rare. In a few cases card-holders are charged a fee of SEK 3 for low value purchases (less than SEK 300). However, in mid 1995 a great many retailers, especially grocers, began to charge a transaction fee on certain card payments. This fee was not charged by the retailers in order to compensate them-selves for their necessary investment in or lease of payment card pro-cessing equipment such as EFTPOS terminals. In most cases the costs of such equipment are relatively moderate.[16] According to the investiga-tion by Karp (1997), the average acquisition cost for a terminal was SEK 5300, while the average leasing cost per terminal was SEK 475 a month.[17] Almost six out of ten retailers leased their terminals. Nor did the retailers introduce the fee because of the percentage charges they have to pay to the card system (network) operator or card issuer. At that particular time, these charges were 2 to 3 per cent of the pur-chased amount.[18] No, the retailers' surcharges on card payments were instead responding to a newly implemented service (interchange) fee that they had to pay to the bank for each card payment transaction.

The new service fee was imposed by two of the larger Swedish banks in the middle of 1995.[19] The banks justified the fee by pointing to their own processing costs for card payments. However, most retailers found it neither fair nor reasonable that they alone should be compensating the banks for these administrative system costs. Consequently, they quite simply passed the new service fee on to the cardholders, that is to those who were using an 'external' payment card and not a retailer card.

The imposed surcharges on card payments were soon debated exten-sively in the newspapers and other media. Were the banks really enti-tled to start charging retailers a service fee for each card payment transaction? And, perhaps even more questionable, should the retailers be permitted to discriminate between payments made by different cardholders? Generally, retailer card payments were still free of charge while payments by bank cards and credit cards, American Express, Eurocard, and so forth, were levied a transaction fee of between SEK 2 and SEK 5. Clearly, in the latter case, the retailers took the opportunity to compensate themselves for their higher costs related to credit card payments.

The imposed surcharges led to a substantial increase in the number of retailer cards in circulation, as more and more card customers switched from using general bank cards and/or traditional credit cards to using the more selective retail cards. From the banks' point of view, this development was not desirable. Consequently, they soon renegotiated the contract with one of the larger grocery chains in Sweden. In the new agreement the service fee was halved in exchange for an immediate withdrawal of the retailer's surcharges on 'external' card payments.[20] Forced by competitive pressure, a majority of the other retailers also tried to renegotiate their contracts with their bank and/or to abandon their surcharges on card payments. As a result, today only a minority of the Swedish retailers is still surcharging card payments.

As is shown in Table 6.3, it is obvious that at least some retailers have managed to get rid of the service charges on bank cards. The table

Table 6.3: Current charges paid by Swedish retailers to bank/network operators (Spring 1997)

Type of payment card/ network operator	Bank/network operator charges (SEK)		
	Average	Min.	Max.
Bank cards	1.17	0[a]	5.50
Delayed debit cards[b]	14.42	2.90	35.20
• Servo, Euroline and others[c]			
percentage fee	3.0%	0.4%	4.1%
flat fee/trans	–	–	–
• BABS[c]			
percentage fee	2.1%	1.2%	2.5%
flat fee/trans	2.81	1.75	5.50
Credit cards (excl Amex and Diners)	13.49	3.58	58.38
• Servo, Euroline, and others			
percentage fee	2.5%	0.4%	4.1%
flat fee/trans	–	–	–
• BABS			
percentage fee	2.1%	1.2%	2.5%
flat fee/trans	2.57	1.75	3.00

Notes:
a. Almost one out of three retailers (32 per cent) did not pay any service charge on bank card payments.
b. Payment cards that are neither linked to a bank account nor offer a credit option (for example, Eurocard). The periodic invoice has to be paid immediately after receipt (normally the end of the month).
c. A majority of the retailers (53 per cent) was linked to BABS, 20 per cent to Servo, and 8 per cent to Euroline. BABS is owned by the savings banks, Servo by the commercial banks and Euroline by SE-Banken.
Source: Based on data from Karp (1997), Tables 3.1, 3.3 and 3.4.

is based on the investigation by Karp (1997) concerning 185 retailers (of which 95 were grocery stores). Furthermore it is clear that the level of infrastructure charges differs substantially between bank cards and other card categories, and it is evident that the network operators apply different fee or tariff structures. This means that a retailer who is selling in small quantities (low value purchases) to many possessors of delayed debit or credit cards will be worse off than is the case of the retailer who is linked to a savings bank. It is, of course, the other way around for those retailers that are selling high value goods or services, albeit less frequently.[21]

6.3   Recent card pricing trends

The described pricing of card payments is by no means unique to the Swedish market. In most countries the costs of the system are financed through service (interchange) fees to the retailers, while the cardholders are usually debited an annual or monthly fee for the possession of a payment card. They seldom have to pay any transaction fees at the point of sale. In the USA, for instance, such fees are prohibited by a majority of the network operators, which was also the case in Sweden until 1995. According to Mitchell (1996), only a few USA network operators allow retailers to impose surcharges at the point of sale. However, they 'only allow merchants to surcharge POS transactions if retailers also surcharge all other card-based purchases' (ibid. p. 14). This reservation is very effective, since Visa and MasterCard do not permit retailers to levy transaction fees on credit card payments. Moreover, the guidelines of the bank card associations prevent surcharges on payments by debit cards.

Lunt (1996) emphasizes the fact that many banks in the USA have found it difficult to supplement the interchange income with monthly or annual fees to cardholders. 'The market does not seem to bear very much.' (ibid. p. 45) Rather the trend appears to go in the other direction, towards no cardholder fees at all. However, the author also puts forward that there do exist alternative ways for the banks to deal with the problem of charging cardholders. One of the approaches is to provide both a fee and a rebate. 'For example, US Bancorp has a UBank Check Card that carries a $1.25 monthly fee and pays a 0.5 per cent rebate on purchases. The typical cardholder uses the card 18 to 20 times a month, receives a $2.85 monthly rebate, and therefore makes money on the card' (ibid. p. 46). Of course, this payment card is by no means loss making business to the bank. On the contrary, it makes

money on the card. The very purpose behind this kind of pricing structure is to encourage cardholders to use their payment cards more frequently. Due to the increased usage of the cards, retailers will be
paying additional interchange fees. Thus, the higher the card activity,
the greater will be the interchange income for the bank.

The combined fee and rebate pricing principle is reminiscent of the
one that seems to be applied by most issuers of co-branded cards. As
mentioned earlier, the cardholder is often offered special rebates or
bonuses if and when the card is used at retail outlets owned by the co-
branded retailer and/or connected to the card issuer. Normally, the
rewards are higher when it is the former case. As for the UBank Check
Card, the card issuers recoup their share of the rewarding costs through
an increased income stream from interchange fees, but they also supplement this income stream with a slightly higher interest rate on the
credits to co-branded cardholders than on other card credits. The retailers are, for their part, supposed to gain from increased sales.[22]
According to a cardholder satisfaction study undertaken by J.D. Power
in 1995, co-branded cardholders used their payment cards almost twice
as often than other cardholders.[23] The study results also imply that the
average purchase amount of a co-branded cardholder is more than
double that of a non-co-branded cardholder.

In their study of how widely accepted payment cards are within the
supermarket industry in the USA, Raphel and Raphel (1995) emphasize
the attractiveness of co-branding to supermarkets (ibid. p. 30):

> Co-branding offers a number of advantages for supermarkets:
> Increased customer loyalty: customers want to receive the benefits
> of the card, so they become more loyal to the chain.
> Competitive advantage: the first store in the market area with a
> good co-branded program will have the best ability to capture
> market share.
> New marketing possibilities: one example is the inclusion of store
> coupons in the bank's monthly statement.
> More information about customers: banks can provide demographic
> and purchase data.

Are then co-branded payment cards to be regarded as a win–win–win
business in which all parties concerned – banks, customers and retailers
– are winners? Vedder (1996) expresses some doubts and raises a
warning finger that this picture may be an idealised description. He
believes there is an obvious risk that the newly issued co-branded cards

will cannibalise older non-co-branded cards. In the case where the cardholder, who receives a new co-branded card already possesses an ordinary payment card of the issuer or the retailer, it is inevitable that the use of the co-branded card will directly affect and reduce the use of the old card. For the retailer it may then be a poor consolation that customers with a co-branded card are more active card users and make higher average purchases than do other card customers. In spite of bonuses and rebates, there is always a risk that co-branded cardholders will turn to other retailers. A reward programme can never fully guarantee customer loyalty. Vedder (1996) demonstrates this using the oil industry as an example, where six of the 15 largest oil companies experienced a slight decline in charge volume in 1995. All six companies had joined a co-branded card programme. This implies that the cardholders may have used the co-branded cards at a rival's petrol station.[24]

Duclaux (1996) reports that the growth rate of co-branding now appears to be falling in the USA and raises the question of whether it has already reached its peak. Three key causes are suggested for this development. First, the existing co-branded cards may have tapped the main part of its potential market. Second, most cardholders seem to be convenience users and do not hold revolving balances. Third, card issuers may find it more and more difficult to detect co-partners that make good sense. On the other hand, other authors maintain that co-branding is here to stay.

6.4   Theoretical guidelines

The current pricing of card payments, of course, may be discussed and analysed from various angles and from different theoretical aspects. In this section we will first of all concentrate on two particular questions. Who should be paying for the administration (system) costs of card payments? How should an efficient pricing of card payments be designed?

By tradition banks have primarily financed payment services through their interest margins, while merchants have allocated their system (administration) costs on all or a great part of their range of goods and services. These policies imply that the 'wrong' customers may have been paying for a major part of the system costs. Undeniably, the users of the banks' payment services and payment cards have not borne the full costs of using these systems. In that respect the retailers' surcharges on card payments appear to be both adequate and justified. The 'right' customers, that is payment card users, will contribute to the system costs in proportion to their usage of it when transaction based flat fees are applied. However, one obvious disadvantage with the implementation of transaction fees is that they may lead to a retrogression in the use of payment cards. Certainly, for both banks and retailers an undesirable scenario would be that customers switched back to cash and cheque payments. These payment media are probably more costly to administer than card payments and, furthermore, are less secure.

Is it then impossible to design and implement an efficient pricing formula for card payments that would lead to a rational usage of existing systems and optimal capacity expansions? Economic theory advocates that an efficient pricing strategy should be forward looking and focus exclusively on future revenues and costs.[25] The reason for this is that the pricing decision will have an impact only on succeeding cash flows. Hence, neither the bank nor the retailer should be paying any attention to historical (accounting) costs. From a decision-making standpoint, these costs are to be regarded as sunk costs: historical costs cannot be undone. On the other hand, one cannot disregard the fact that earlier decisions may have a major impact on later decision-making and, occasionally, severely restrict the range of future actions. For example, the costs of huge infrastructure investments may for a long period restrict the future actions of a business that is applying an efficient pricing. In the worst case these historical costs may never be recouped at all by the company. Therefore, it is of utmost importance that pricing and investment decisions are made in congruence with each other. This is especially true for payment systems since services are not storable and have to be produced and consumed simultaneously. Assuming an efficient pricing, that is each customer has to pay a price in accordance with marginal costs, congruity will be obtained if new investments are accomplished only when the price covers their marginal capacity costs as well as operative marginal costs.[26]

In practice it is much easier to advocate the marginal cost pricing principle than it is to implement it. Uncertainty and measurement problems make it difficult not only to forecast customers' price elasticity and future system marginal costs, but also to determine the corresponding elasticity and costs of today. Therefore, the risk is evident that an application of the marginal cost-based pricing rule will either over- or underestimate the future capacity cost, which in turn will lead to a system that is either being under- or overdimensioned. In the latter case, capacity costs will be uncovered. For an automated payment system, such as the ATM system, the optimal solution in this situation would not be to switch to an average cost-based pricing rule, like the so-called cost plus pricing principle. Clearly, prices based upon average costs would not be a guarantee either for full cost coverage or for an efficient utilization of the existing system capacity.

Regarding the banks' manual payment services, such as cheques and ordinary cash withdrawals at their teller desks, it is possible to distinguish a relationship between resource usage, that is the occupying of bank personnel, and the number of performed transactions (cheque clearings and/or cash withdrawals). This indicates that the corresponding indirect costs are dependent on the transaction volumes. Hence, a flat, average, cost-based, transaction fee may be adequate for manual payment services, and even in accordance with an efficient pricing of them. A change in the use of these services will lead to a corresponding change of indirect costs.

For automated payment services, like ATM services, the time dimension becomes interesting and of vital importance. Here, the flexibility is far more confined than it is in a personnel intensive system. As a consequence, in an automated system the demand for capacity, and therefore also a major part of the indirect costs, will be determined by the point in time that the customers' demand for payment services is at its maximum. This implies that a customer that is a frequent user of ATM services is not necessarily more costly to the bank than a customer that rarely or hardly ever requires them. The determining factor is when the customer demands a payment service. Indirectly, it is the peak users that are dimensioning the capacity of a payment system and thereby also an essential portion of its capacity costs. Theoretically, these circumstances point towards an application of the peak-load pricing concept, that is, varying prices over time in accordance with short-run marginal costs.[27]

How should we then characterise the EFTPOS systems? From an outside perspective the cost structure of an EFTPOS system appears to be very similar to that of an ATM system. Variable processing costs tend to be rather low, whereas system capacity costs are quite dominant. Thus, provided the capacity of the system is not fully utilized, the marginal costs of processing an additional card payment are almost insignificant.[28] Hence, the flat, transaction based, service fees that most Swedish banks and/or network operators are applying and charging their associated members (retailers) cannot be justified by the cost structure of EFTPOS systems.[29] In that respect the fixed annual fees to cardholders are more adequate, that is as long as the fees do not discourage customers from applying for and possessing payment cards.

In the case where retailers are not permitted explicitly to pass the flat service fees on to card payments, these fees are not necessarily wrong from an efficiency point of view. At least, the fees will not influence the volume of card payments since it is up to the individual cardholder, not the retailer, to decide whether the payment card or another means of payment should be used to settle a purchase. The picture will be quite different if the retailers are able to surcharge card payments and, thus, pass the service fees on to their card customers. Then the cardholders will no longer be indifferent to the fees and they may become more reluctant to use their payment cards. Assuming that the fees are based on average costs, the decreasing number of card payment transactions will lead to an ever-ceasing flow of revenue to the banks without producing any significant cost savings. Because capacity costs are fixed, average costs will by definition become higher than before.[30] The banks' immediate, but uncritical, response is, therefore, likely to be an increase of the service fees in accordance with the new and higher average costs. Presumably the retailers will then, in turn, adjust their surcharges to the new levels and the merry-go-round begins to spin. Needless to say, this turn would definitely lead the development in the wrong direction, that is away from the use of electronic money in the retail sector instead of leading it further towards the cashless society.[31]

Is it then erroneous for retailers to try to impose surcharges on card payments? If we disregard the fact that the existing alternatives to such payments are also costly to retailers, the answer is not necessarily affirmative. As long as the surcharges are equal to the banks' transaction-based service fees, the retailers are in line with the marginal cost pricing principle.[32] Furthermore, for those retailers that have issued retailer cards, the surcharging of payments made by 'external' cardholders only may serve to increase the number of their own payment cards in circulation, as was the case in Sweden. However, according to the Swedish experience, there also exists another important factor to take into consideration. Due to competition, it may be a risky enterprise for a retailer to surcharge card payments. If its competitors refrain from doing likewise, it may lose customers to them even when it has issued a retailer card. Hence, confronted with the prospect of losing market share, it was logical for most of the Swedish retailers to abandon their newly implemented surcharges, irrespective of whether or not they had a retail card programme of their own.

6.5   Conclusions

At the beginning of this chapter we draw attention to the fast growth of the use of payment cards, particularly in Sweden, but also world-wide. We may conclude that a prerequisite for this growth is a well functioning and cost-efficient network or settlement system. EFTPOS systems are mostly considered to fulfil these requirements. During the 1990s the EFTPOS systems in Sweden, as well as in many other countries, have rapidly increased in terms of terminals available at different retail outlets. The improved accessibility of relatively speedy processing equipment has in turn laid the basis for the remarkable rise of the number of payment cards in circulation. These payment cards may be of various kinds and have different origins and, recently, we have been witnessing the launch of new types of payment cards, the retailer cards and the co-branded cards. Both these types of payment cards may serve as a means to increase the sales for retailers through improved customer loyalty.

In this chapter we have emphasized the fact that the card payment systems, like the EFTPOS systems, incur considerable capacity costs. Especial attention has been paid to the problem of pricing payments by cards efficiently. Economic theory tells us that a rational utilization of a capital intensive system, like an EFTPOS system, will be achieved when the final users (customers) are meeting prices in accordance with marginal costs. The dilemma is that the marginal cost pricing rule is difficult to implement in practice: bear in mind that it requires prices that constantly balance demand to available system capacity. However, average cost-based prices, which apparently are applied in practice, are seldom a recommendable substitute for prices based on marginal costs. Such pricing may lead to a reduced use of the cost-efficient EFTPOS systems. This may explain the reason why card payments generally are free of charge for customers, whereas retailers are debited a transaction-based flat service fee. As long as the latter fee is not passed on to the customers, it will have no impact on the demand for card payments.

Despite the difficulties of surcharging payment card customers, the importance of payment cards for the income of retailers appears to be indisputable. According to Raphel and Raphel (1995), many retailers within the supermarket industry in the USA believe that they would not be competitive if they were not able to accommodate card customers. Studies show that sales have increased on average by more than 2 per cent for those outlets that welcome payment cards.

Furthermore, cardholders tend to purchase higher margin items to a greater extent than do other customers.

Under the presumption that such sales effects are general, these revenue improvements for retailers, together with the negative impact of surcharges on customers' use of payment cards, speak in favour of card payments being free of charge for the user.[33] The question whether or not banks (or network operators) should also avoid transaction-based service fees to retailers will then be of minor interest. As long as card payments are free of charge, these fees will not affect the usage of payment cards anyway. The way infrastructure costs should be allocated is, therefore, an issue only for the two counterparts, retailers and banks, to discuss and come to an agreement.

Possibly a transaction fee to cardholders may be adequate if it is coupled to a reward programme, like the one applied by the UBank Check Card in the USA. Depending on the design of this kind of pricing, it may very well stimulate the use of payment cards. From an efficiency point of view, an increased use of payment cards may be positive as long as the demand for system capacity is unaffected. However, because of the additional interchange or service fees that are likely to be debited by the banks (or network operators), the risk is obvious that retailers will try to compensate themselves with an increased general price level on their offered goods and services. The co-branded cards may be a solution to this problem. Certainly the retailer would then, to a great extent, have to contribute financially to the reward programme as well, but this extra spending could be more than worthwhile for the retailer if it, as Raphel and Raphel (1995) are emphasizing, results in an increased customer loyalty, a competitive advantage, new marketing possibilities and more accurate information about customers regarding their habits and preferences, and so forth.

Notes

*   Presented at the 1997 Annual Seminar of the European Association of University Teachers in Banking and Finance, Amsterdam, the Netherlands, 3–7 September 1997.

** The author wishes to express special thanks to Irené Andersson for her assistance with the collection of data concerning the pricing applied by Swedish card issuers.

1. The development is similar for other European countries, albeit the use of cards as a percentage of total number of cashless transactions may be higher or lower. The latter is very much dependent on the relative importance of

the other cashless payment instruments, that is, cheques, credit transfers and direct debits (see, for example, Bank for International Settlements (BIS) (1993), Table 8 in Annex 1, and European Monetary Institute (EMI) (1996), Table 9 in Annex 2).

2. On the other hand, according to the data in EMI (1996), the development of the volume and value of transactions is not extreme in Sweden (see Table 6).

3. EMI (1996), Table 7 p. 601.

4. According to the statistics presented in EMI (1996), Table 7 p. 601, payment cards with a debit function have increased more than eight times between 1990 and 1994. In total there were 10.4 million debit cards in 1994 but only 1.7 million credit cards.

5. Lunt (1996) reports that the use of debit cards has finally grown in the USA. In particular the so-called off-line debit card has gained acceptance by customers, banks and retailers. It rose by 75 per cent in 1995. The off-line debit cards are similar to the ordinary Swedish debit cards (bank cards). They are linked to a demand deposit account (DDA) but, in contrast to the Swedish bank cards, purchases at the point of sale are not debited to the DDA directly. As a consequence cardholders gain a float while retailers do not need to acquire an on-line EFTPOS terminal. Finally, the banks are attacked by the off-line debit cards because of the relatively higher interchange fees. These fees are set by the network operator and paid by the retailers.

6. For the majority, this bank or DDA is a pay account. When the pay account is provided with an overdraft facility, the debit card also may be regarded as a credit card.

7. See EMI (1996), p. 583. It should be noted that none of the bank cards are linked to American Express. According to Oliver (1996), the former management of American Express was very reluctant to share its payment system with other organisations. This reluctance led to a serious loss of market share.

8. The retailer card is sometimes backed up by a bank or some other financial institution. However, this kind of arrangement is not shown on the front of the card. The co-branded card is mostly issued on the initiative of the bank or credit card issuer (see also Kiley 1996).

9. Another type of payment card that is expected to grow in importance is the cash card or so-called smart card that is pre-paid by the user. Cash cards are still rare and mainly used in public telephones. However, more general cash cards are being tested in some towns that may be used for shopping and other payments (see, for example, Karp 1997).

10. According to articles in journals and magazines about co-branded cards in the USA and EU markets, it is common that possessors of such cards are offered a rebate of as much as two to five per cent on purchases made at the retailer (see, for example, O'Connor (1996) and Raphel and Raphel (1995), Britt (1996), Gandy (1996)).

11. During our on-going investigation at Gothenburg School of Economics we have found examples of retailer card rebates of up to as much as 10 per cent of the purchased amount.

12. See for example, O'Connor (1996), Raphel and Raphel (1995) and Vedder (1996).

13. Kiley (1996) reports that more than four out of ten MasterCards are co-branded, while Britt (1996) refers to Visa officials expecting every second Visa card to be co-branded or affinity by 1998.
14. See for example, EMI (1996), p. 584.
15. In Karp (1997), a questionnaire was sent to 240 retailers of which 208 responded. However, since seven of them did not accept cards, six were no longer in business, and ten used only a manual terminal, the results are based on the replies from 185 of the respondents. Our own investigation covers the existing payment cards in Sweden. Questions have been put to the card issuers about their pricing, credit limits, interest rates and reward programmes. To date we have received data concerning 57 payment cards.
16. Naturally, there are exceptions. Whittelsey (1997) reports that small firms in particular may be heavily overcharged for payment card processing equipment in the USA. In some cases the retailer has paid five to six times as much as the suggested list price for such equipment.
17. See Karp (1997 p. 7).
18. See, for example, Huldén (1995).
19. EMI (1996), p. 584.
20. See Rosengren (1995) and Törnroth (1995).
21. It should be stressed that the study by Karp (1997) refers to period February to April in 1997. According to our own investigation during summer 1997, Euroline has now a two-part tariff, that is a percentage charge and fixed transaction based charge.
22. The pricing of co-branded cards may be regarded as a form of price bundling, where the rebates or bonuses are the 'leader'. For a discussion about price bundling see, for example, Guiltinan (1989).
23. See Kiley (1996).
24. It should be mentioned that Vedder (1996) also refers to a study of card payments in the oil industry, which suggests that oil co-branded cards are more frequently used than other co-branded cards.
25. See for example, Lindblom (1990).
26. From the standpoint of economic theory, it would seem reasonable that the pricing of retail services should approach marginal costs because of the apparently increasing competitive pressure in the banking industry, but this is still not the case. This may be explained by customer search costs and switching costs. Evidently, these costs can have an injurious effect on competition (c.f. Calomiris (1995)).
27. The concept of peak-load pricing is presented and discussed in, for example, Lindblom (1990). It should be noted that the concept is used in practice, at least partly, in the pricing of phone calls. Call charges vary between daytime on weekdays and other times because of the more intensified use on weekdays.
28. There may be a 'telephone charge' for the transmitting of information in order to verify that the card is valid, and so forth. Although this charge is variable to the retailer (or card issuer), it usually entails an almost zero marginal cost for the transmission company, that is as long as the transmitting capacity is not fully utilized.
29. The percentage charges may be justified by other reasons. First and foremost the banks take on a credit risk.

30. By definition, fewer payment transactions are bound to lead to a lower number in the denominator, whereas the numerator, that is total costs, would still be almost unchanged.
31. Also bear in mind that the progress of payment systems has already more or less overcome three of the four natural barriers stated by Hoenig (1995) for the implementation of a new technology. The four barriers are cost efficiency, achieving a technical standardisation, adequate pricing, and consumer acceptance. Surely, to take a step backwards because of the pricing dilemma today makes no sense.
32. By definition, the average cost-based transaction fees paid by the retailers become marginal costs to them.
33. This remark is particularly valid for average cost-based fees. Transaction fees based on marginal costs according to the peak-load pricing principle are still desirable, at least from a theoretical point of view. Of course, the problem is considerable to implement marginal cost prices in practice.

References

Bank for International Settlements (1993), *Payment Systems in the Group of Ten Countries*, Basle: BIS

Britt, P. (1996), 'An affinity for affinity credit cards', *America's Community Banker*, **5** (4), p. 42

Calomiris, C.W. (1995), 'Pricing margins: competition is the driver', *Journal of Retail Banking Services*, **17** (3), pp. 59–62

Duclaux, D. (1996), 'Has the co-branded boom gone bust?', *ABA Banking Journal*, **88** (7), p. 69

European Monetary Institute (1996), *Payment Systems in the European Union*, Frankfurt am Main: EMI

European Monetary Institute (1997), *Payment Systems in the European Union: Addendum incorporating 1995 figures*, Frankfurt am Main: EMI

Gandy, T. (1996), 'Buy drive', *Banker*, **146** (841), pp. 76–7

Guiltinan, J.P. (1989), 'The price bunding of services: a normative framework', in J.E.G. Bateson, (ed.) *Management Service Marketing*, Chicago: The Dryden Press

Hoenig, T. (1995), 'The evolution of the payments system: A US perspective', *Economic Review Federal Reserve Bank of Kansas City*, **80** (3), pp. 5–9

Huldén, U. (1995) 'Prisvärt snuva banken', *Dagens Industri*, 25 October, p. 56

Karp, R. (1997), *Avgifter på bank-och kreditkort – en kostnadsstudie*, AB Handelns Utredningsinstitut (HUI), May, Stockholm

Kiley, K. (1996), 'Branded!', *Catalog Age*, **13** (6), pp. 77–80

Lindblom, T. (1990), *Pricing strategies on payment services*, Institute of European Finance, RP 90/16, Bangor: IEF

Lunt, P. (1996), 'Is it first and goal for debit cards?', *ABA Banking Journal*, **88** (9), pp. 44–8

Mitchell, R. (1996), 'Get ready for surcharges', *Credit Card Management*, **9** (5), pp. 14–18

O'Connor, R. (1996), 'Thumbs up for co-branding', *Credit Card Management*, **9** (6), pp. 150–4

Oliver, S. (1996), 'The battle of the credit cards', *Forbes*, **158** (1), pp. 62–6

Raphel, N. and M. Raphel (1995), 'Make room for credit cards', *Progressive-Grocer*, **74** (6), pp. 29–30

Rosengren, Å. (1995), 'Ras för kortköp hos Billhälls', Fri Köpenshap, 25 August, p. 4

Törnroth, G. (1995), 'Bankerna tog hem första ronden', *Fri Köpenskap*, 15 September, p. 2

Vedder, K.J. (1996), 'Sibling rivalry in the oil patch', *Credit Card Management*, **9** (4), pp. 14–20

Whittelsey, F.C. (1997), 'The minefield of merchant status', *Nation's Business*, **85** (1), pp. 38–40

7

The Unified European Banking Market and the Convergence of National Banking Sectors*

Elisabetta Montanaro, Claudio Scala and Mario Tonveronachi

7.1 Introduction

The rationale for public regulation springs from the need to overcome the more severe effects of some form of market failures. However, regulation is costly and may produce unwanted negative side effects. A public framework of regulatory measures needs to be justified on the ground of net gains for the community.

Since real economic systems with market and co-ordination failures do not possess the well-behaved conditions required for the Pareto optimality, these systems are the locus of conflicting interests that do not permit us to define an objective or generally accepted social welfare function. The evaluation of the potential net benefits accruing from a regulatory framework is then determined by structural and political aspects of economic societies, therefore possessing country-specific characters and being subject to change with the passing of time.

Different traits in the morphology of financial systems are clearly *per se* causes and consequences of differences in their regulatory frameworks. On the contrary, international relations and technological progress are powerful agents pushing towards harmonisation, if not towards convergence. Whether economic development is conducive to a single structural model (structural convergence) it remains one of the hot topics for historians and theoreticians of financial systems.

The countries now belonging to the European Union (EU) experienced quite distinct secular evolutions in their financial systems and in their financial regulatory frameworks. For more than twenty years these countries have been facing an increasingly rapid process aiming at the creation of a common financial market and the harmonisation of their regulatory schemes.

These political measures did not follow from an endogenous and spontaneous process of convergence among the EU countries. On the contrary, they were part of the more general political design aimed at creating a unified Europe. The general political process was condemned to produce quite different velocities of harmonisation and convergence in the various fields, since the starting point was characterised by a wide set of national differences in well-rooted social, political, institutional and economic features. Especially in the last years, an inter-European burst to competition was seen as a major step forcing economic convergence, the latter somehow considered as a discipline device for the more general political process of convergence (Bruni 1995). The result is that much of the economic harmonisation is still confronted with strong and, to a certain extent, unavoidable differences in non-economic aspects. Since the interactions between economic and non-economic features, and among the different aspects of economic life are quite powerful, and the financial system constitutes a particularly crucial junction, some difficulties in the process of financial convergence were to be expected.

It is then not surprising that the solution adopted at the European level was a minimum harmonisation in the national regulatory schemes. This does not mean that the required adjustments were irrelevant. Quite the opposite. For some countries the process meant a complete change in the nature of their financial regulation and/or an increase in the weight of regulation. The interesting problem is how much and in which directions these policy changes have affected, and can affect in the future, the substance of European finance.

The main stages in the convergence process of the European banking regulations were completed at the end of 1992, following the guidelines of the Second Banking Directive. The removal of the legislative barriers to freedom in banking competition within Europe was in reality only one of the objectives of the more ambitious design aiming at the creation of the European banking internal market from 1 January 1993.

The full integration of previously segmented banking markets was realized through the harmonisation of regulatory constraints and the adoption of common minimum standards of prudential regulation. These measures were necessary to put into practice the principles of mutual recognition and of the home country control, and for the adoption of the single banking licence.

Although with different intensities, many European countries had been subject to deregulation from the beginning of the 1980s. The need to prepare their financial institutions for the new market discipline characteristic of the adopted principles of unification, accelerated deregulation in those European countries that had been subject to a long tradition of state intervention and protectionism, like Italy, France, Belgium and Spain. The disparities in regulation that, in the past, protected the least advanced systems from external competitive pressures and had contributed to the segmentation of national banking markets, were in the same period progressively relaxed or eliminated.

The regulative convergence and the homogenisation of instruments of supervision are the bases of the project for European banking integration. Their foundations were ascribed to the necessity to create a 'level-playing field' that would have secured a fair and symmetric distribution of the costs and benefits of deregulation for the participating national systems.

It was expected that the elimination of regulatory disparities would have created the necessary and sufficient conditions to obtain the convergence both in financial structures and in bank performances. Moreover, the demolition of the barriers to entry was seen as the correct way to improve the efficiency of the financial services industry. It should also have favoured consumers through the demolition of the oligopolistic rents that were thought to derive from regulatory measures aimed at protecting this industry from competitive risks. The convergence in managerial models, in the allowed price and product strategies, in the opportunities for banks to grow and to make profits, would also have created the conditions for a homogeneous trade-off between efficiency and stability for all European banking systems.

This chapter will try to show that the greater part of these expectations, especially the ones regarding convergence, were based on weak foundations while there were good theoretical reasons to be at least more cautious. An analysis drawing on market power approaches suggests that the presence of dynamic oligopolistic barriers may produce quite distinct results (Section 7.2). On these premises, we will show that, contrary to expectations, recent experience points to a lack of convergence in the structural models of banking and to significant processes of polarisation and divergence in the performance of the European national banking sectors (Section 7.3).

7.2   Regulation, competition and convergence

The approach taken by (de)regulators considered the degree of competition in banking too low to permit a satisfactory performance. In a certain sense regulators followed the structure–conduct–performance paradigm connecting *free* competition to a structure where the legal and administrative constraints were absent. The deregulation on competition was, however, the result of a more general approach. As the theory suggests for 'apples and pears', competition does not only derive from the confrontation of firms inside the national banking sector; its degree also depends on the pressures deriving from foreign financial firms and from the stock market. This explains the three characteristics of deregulation in competition: the abolishing of regulatory constraints on the birth of new banks and on the creation of new branches; the opening up to foreign competition; the abandoning of the forced specialisation between commercial banks and organised markets. As already stated, the expected results were decreased bank margins and a push towards a higher operating and allocative efficiency. Some more disenchanted observers pointed, however, to an increased fragility due to the attempt to regain the lost profitability through the assumption of higher risks (Hellwig 1996).

The first weakness of this approach is to mix together liberalisation, free competition and perfect competition (defined as the maximum and optimum degree of competition). As one of the founding fathers of the 'old' Chicago School argued, since a deregulated economy tends to create monopolistic powers, competition is the result not of *laissez-faire* but of an active intervention by the state (Knight 1923). The theory of oligopoly based on classical premises (Sylos Labini 1967) and the theory of contestable markets suggest that the cancellation of legal and administrative barriers leaves economic barriers untouched. Consequently, the result is not necessarily one of increased competition once the sector finds its new oligopolistic truce. It might well be that, under the strain of the adjustment process, new and/or higher economic barriers are created. The new oligopolistic structure could then produce higher and not lower profit margins. In general, without an analysis of the relevance and the dynamics of economic barriers it is not possible to get a clear idea of the direction of the process.

Recent work drawing on the industrial organisation approach (for example Neven 1993) confirms that the banking sector possesses the distinctive features of an imperfect market. Due to product differentiation, consumers do not respond to low price differentials; long-term relationships favour consumers' capture by banks; geographical market fragmentation has important implications for branching; the low number of banks favours collusive behaviour; weak bankruptcy and hostile takeover threats lower the pressure on managers to reach productive efficiency. Prior to 1990 these characteristics were reinforced by regulation, leading to a lack of price competition and to different degrees and types of competition in the European countries. Neven states that deregulation will make price competition more intense and goes on to examine its consequences for banks' strategy and market structure. His opinion is that deregulation will affect allocative efficiency (lower margins) but not productive efficiency, even if some job reductions and salary cuts are to be expected. Regulation will also favour those country systems already accustomed to more intense price competition, having negative effects on the systems that adopted quality competition. Moreover, deregulation will foster mergers and acquisitions and will favour geographical dispersion and a lower branch density.

The crucial passage in this type of analysis is the link between deregulation and higher price competition. We have already expressed our opinion that structural features coherent with oligopolistic markets render spells of price wars possible, especially when the oligopolistic truce is disturbed and a new structural equilibrium must be reached. We are, however, not convinced that a higher degree of price competition will be a stable character of the 'new European order', given the capacity of firms to strengthen barriers to entry and exit. The German experience may be a good example of a financial sector that, notwithstanding being subject to no explicit legal and administrative prohibitions, was far from being the theatre of a vivid internal, foreign and stock market competition. Furthermore, quality competition does not constitute a drawback but one of the best ways to strengthen economic barriers. This different perception may also be the result of differences in what constitutes banking activity. Neven seems to play down asset specificities in banking, that we know are mainly related to human capital; he focuses his attention on the liability side of retail banking and seems not to evaluate the consequences of the increased complementarity and competition between banks and stock markets stemming from deregulation. In our view, banking is going to become an increasingly complex activity in which, if successful, labour costs will constitute a positive leverage for performance.

As we saw before, the problem must not be confined within the boundaries of the traditional banking sector. Much of the emphasis of deregulation is placed on the primary role that will be played by the stock market once the competitive privileges reserved to banks disappear. The so-called Anglo-Saxon market-based model has substantially moved towards a system of large financial firms acting as dealers in internalised markets. The result is significant erosion of what is normally intended as a flex price market (Kregel 1993). Bank-based systems are moving towards a wider set of marketable assets, where banks are, however, going to exert an increasing influence on the market. For at least some financial systems this will mean a shift towards an overall portfolio with an increased weight of flex price assets. The consequences of this shift on the generation, dissemination and coverage of risks are already significantly influencing banks' activity, increasing the importance of an advanced risk management.

All these factors concur to strengthen banks possessing higher specificities, giving them the possibility to reinforce their market power. At the outset of the European deregulation these specificities were not equally distributed among the national banking sectors, and those systems possessing them had different types of specificity. We, therefore, had to expect a process of entrenchment in specificities as a basis for further expansion and the absence of convergence towards a single banking model.[1] Moreover, the new European prudential regulation based on capital ratios does not produce neutral results. In the new European context, banks' ability to grow successfully with internal and external strategies is linked to strong capabilities in deriving profits from specificities and high market power, to lower capital costs and/or to easier access to capital markets, and to a higher initial capitalisation in terms of market value. A simplified expression of the rate of growth based on internal funds may illustrate the point.

The return on equity (ROE) of a bank may be written as

$$ROE = i_a + (i_a - i_d)L + \frac{NII}{K} - \frac{OE}{K} - \frac{PR}{K} \tag{1}$$

where i_a is the average return on assets, i_d is the average cost of debt, L is the leverage, NII is the non interest income (net), OE are operative expenses, PR are provisions (net), K is capital and reserves.

Denoting with g the rate of growth of capital permitted by internal funds and with i_k the dividend per unit of capital we obtain:

$$g = i_a - i_k + (i_a - i_d)L + \frac{NII}{K} - \frac{OE}{K} - \frac{PR}{K} \tag{2}$$

If with respect to a risk-free rate of interest (i_f) we define a mark-up ($mu = i_a - i_f$), a mark-down ($md = i_f - i_d$), and a dividend spread ($ds = i_k - i_f$), we can write:

$$g = mu - ds + (mu + md)L + \frac{NII}{K} - \frac{OE}{K} - \frac{PR}{K} \tag{3}$$

L is strongly influenced by the regulatory capital ratio and by risk management. Market power affects *mu* and *md*, while the cost of capital affects *ds*. Apart from changes in the risk composition of assets, regulation on capital ratio forces assets to grow in tune with capital.

Banking systems possessing higher *mu* and/or *md* and lower *ds* receive from the regulation on uniform capital ratios a further 'competitive' advantage, being in a position to grow at a higher rate and to dynamically strengthen their specificities and market powers. On the other hand, a good risk management lessens the regulatory constraint permitting higher leverages and lower provisions.

Equation (3), together with the recent explosion of mergers and acquisition in the European banking industry, shows that the impact of the European banking (de)regulation on the convergence of capital adequacy standards cannot be seen only in terms of fair competition, more efficiency, and more safe and sound banking. In reality, this so-called prudential regulation may foster important structural changes in banking with uneven consequences on the cost-benefit balance for the different national systems (Kapstein 1994).

Evidently our doubts concern deregulation considered as a necessary and sufficient condition for convergence. According to a widely held opinion, liberalisation and the European unification would have reduced banks' market power and hence their interest margins (Conti and Maccarinelli 1993; Gardener 1995; Neven 1993). Recent experience does not seem to support this claim. As Figures 7.1 and 7.2 show, interest margins do not follow a general downward tendency. Where it occurs, the tendency starts before the unification of the European banking market. Bank spreads show an even lower general downward tendency, with notable opposite patterns for Germany and the UK. If banks' spreads are deemed as more representative of market power than interest margins, strongly influenced by balance sheet composition, and with the cautions due to cross-countries heterogeneity of data, figures 7.1 and 7.2 show no distinctive sign of a general decrease in market power.

The impact of deregulation on financial structures and on bank profitability is largely controversial, even assuming a strong tendency towards integrated markets. The strategies that banks may adopt in reaction to the new market order depend on a set of diversified options, so that it is difficult to foresee what will change in their conditions of stability and productive efficiency. The situation becomes even more complex when strongly segmented markets are subject to deregulation with different intensity and with different starting times. As we said

Figure 7.1: Interest margin (yield on assets–cost of debt)

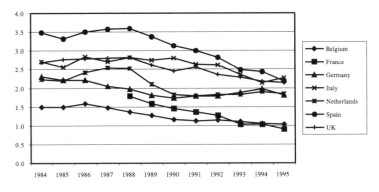

Source: OECD, *Bank profitability: financial statements of banks*, 1997.

Figure 7.2: Bank spread

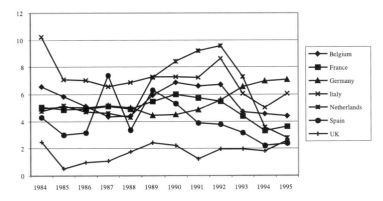

Source: IMF, *International Financial Statistics*, CD, January 1998.

before, the European banking market is to a large extent a virtual phenomenon, built in few years through the adjustment of national regulations to the European directives, but still devoid of a precise identity.

Consequently, the effects of European banking integration are not to be evaluated with exclusive reference to deregulation. The project to unify the European banking systems into a single internal market 'politically' presupposes the possibility of overcoming the differences in structure and performance already existing among the countries belonging to the EU. The risks and the opportunities deriving from the new competitive environment will, however, be distributed according to the directions imposed by forced harmonisation and, in particular, according to the models of banking structure that will become dominant. The new models of regulation (and deregulation), with which the single countries have accommodated the European directives had in the recent past, and will have in the future, very different effects on structures and performances of banks belonging to different national realities. Uniform regulations applied to financial systems with substantial differences create instability for the weaker systems. With instability affecting national systems, financial harmonisation does not in itself render more credible the threat of exit for the inefficient banks, and is not a guarantee of an increased accountability for individual country financial regulators (Kane 1991). More importantly, a uniform regulation generates conditions of competitive advantages both for banks belonging to countries like Germany, that have a regulatory framework more similar to that adopted at the Community level and for banks, like the UK and the Dutch ones, possessing a longer experience of risk management and of opportunities for liberalisation and innovation.

The hypothesis that we intend to test in the next section is that deregulation and the harmonisation of the national banking regulations are not sufficient conditions to promote a process of convergence characterised by equal competitive opportunities and by a symmetrical distribution of costs and benefits of liberalisation.

7.3   The recent experience

The empirical analysis presented in this section constitutes a preliminary evaluation of the modifications experienced by the European banking systems following the creation of the 'unified market'. We will verify whether the differences in banking structure and performance have been modified as a result of the strategies adopted by banks in each individual country to meet the European challenge. The analysis concerns the banking sectors of seven European countries: Belgium, France, Germany, Italy, the Netherlands, Spain, and the UK. The two periods in which the divergences are measured and compared respectively reflect the four years of the preparatory phase to the unified European market, from 1989 to 1992, and the following three years, 1993 to 1995, for which the aggregate balance sheet data published by the OECD are available. The variables that have been used to define the characteristics of the structure and performance of each single banking sector and to measure national divergences before and after 1992 are reported in Tables 7.1 and 7.2.[2]

Table 7.1: Variables of banking performance

Variables	Definitions	Symbols
1 Profitability	Profit before taxes/capital and reserves (%)	ROE
2 Risk	Standard deviation of ROE	VAR
3 Productive efficiency	Gross income (Operating expenses + net provisions)	PE

Note: Data refer to 'all banks', with the exception of the UK whose data refer to 'commercial banks'.
Source: OECD, *Bank profitability: financial statements of banks*, 1997.

Table 7.2: Variables of banking structure

Variables	Definitions	Symbols
1 Price competition	Lending rate-deposit rate [1] (%)	S
2 Monetary stability	Consumer price inflation [2] (%)	INFL
3 Degree of openness	Cross-border bank deposits of non banks by residence of borrowing bank/cross-border bank deposits of non banks by residence of depositors [1]	OPEX
4 Monetary function	Reserve money/demand + time deposits of banks [1]	MB/D
5 Weight of banks in credit to the private sector	Banks' claims on private sector/GDP [1]	CR/GDP

Source: (1) IMF, *International Financial Statistics*, CD, January 1998.
(2) OECD, *Economic Outlook*, December 1997.

A first evaluation of the convergence level is obtained computing for performance and structure variables and, for both periods, the matrices of the Euclidean distances among the European banking systems (Appendix, Tables 7.A13 and 7.A14). The average level of distance increases from 5.81 to 10.79, that is 85.63 per cent, showing that the divergences among the countries widened after the European integration. From the Euclidean distances of the complex of all variables we can derive the relative dendograms of clusterisation for the two periods (Figures 7.3 and 7.4). For both periods the UK appears as a separate model. The 'continental' model, in which the other countries are grouped together in the first period, splits into two separate models in the second period: a north continental model, composed of Germany, Belgium and the Netherlands, and a south continental model, with France, Italy and Spain.

Figure 7.3: Typology of banking models of the selected European countries (1989–92)

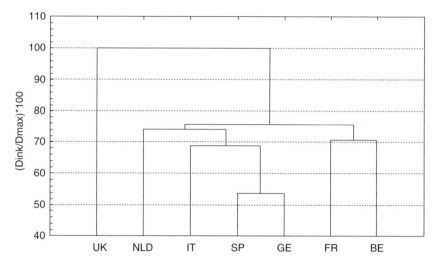

Figure 7.4: Typology of banking models of the selected European countries (1993–95)

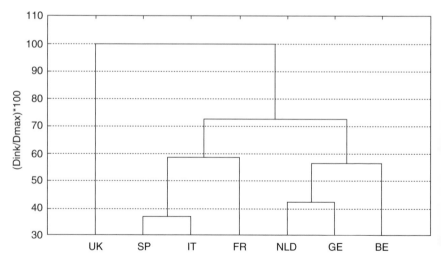

The increased divergences must be interpreted taking into account the different interactions between banking structure and performance in the selected countries. To this end we need a comparative methodology that permits us (a) to represent and to interpret the divergences among the seven European countries in the two periods, before and after unification; (b) to compare the relative position of each country for the two periods in order to verify which have been the 'successful' and 'unsuccessful' countries in the new competitive environment generated by European integration.

The chosen methodology is based on the principal components analysis that permits us to synthesise in two dimensions (C_1 and C_2) the set of variables that have been used to define the characteristics of structure and performance of the various European banking systems.[3] Tables 7.3 and 7.4 contain the results of the principal components analysis. The percentages of the total variability captured by the first two components confirm that it is possible to represent and to interpret in two dimensions the configuration of the system composed by the seven European countries, suffering only a moderate loss of information.

The values of the components C_1 and C_2 are transferred for each period in a map in which the relative position of the different countries is represented. Each quadrant of the map constitutes a different set of levels of the variables referring to banking structure and performance. In order to give a specific meaning to the quadrants it is necessary to define the prevalent informative content synthesised in C_1 and

Table 7.3: Country co-ordinates in terms of principal components

Countries	1989–92		1993–95	
	C_1	C_2 [1]	C_1 [1]	C_2 [1]
Belgium	−3.77134	3.81995	1.74548	−3.04972
France	−0.88268	1.19831	−9.19335	−2.86172
Germany	2.59476	−0.96744	0.59483	2.81300
Italy	1.13379	0.06321	−6.67626	2.29272
Netherlands	4.63881	1.34070	4.44311	1.71673
Spain	1.28655	−2.47988	−4.60356	0.13712
UK	−4.99989	−2.97486	13.68974	−1.04812

Note: (1) These co-ordinates are used with inverted sign in order to maintain for both maps the same qualitative direction of the axes.

Table 7.4: Principal components: percentages of total variability (variance–covariance matrix)

Components	1989–92	1993–95
C_1	56.76850	84.55015
C_2	26.92381	8.13656
Cumulative	83.69231	92.68671

Table 7.5: Explicative variables for C_1

Variables	Definitions	Symbols
1 Labour costs	Staff costs/total assets (%)	LC
2 Capitalisation	Capital and reserves/Total assets (%)	CAP
3 Return on assets	Profit before tax/Total assets (%)	ROA
4 Provisions	Provisions/Total assets (%)	P/A

Note: Data refer to 'all banks', with the exception of the UK whose data refer to 'commercial banks'.
Source: OECD, *Bank profitability financial statement of banks*, 1997.

C_2. To this end each component has been regressed to a set of explicative variables throughout in which it is possible to identify the prevalent economic meaning of each component. The best explicative variables for C_1 and C_2 are shown in Tables 7.5 and data refer to 'all banks', with the exception of the UK whose data refer to 'commercial banks'.

These explicative variables, with their signs and weights as measured by the Mexvals,[4] allow us to trace back the variables of structure and performance that exert the main influence on the distribution of the countries along the two axes of the maps. The values of the variables and the results of the regressions for the two periods are reported in the Appendix Tables 7.A5–7.A8 and Tables 7.A9–7.A12. The results show that the component C_1 mainly synthesises the performance variables in terms of profitability (ROA and CAP) and efficiency (LC for operative efficiency and P/A for efficiency in risk management). The component C_2 mainly synthesises the structure variables affecting market power (and INT) and securitisation activity (NI).

Table 7.6: Explicative variables for C_2

Variables	Definitions	Symbols
1 International market share of the banking sector(*)	Foreign assets of banks in individual countries/total international assets of banks in industrial countries (%) (2)	INT
2 Mark-up	Lending rate – money market rate (%) (2)	MU
3 Mark-down	Money market rate – Deposit rate (%) (2)	MD
4 Financial innovation	Non interest income/Net interest income (1)	NI

Notes: (*) The definition of the variable is taken from Bruni (1993).
Source: (1) OECD, *Bank profitability financial statements of banks*, 1997. Data refer to 'all banks', with the exception of the UK whose data refer to 'commercial banks'.
(2) IMF, *International Financial Statistics*, CD, January 1998.

Table 7.7: Qualitative values for C_1 and C_2

E = low	E = high
P = low	P = high
M = high	M = high
S = low	S = low
E = low	E = high
P = low	P = high
M = low	M = low
S = high	S = high

E = efficiency; P = profitability; M = market power; S = securitisation.

Table 7.7 shows how the position of a country in one of the four quadrants of the map is characterised in terms of the qualitative values of the main determinants of the two components. To interpret the divergences and the competitive strategies adopted by the different banking systems to react to the European unification let us compare the maps for the two periods (Figures 7.5 and 7.6).

The considerable improvement between the two periods of the UK performance is the most impressive result. UK banks appear to have gained from their longer experience with open competitive markets to the point that their performance shifts from the last to the first position. Probably an important role has been played by the stimulation of the productive efficiency derived from the 'market selection' that facilitated the exit of the inefficient banks. However, as we will see at the end of the section, this strong repositioning may be partly related to the UK's real cycle not being in phase with those of continental Europe, together with an accentuated cyclical sensibility.

Figure 7.5: Mapping of the two principal components (1989–92)

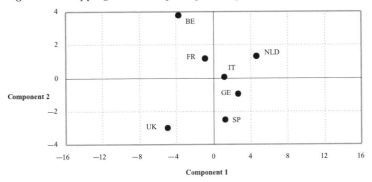

Figure 7.6: Mapping of the two principal components (1993–95)

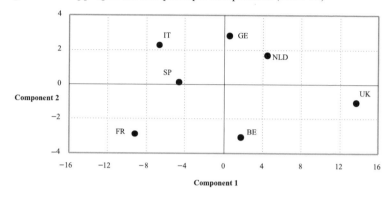

The Belgian system, too, shows important progress, even if it was subject to accentuated competition. The German and especially the Dutch systems are confirmed stable and with high performance. All the other countries, in particular France and Italy, move backwards. The results show that the costs and benefits of deregulation have not been evenly distributed among the countries with an inevitable consequent increase in their divergences. As we said before, this was to be expected.

As the regressions for the component C_1 on the CAP variable suggest, the productive and managerial choices with which banks tried to limit their capital needs became a crucial element. This element was stronger in the second period. The efficient risk selection appears to have been the winning strategy. The sign of the regression coefficient of P/A on C_1 confirms that the changes in performance between the first and the second period, increasing for the UK and Belgium and decreasing for Spain and France, are strongly related to changes in the opposite direction of the risk index.

The relation between performance and labour costs, as measured by LC, is weak and always positive. Contrary to the opinion prevalent among banks' managers and experts (Altunbaş and Molyneux 1993), strategies directed to the simple control of labour costs rarely appear as the winning solution in the competitive fight. Furthermore, empirical evidence does not seem to confirm the expectations of increased efficiency in conditions of higher banking competition. For example, while the UK banking system is normally considered as the most open to competition in Europe, its labour costs are among the highest, comparable to those of the banking systems generally taken to be the more closed and inefficient, like Italy and Spain.

The divergences among the banking systems due to the structure variables are synthesised in the component C_2. In the period following integration, the divergences among the European banking systems are to a lesser degree due to the structure variables than appears to hold for the first period. This is confirmed by the lower global variability explained by C_2, 8.14 per cent with respect to 26.92 per cent in the first period (see Table 7.4).

In the first period the vertical positioning on the map singles out three blocks, as is even more clearly shown by the clusters of Figure 7.5. The first block, composed of the Netherlands, Italy, Germany and Spain, derives its market power mainly from a strong control of the domestic market which is scarcely contestable and competitive. A strong domestic market power allows banks to act as price makers and to maintain high interest spreads that are mainly due to high mark-ups, as in Germany and the Netherlands,[5] and/or high mark-downs, as in Italy, the Netherlands and Spain.

The second block is composed of Belgium and France, in which a strong domestic market power is coupled with high internationalisation. This power mainly derives from the barriers to entry resulting from regulation and state control in the French case (de Boissieu 1993), and from high concentration and a solid custom base favouring niche strategies in Belgium (Abraham and Lierman 1991).

The third block is represented by the UK. It is located in the lower part of the map mainly due to a high level of securitisation (as shown by the strong weight of the NI variable possessing a negative regression coefficient). This reflects financial innovation and the increased weight of non-interest returns when the banking industry acts in a strongly competitive market characterised by important processes of securitisation.

The much lower variability explained by the component C_2 in the second period may be seen as an important indication of the impact of European banking integration. It shows that the divergences among the country systems due to the interactions between the variables of structure and the levels of performance became less perceptible, hence harder to read in terms of systemic regularities.

Note that the two banking models showing the neatest structural differences and the most accentuated specificities (those of the Netherlands and Germany on one side and UK on the other side) are the ones that benefited most from the challenge posed by the integration process. They could join high market power with high performances. These results offer an empirical contribution to the debate on the relative efficiency of relationship-based systems (Germany) compared to transactionship-based competitive systems (UK). In particular, they seem to confirm the analysis offered by Rajan (1992, pp. 1392–3), according to whom 'relationship and transactionship reflect two extremes of the control-rent trade-off', each of which has its own virtues. The result is that 'unidimensional comparisons are misleading'.

In the other countries, especially in France, Italy and Spain, the adjustment strategies to the new competitive environment have magnified the factors of structural weakness and the weight of the inefficiencies inherited from the past. For Italy, the recent passage from a transactionship-based system to a relationship-based one was done without having first acquired the necessary expertise in risk management in a context of decreasing interest margins. This may help to explain the deterioration of the portfolio risk and the consequent decline of banking performance. The same result is observable in Spain where the passage was, however, in the opposite direction.

The actual phase of transition shows an increased fragility of the weaker systems. Compared with the more successful banking systems of Germany, the Netherlands and the UK, the more unstable systems of France, Italy and Spain still appear in search of a specific repositioning inside the European market. The outcome of European banking integration in a competitive deregulated scenario is hard to predict.

The above analysis may be supplemented in two aspects. The first concerns the relevance assumed by the efficient allocation of capital, mainly as a consequence of the new prudential regulatory approach. In the new context banks must reposition their pricing and portfolio policies in order to produce profits in line with the net returns required by shareholders (Foss 1992; Jorion 1996). From this point of view a better indicator than ROE could be the entrepreneurial return (ER), defined as ROE minus the long-term risk-free interest rate. The second aspect refers to the different cyclical patterns experienced in the 1989–95 period by the economies of the selected countries, capable of somewhat distorting their relative position due to performance divergences.

It might then be useful to perform a rough exercise using the ER corrected for the real cycle in order to test the strength of our results. We assume that the main influence of the real cycle on ROE is felt through the cyclical changes in the ratio of provisions on loans/loans. This is particularly evident for systems, like the UK one, that are effectively compelled by regulation to account for bad loans in the very short period. Accordingly, we can adjust ROEs for the real cycle (ROEc) replacing the actual (a) values of provisions on loans/loans (P/L) by the trend ones (t):

$$ROE_c = ROE - \left(\frac{P_t}{L_t} - \frac{P_a}{L_a} \right) \frac{L_a}{K_a} \qquad (4)$$

The trend was computed for the longer 1984–95 period.[6] We are aware that some cyclical influences remain on the trend, thus over emphasizing the correction. In addition, other components of ROE are influenced by the real cycle in not quite homogeneous ways across the countries. ER is then computed using the corrected values of ROE.

With the above provisos, Figures 7.7 and 7.8 and Table 7.8 show that ER is characterised by an increased dispersion in the second period that is mitigated, but not eliminated, when correcting ROE for the real cycle. The most notable effect of the correction is on the relative position of the UK.

Figure 7.7: ER: deviations from countries averages

Figure 7.8: Corrected ER: deviations from countries averages

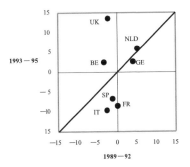

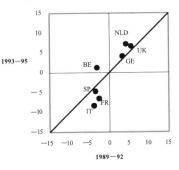

Table 7.8: ER and corrected ER

Countries	ER		Corrected ER	
	1989–92	1993–95	1989–92	1993–95
Belgium	−2.53746	5.99046	−1.38276	4.02456
France	0.96172	−4.95374	−0.90021	−3.71089
Germany	4.82886	6.15988	4.95586	6.85117
Italy	−1.91065	−6.17657	−2.16423	−5.52319
Netherlands	5.96462	9.37775	5.98417	9.90301
Spain	−0.33199	−3.25635	−1.86368	−1.90076
UK	−1.49897	17.02219	7.26342	9.44495
Stand. Dev.	3.36605	8.57718	4.15939	6.40633

The increased country dispersion obtained with the principal components analysis tends, therefore, to be confirmed.

7.4 Conclusions

The empirical results presented in the previous section should evidently be read with due caution. In particular, it is well known that balance sheet indicators of banks belonging to different systems, with different fiscal regimes and different traditions on disclosure and on accounting rules, are not fully comparable. In addition, mainly due to the different incidence of the reserve requirements and the different fiscal treatment of financial instruments, interest rates on deposits and loans offered by international statistics do not homogeneously reflect the real returns and costs of intermediation in different countries. Furthermore, the divergences in profitability measured by ROEs may be somewhat distorted by differences in the inflation rates and by significant differences in the deviations between book and market values of banks' capital. Another motive for caution is given by the shortness of the second period that impedes a fuller evaluation of the impact of banking integration.

The results appear, nevertheless, sufficiently meaningful to confirm that there are no indications of convergence. On the contrary, as was to be expected following the theoretical premises of Section 7.2, the divergences in structure and performance have become more accentuated.

Our analysis does not intend in any way to cast doubts on the unification of the European banking market. Our aim is to evaluate its effects in order to offer a contribution for a better understanding of the necessary regulatory adjustments and of the more effective strategies with which the banks will have to reposition themselves inside the new unified European market. Reflecting on these aspects appears even more relevant when we realize that the transition to the European single currency will accentuate and put in a new perspective the competitive process initiated by the liberalisation of capital movements and by the unification of the banking markets (De Grauwe 1996).

With the implementation of EMU, the European national financial systems will face a third institutional shock of no lesser relevance than the former shocks with regard to their operational and technological aspects. In addition, the third shock must be confronted when the full effects of the previous ones are far from being fully digested. The disappearance of the currency barrier will inevitably redesign and reshuffle the national markets, destined to assume regional characters, changing the complementarity between economic and financial localisms. A deep redesign of the still national banking systems remains on the agenda.

Methodological appendix

These notes elucidate the methodological criteria followed in this chapter. To minimise the risk of misunderstandings, we have to clarify that the aim of the chapter is to examine the system composed by the selected countries in two distinct historical periods. Accordingly we use a comparative static approach in order to perceive their autonomous multivariate complexity in each period. It is not our intention to examine the evolutionary trajectories in the course of time. Therefore, our distinct examinations of the relative positioning of the countries in the two periods must be understood as absolutely independent. The interpretations (reifications) in which we proceed for the two distinct historical periods, therefore, have to be considered as independent.

To better express, and justify, the methodological choices made in the chapter it is useful to recall some elementary notions on the technique of Principal Components, although often confused with Factor Analysis it has quite a different conceptual foundation.

The technique of multivariate analysis known as 'method of Principal Components' (PCs) is nothing else, in its elementary geometric formulation, than a rigid rotation, suitably defined, of the orthogonal Cartesian system in an Rk space in which is located a system of points P1, P2, ..., Pn, the relative positioning of which we want to investigate. In general, the study of this positioning tends to discover the existence of structures that, living in a k dimensional space, are not easily perceivable. The first objective of the PCs method is to reduce the dimensionality of the phenomenon (system of points) from the Rk space to a smaller and more easily perceivable space (for instance of three or two dimensions). If this reduction implies an acceptable loss of information, the use of this technique makes it possible to investigate the phenomenon in a more familiar space, like a plane, if the reduction leads to a two dimensional space. This objective may be pursued suitably transforming the original variables x1, x2, ..., xk into other variables C1, C2, ..., Ck defined by the orthogonal transformation C = A x.

If a is a column of the matrix A, each Ci can be written as: Ci = ai1 x1 + ai2 x2 + ... + aik xk. This linear combination expresses the new variables C1, C2, ..., Ck. If the coefficients a of the original variables x1, x2, ..., xk are chosen according to appropriate criteria, the new variables simply constitute the coordinates of the original points P1, P2, ..., Pn in the new space Rk so defined, that is simply the original space in which we have operated a rotation of the axes. Obviously, up to now we have not reached any dimensional reduction. However, if the coefficients a1, a 2, ..., ak are such that: (a) for each linear combination the sum of their squares is one; (b) the combinations of the coefficients are such that C1 has the highest variance; (c) among all the combinations from which the Ci are derived, C2 is the one that among the Ci not correlated with C1 has the highest variance; (d) C3 is the combination with the highest variance among all the Ci not correlated with C1 and C2, etcetera, we obtain a system of variables Ci capable of being clearly geometrically interpreted. These variables can be read as a support that can be progressively reduced in order to allow the projections of the points expressing the phenomenon fully contained in Rk in a reduced space (for instance R2). Furthermore, the variables Ci are so constructed as to produce the widest possible projections or, if we like, constitute the support that reduces at their minimum the distortions that are inevitable in every projection. In other words, the points P1, P2, ..., Pn belonging to Rk but seen in the system R2 with axes C1 and C2, constitute a 'shadow' of the original points that is as large as possible, preserving in this way the maximum possible structural detail proper of the original Rk space.

The objective of a reduced dimensionality is gained at the price of a certain (measurable) loss of information (the shadow of an object is not certainly the object in its entirety). If the loss of information is tolerable, the dimensional reduction is acceptable and useful.

In order to further clarify this concept, let us imagine that k = 3 and that the system of points in this space constitutes an ellipsoid with three axes, A, B and C in decreasing order of magnitude, that are not parallel to the axes X1, X2, X3. Now, let us proceed to a reduction of dimensionality from R3 to R2. The axes X1, X2, X3 are being rotated in terms of the PCs method, obtaining a new system of axes C1, C2, C3. The points that in the 'true' space were defined by the three coordinates x1, x2, x3 can now be read in the reduced space C1, C2 and will be nested in the ellipse with axes A and B. The loss of information is related to the third axis of the ellipsoid. The loss has been, however, minimised by shrewdly choosing the system C1, C2, C3 (rigidly rotating the system X1, X2, X3) in such a way that the new axes C1, C2, C3 are parallel to the axes of the ellipsoid. The axis C1 has been built so as to be parallel to A; the axis C2 parallel to B; etcetera.

We have dwelt on these really elementary considerations in order to remark that the purpose of the PCs method is to realize, wherever possible, an optimum in the correspondent projections that permit us to read the structures, of which it is a reflection, with the highest possible degree of detail.

In concrete terms, if V1 is the variance–covariance matrix of the original system S1 with points P1, P2, …, Pn in Rk, the vector a (of the coefficients of the PCs) is the one that maximises the quadratic form a'V1a under the constraint that a'Ia = 1 (I = identity matrix). In view of the discussion that follows, let us carefully consider the essential role played by the matrix V1. It is evident that a covariance matrix V2, that is different from V1 since it corresponds to a new system S2 and, therefore, to a distinct configuration of the points in Rk, is the result of a different rigid optimal rotation of the projections. Hence it is relative to a distinct structure of the PCs with a (probable) different loss of information. If S1 and S2 are the two systems of points to which correspond the two covariance matrices V1 and V2, and we proceed separately to the rigid rotations relative to V1 and V2, we obtain two maps M1 and M2 in terms of C1 and C2. If in the two maps the loss of information is acceptable, each map constitutes, for each system separately, the optimal reduction of dimensionality, that is the reduction that permits the maximum preservation of the detail for the structure of the two systems of points S1 and S2.

We must then ask if the two maps, each optimal by itself, are comparable if our aim is the recognition of the relative position of the points included in them. The answer is undoubtedly a positive one, notwithstanding the different structures of the two vectors a1 and a2 that maximise the quadratic forms.

We must clarify the terms in which the maps, autonomously optimal, are comparable if the aim is to interpret the relative position of the points represented in the optimal cartography. The problem is one of 'reification', that is of attributing to the axes C1 and C2, separately and autonomously for each map, a meaning surpassing the simple linear combination of the original variables. We must not forget that in a single map the vector of coefficients a is different for the abscissa and the ordinate and, what is more important, that the vectors a are different for the two maps. Basically, the reification wants to surpass the arithmetics associated to the optimising geometry and the merely instrumental and utilitaristic intrinsic heterogeneity of the axes of the two maps. Its purpose is to propose an interpretation of the points in the cartography by means of variables that are different from the x1, x2, …, xk that allowed the allocation of points in the original space Rk. To the question concerning the comparability of the maps we must again give a positive answer if the reification is done homogeneously for the two maps. In the reification process, in fact, the geometrical device (the technique of PCs) is over and the vectorially different nature of the two axes in M1 and M2 becomes irrelevant: the reificated maps acquire the right to comparability. Let us observe, for example, that a specific proposal of reification connected to a multiple regression (for example, C1 versus external variables) would remain unchanged in terms of its capability to 'explain' the variability also in presence of linear transformation of the PCs (for instance standardising them). The regression coefficients would change but R2 would not change.

It is true that we arrive at the positioning by means of deliberate different arithmetics for each map: the axes are deliberately 'different' since they come from different vectors of the coefficients. There is, however, no obstacle to an independent reading of the relative positioning of the points in the cartography through variables that are different from the ones utilized in the construction of the PCs. Now, since we have generic latitudes and longitudes of the points in the maps, that we can imagine being imposed by new variables, PCs do not exist any more. These variables are obviously the same for the two maps but they act differently in each of them, producing a different structure of points. The search for these new variables constitutes the essence of reification.

At first sight it could appear logically more persuasive to locate the two systems of points S1 and S2 in the same space Rk and to define the PCs for the mixed system (S1&S2), that is, for a variance–covariance matrix V3 computed for the mixed system S1&S2. We would obtain in this way a simultaneous mapping of the points in S1 and in S2, that is a unique map instead of two distinct maps. In this case there is clearly no problem connected to the different composition of the vectors of abscissa and ordinate (coefficients of PCs) as we have in the two maps distinctly built. The reification would be done with reference to a single map and not separately (even if in a homogeneous way) on two distinct maps. The point is whether this procedure is more rational than the one adopted in the present chapter.

To answer the question we must reiterate the aim of the analysis: to interpret the different positioning of the points in the two systems S1 and S2, each with its structure and its variance–covariance matrix, attributing the different positioning to new variables, distinct from the PCs.

Working with one single space Rk, instead of two distinct matrices, we have to work with one matrix, V3, which takes into account the co-ordinates of all points ignoring that they pertain to two systems S1 and S2 that are historically and structurally different and that are worth studying just because they are different. We introduce in this way a first degrading of information since the optimum of the projection of S1 and S2 on the plane C1, C2 cannot be attainable. The attainable optimum will refer to the mix S1&S2, which is not what we are interested in.

A further element causing distortions in the relative positioning is represented by the fact that the variances of the mix S1&S2 depend also on the mean values of the variables representing the coordinates of points in S1 and S2. These mean values are of no interest for the mapping since the aim of mapping is the understanding of the relative positions of the points and nothing else. In fact, given a variable Y, the variance VAR3 of a mixture of elements of Y, representing two distinct sets with numerosity n1 and n2 characterised by variances VAR1 and VAR2 and by means W1 and W2, is:

$$VAR3 = p1VAR1 + p2VAR2 + p1(W1 - W)2 + p2(W2-W)2$$

where p1 = n1/(n1+n2); p2 = n2/(n1+n2); W = p1W1+p2W2.

Evidently, VAR3 is being inflated by the (for us) irrelevant differences between the means. Furthermore, when there is a strong prevalence of one VAR on the other, the entire system of PCs is heavily conditioned by it, darkening just what we are looking for, that is, the positioning of the points in the two systems, and producing a seriously distorted cartography. The optimum representation, which is the characteristics of PCs and that is obtained starting from VAR3, is purely formal and illusory having destroyed the really useful optimality attainable through the distinct mappings of S1 and S2 in terms of PCs.

This is just the case for the present chapter. Let us compare the variance–covariance matrices for the two distinct periods Appendix, Tables 7.A15 and 7.A16 with the variance–covariance matrix obtained combining the information of the two periods (Appendix, Table 7.A17). Comparing the principal diagonal of the latter matrix with those of the matrices for the two distinct periods, the mixture solution is dominated by the second of the two, in particular obscuring the relative positions of the countrypoints in the first period.

If the simultaneous mapping of S1 and S2 had been the goal or the prerequisite of the investigation, it should have, however, been reached using the different frame of the well known CPC model (Flury 1988) which is a generalisation of PCs to several groups. Even in this case, the optimality of mapping is not granted (though worth exploring).

APPENDIX

Table 7.A1: Performance variables (mean values 1989–92)

Country	ROE	VAR	PE
Belgium	6.6171	1.1616	1.1481
France	10.0596	2.3842	1.1909
Germany	12.9709	1.0833	1.2464
Italy	10.2595	2.0679	1.2724
Netherlands	14.2092	2.5785	1.3062
Spain	12.9136	1.8063	1.3694
UK	8.4273	4.5536	1.0917

Table 7.A2: Performance variables (mean values 1993–95)

Country	ROE	VAR	PE
Belgium	13.4180	0.6377	1.2405
France	2.3288	1.6388	1.0481
Germany	12.6435	0.9079	1.2630
Italy	5.1840	3.1806	1.1485
Netherlands	16.3441	0.5785	1.3511
Spain	7.0398	2.8861	1.2124
UK	25.0783	5.0796	1.3320

Table 7.A3: Structure variables (mean values 1989–92)

Country	S	INFL	OPEX	MB/D	CR/GDP
Belgium	6.5521	3.0250	5.2888[1]	0.1775	0.3687
France	5.6763	3.1500	3.5217	0.0867	0.9518
Germany	4.8467	3.5500	0.4969	0.1884	0.9082
Italy	7.6248	6.1250	0.5162	0.2623	0.5396
Netherlands	8.6135	2.5000	1.0831	0.1140	0.8398
Spain	4.8356	6.3250	1.8520	0.2890	0.7094
UK	1.9585	6.7250	4.6241	0.0440	1.1486

Note: (1) Belgium plus Luxembourg.

Table 7.A4: Structure variables (mean values 1993–95)

Country	S	INFL	OPEX[1]	MB/D	CR/GDP
Belgium	4.5472	2.2333	6.0288[2]	0.1456	0.3611[3]
France	3.7806	1.8333	4.3920	0.0653	0.8760
Germany	6.8919	3.0000	0.5783	0.1651	0.9839
Italy	5.7061	4.5000	0.3678	0.2022	0.5618
Netherlands	4.5625	2.4333	0.9341	0.1178	0.9343
Spain	2.5878	4.6667	1.6370	0.2366	0.7031
UK	2.1158	2.5000	3.6441	0.0416	1.1369

Notes: (1) 1993–94.
   (2) Belgium plus Luxembourg.
   (3) Due to a 1992 change in reporting criteria, the 1993–95 data were reconstructed taking as constant the 1992 ratio between the old and the new value.

Table 7.A5: Explicative variables of the 1st principal component C_1 (mean values 1989–92)

Country	LC	CAP	ROA	P/A
Belgium	0.66928	3.72225	0.24479	0.3433
France	0.85886	3.65745	0.36217	0.3163
Germany	1.10961	4.10222	0.53228	0.4181
Italy	1.75281	8.82892	0.89689	0.2475
Netherlands	1.03492	4.38762	0.62737	0.6162
Spain	1.80062	10.07007	1.29478	0.6143
UK	1.79141	4.77951	0.39798	1.2751

Table 7.A6: Explicative variables of the 1st principal component C_1 (mean values 1993–95)

Country	LC	CAP	ROA	P/A
Belgium	0.74912	2.57366	0.34539	0.2068
France	0.78722	4.27874	0.09898	0.6099
Germany	1.01805	4.41009	0.55715	0.4516
Italy	1.56736	9.35729	0.48185	0.1918
Netherlands	1.00650	4.31619	0.70559	0.7852
Spain	1.47454	9.32533	0.65087	0.9002
UK	1.48776	4.06586	1.02362	0.5013

Table 7.A7: Explicative variables of the 2nd principal component C_2 (mean values 1989–92)

Country	INT	MU	MD	NI
Belgium	3.80459	3.97708	2.57500	0.26403
France	9.08555	0.48608	5.19017	0.35291
Germany	7.50655	3.70417	1.14250	0.33496
Italy	2.10090	1.67009	5.95470	0.26643
Netherlands	3.62135	3.52125	5.09229	0.41268
Spain	0.96944	1.27229	3.56333	0.23142
UK	20.39032	0.05125	1.90729	0.66792

Table 7.A8: Explicative variables of the 2nd principal component C_2 (mean values 1993–95)

Country	INT	MU	MD	NI
Belgium	3.97959	3.63861	0.90861	0.38910
France	10.47001	1.36944	2.41111	0.71764
Germany	8.38914	5.97694	0.91500	0.27039
Italy	2.29502	2.79989	2.90622	0.30627
Netherlands	3.51143	3.14389	1.41861	0.47007
Spain	1.40151	0.89083	1.69694	0.30745
UK	19.93097	0.62861	1.48722	0.77041

Table 7.A9: Regression of the 1st principal component C_1 versus its explicative variables (1989–92)

Stat. Multiple Regression	Regression Summary for Dependent Variable: C_1 $R^2 = 0.8801$			
N = 7	B	BETA(1)	MEXVAL	Partial det. Coeff. (%)
Intercept	2.500			
LC	5.738	0.804	17.203	35.91
CAP	−3.565	−2.743	76.803	76.12
ROA	23.280	2.463	117.172	84.78
P/A	−7.721	−0.787	39.120	58.38

Note to Tables 7.A9–7.A12 To avoid misunderstandings, it is worth noting that we are dealing with populations and not with samples. Since we face descriptive and not inference problems, we need neither theoretical assumptions concerning the (stochastic or deterministic) nature of the variables involved, nor postulates about distributional frames (normality, etc.). A consequence of our descriptive analysis is that the BETA coefficients, that is, the regression coefficients associated with the standardised variables, are not obliged to lie in a defined (−1; +1) range.

Table 7.A10: Regression of the 1st principal component C_1 versus its explicative variables (1993–95)

Stat. Multiple Regression	Regression Summary for Dependent Variable: C_1 $R^2 = 0.9910$			
N = 7	B	BETA (1)	MEXVAL	Partial det. Coeff. (%)
Intercept	–3.000			
LC	1.225	0.054	0.564	1.67
CAP	–1.688	–0.590	79.367	76.88
ROA	22.695	–0.852	169.689	90.39
P/A	–3.273	–0.114	22.478	42.86

Table 7.A11: Regression of the 2nd principal component C_2 versus its explicative variables (1989–92)

Stat. Multiple Regression	Regression Summary for Dependent Variable: C_2 $R^2 = 0.7862$			
N = 7	B	BETA (1)	MEXVAL	Partial det. Coeff. (%)
Intercept	–5.6			
INT	0.691	1.936	33.174	53.71
MU	1.823	1.248	67.737	73.12
MD	1.328	1.029	49.336	64.85
NI	–21.467	–1.344	27.367	48.27

Table 7.A12: Regression of the 2nd principal component C_2 versus its explicative variables (1993–95)

Stat. Multiple Regression	Regression Summary for Dependent Variable: C_2 $R^2 = 0.5414$			
N = 7	B	BETA (1)	MEXVAL	Partial det. Coeff. (%)
Intercept	0.874			
INT	0.228	0.618	7.496	18.92
MU	0.299	0.233	1.783	5.12
MD	1.273	0.394	7.720	19.39
NI	–11.753	–0.997	13.793	30.66

Table 7.A13: Euclidean distances (1989–92)

Country	BE	FR	GE	IT	NLD	SP	UK
Belgium	0.0						
France	4.20	0.0					
Germany	8.17	4.49	0.0				
Italy	6.90	4.69	4.78	0.0			
Netherlands	9.06	5.68	4.41	5.51	0.0		
Spain	8.12	4.71	3.18	4.09	5.6	0.0	
UK	7.12	5.49	8.26	7.70	10.6	6.64	0.0

Table 7.A14: Euclidean distances (1993–95)

Country	BE	FR	GE	IT	NLD	SP	UK
Belgium	0.0						
France	11.3	0.0					
Germany	6.1	11.5	0.0				
Italy	10.6	6.1	8.0	0.0			
Netherlands	5.9	14.5	4.4	11.7	0.0		
Spain	8.7	6.4	7.6	3.9	10.1	0.0	
UK	13.0	23.1	14.3	20.7	10.5	18.4	0.0

Table 7.A15: Variance–covariance matrix (1989–92)

	S	INFL	OPEX	MB/D	CR/GDP	ROE	VAR	PE
S	4.7313							
INFL	−2.1688	3.3035						
OPEX	−1.8782	−0.0730	3.9511					
MB/D	0.0628	0.0470	−0.0917	0.0082				
CR/GDP	−0.3451	0.0723	−0.0012	−0.0159	0.0695			
ROE	1.7580	−0.6690	−4.4900	0.0632	0.1969	7.4611		
VAR	−1.2601	0.9823	0.7522	−0.0699	0.2108	−0.5445	1.3677	
PE	0.1028	0.0036	−0.1461	0.0061	−0.0062	0.2111	−0.0497	0.0091

Table 7.A16: Variance–covariance matrix (1993–95)

	S	INFL	OPEX	MB/D	CR/GDP	ROE	VAR	PE
S	2.7994							
INFL	0.1022	1.2573						
OPEX	−1.5871	−1.5394	4.7960					
MB/D	0.0394	0.0665	−0.0773	0.0049				
CR/GDP	−0.0901	−0.0857	−0.1652	−0.0106	0.0716			
ROE	−3.5747	−2.8749	2.0778	−0.2567	0.9736	59.3971		
VAR	−1.6581	0.6596	−0.1558	−0.0199	0.1425	3.7955	2.7907	
PE	−0.0154	−0.0111	−0.0424	−0.0008	0.0099	0.7158	0.0079	0.0110

Table 7.A17: Variance–covariance matrix (1989–95)

	S	INFL	OPEX	MB/D	CR/GDP	ROE	VAR	PE
S	2.9678							
INFL	-0.9879	1.9797						
OPEX	-1.9241	-0.4209	2.8075					
MB/D	0.0524	0.0559	-0.0881	0.0066				
CR/GDP	-0.2370	-0.0042	0.0648	-0.0137	0.0696			
ROE	-1.7003	3.4027	-0.9972	0.0387	0.1268	11.6778		
VAR	-3.9886	0.8004	3.6466	-0.1560	0.3721	2.1740	8.0175	
PE	0.0308	0.0174	-0.0775	0.0026	0.0002	0.0007	-0.0604	0.0047

Notes

* The study is a substantially revised version of a previous work published in *Europe in Transition*, ed. by H. Peeters and M. Tonveronachi, Tilburg University Press, 1977.
1. The traditional distinction between commercial and universal banking does not fully capture the differences in risk management models that characterise the most recent experience.
2. The data are reported in Appendix, Tables A7.9–A7.12. In the whole period, except for the inflation rate, none of the variables related to the Maastricht criteria were useful to discriminate among the selected countries. This might mean that a significant and systematic association between the Maastricht criteria and the variables of bank structure and performance does not exist, or that it might not be shown by the adopted statistical method.
3. A concise discussion of this statistical method is presented in the Methodological Appendix.
4. 'The Mexval, or marginal explanatory value, of each variable is simply the percentage by which the standard error of estimate of the equation would increase if the variable were omitted from the equation and the coefficients of the remaining variables were adjusted to give the best possible fit without that variable. It helps us to see how important each variable is for the fit of the whole equation.' Almon (1988), p. 40.
5. Since mark ups and mark downs are computed with reference to different records of inflation and country risk, these nominal margins undervalue the real power of banks pertaining to countries with a long history of strong currencies.
6. Due to data availability, provisions/total assets is used for Belgium, the Netherlands and UK.

References

Abraham, J.-P. and F. Lierman (1991), *European banking strategies in the Nineties: a supply side approach*, Research Papers in Banking and Finance 91/8, Bangor: Institute of European Finance
Almon, C. (1988), *The Craft of Economic Modelling*, Department of Economics, University of Maryland, Needham Heights: Ginn Press
Altunbaş, Y. and P. Molyneux (1993), *Scale and scope economies in European banking*, Research Papers in Banking and Finance, 93/11, Bangor: Institute of European Finance
Bruni, F. (1993), 'Banking and financial regulation: the Italian case', in J. Dermine, (ed.), *European banking in the 1990s*, 2nd edn, Oxford: Blackwell
Bruni, F. (1995), 'Prudential regulation in an integrated financial market: issues of optimality and credibility', in G. Ferrarini, (ed.), *Prudential regulation of banks and securities firms: European and international Aspects*, London: Kluwer Law International

Conti, V. and M. Maccarinelli (1993), *Deregulation and profitability in different OECD banking systems*, Research Papers in Banking and Finance, 93/18, Bangor: Institute of European Finance

de Boissieu, C. (1993), 'The French banking sector in the light of European financial integration', in J. Dermine, (ed.), *European banking in the 1990s*, 2nd edn, Oxford: Blackwell

De Grauwe, P. (1996), 'The dynamics of convergence towards European Monetary Union', in, *European Monetary Union: the problems of the transition to a single currency*, Banca Nazionale del Lavoro Quarterly Review, Special Issue, March

Flury, B. (1988), *Common principal components and related multivariate models*, Wiley Series in Probability and Mathematical Statistics, Wiley: New York

Foss, G. (1992), 'Capital allocation and pricing credit risk', *Journal of Commercial Lending*, October

Gardener, E.P.M. (1995), *Banking strategies in the European Union: financial services firms after the Cecchini report*, Research Papers in Banking and Finance, 95/7, Bangor: Institute of European Finance

Hellwig, M. (1996), 'Financial innovations and the incidence of risk in the financial system', in F. Bruni, *et al.* (eds), *Risk management in volatile financial markets*, Dordrecht: Kluwer Academic Publishers for the Société Universitaire Européenne de Recherches Financières (SUERF)

Jorion, P. (1996), *Value at risk*, Chicago: Irwin

Kane, E.J. (1991), 'Incentive conflict in the international regulatory agreement on risk based capital', in S.G. Rhee and R.P. Chang (eds), *Pacific-Basin capital markets research*, vol. 2, Amsterdam: North Holland

Kapstein, E.B. (1994), 'Supervising international banks: origins and implications of the Basle Accord', in C.A. Stone and A. Zissu (eds), *Global risk based capital regulations Vol. I: Capital adequacy*, New York: Irwin

Knight, F. (1923), 'The ethics of competition', *Quarterly Journal of Economics*, August

Kregel, J. (1993), *Financial fragility and the structure of financial markets*, Università degli Studi di Bologna, Dipartimento di Scienze economiche, Collana Rapporti Scientifici, No. 157, February

Neven, D. (1993), 'Structural adjustments in European retail banking: some views from industrial organisation', in J. Dermine (ed.), *European banking in the 1990s*, 2nd edn, Oxford: Blackwell

Rajan, R.G. (1992), 'Insiders and outsiders: the choice between informed and arm-length debt', *Journal of Finance*, XLVII, 4

Sylos Labini, P. (1967), *Oligopoly and technical progress*, 2nd edn, Cambridge: Harvard University Press

8
Product Mix of the Spanish Banking Firms: Do Competition Clubs Exist?[1]

Francisco Pérez and Emili Tortosa-Ausina

Abstract

The expansion and intensification of banking competition, which has occurred in Spain during the last ten years, has allowed banks and savings banks to define their competitive strategies with more freedom. This chapter analyses the similarities and the differences in the product mix of the firms and their time evolution. In particular, it aims to identify the different kinds of firms and, on this ground, to analyze whether competition leads to the homogenisation (convergence) of product mixes between firms or groups of firms (clubs). The empirical success is higher when specialisation clubs are considered, finding increased heterogeneity within the banking system as a whole but also increased homogeneity within certain clusters of banks and savings banks.

8.1   Introduction

During the last decade, many European countries have witnessed great changes in the conditions surrounding the banking industry. A new financial environment, deregulation, technological change and internationalisation of the economies are some of the outstanding features of such transformations. Banking firms have been impelled to modify their competitive strategies into a wider context for both products and markets. One of the more important components of such strategies has been the choice of a certain specialisation in their production or product mix.

Bearing in mind that these are multiproduct firms, this study attempts to identify the lines of specialisation of banking firms in these circumstances, along with the evolution of such a specialisation. The analysis is carried out through a database of Spanish banking firms. However, the exercise is also interesting because it tries to capture the usefulness of applying some of the frequently used techniques in the economic growth and inequality literature to the study of the specialisation of multiproduct firms.

In order to analyse the banking product mix, a measurement of banking output is required. This question has often been involved in debate and controversy.[2] According to our objective, it is necessary to use an output measure which allows us to identify product diversity. This is the reason underlying the use of the balance sheet items as output indicators, although this choice has well-known shortcomings.[3]

The approach used in this paper to analyse the evolution of specialisation in the banking industry has been considered in different studies.[4] Pastor and Pérez (1999) for example, seek to analyse the differences in the product mix patterns between the aggregate of banks' and savings banks', considering each aggregate as the representative firm. In an approach similar to the one pursued in this chapter, their study provides an overview of the changes faced by the banks' and savings banks' balance sheet structures over the last decade. They find that there is a tendency for both types of institutions to narrow or widen their product mixes throughout this period, during which the increase in competition has allowed them to choose less regulation-conditioned competitive strategies. The overall conclusion of their study is that, while there appears to be a convergence of product mix for certain balance sheet items, no clear pattern exists for the overwhelming majority of asset and liability items.

However, it is not possible to reach a conclusion as to whether the widening of markets and products has resulted in increased homogeneity (or diversity) within the banking sector or not from the exercise developed in the Pastor and Pérez (1999) study. First, results tend to be ambiguous. Second, competitive strategies must be studied, considering the individual firm rather than any type of institution aggregate. For that reason, possibilities of developing an analysis of the aforementioned problem in relation to the banking firms are exploited in our study.

As we try to study banking firms, both statistical and instrumental difficulties emerge. The former refers to the individual available data[5] which do not offer the same level of detail as the aggregate data published by the Bank of Spain, which forces us to use slightly different product mix indicators.[6] The instrumental difficulty is more substantial, as it deals with the way of building product mix indicators which synthesize the behaviour of multiple firms and multiple product lines. That will be the main goal of this chapter.

8.2 Basic product mix indicators

The starting point lies in defining some basic product mix indicators from the chosen output measures. Let X_{ij} be firm j's balance sheet's item i. When the items are asset items, they will be denoted by A_{ij} and by L_{ij} when they are liability items. Let $X_j = A_j = L_j$ be the total value of such firm assets and liabilities. In the same way, let X_i (A_i, L_i) be the aggregate value of item i for a group of firms.

The output of a firm is defined by its assets and liabilities vector:

$$X_j(A_{ij}, L_{ij}) \tag{1}$$

The vectors of the firms as a whole make up a matrix:

$$X(X_j) = X(A_{ij}, L_{ij}) \tag{2}$$

This type of matrix, which includes the output of the firms in its rows, is available in every period. In the same way, we have two aggregate vectors: each firm's aggregate vector (X_j) and each product aggregate vector (X_i).

The basic group of product mix indicators is obtained through:

$$x_{ij} = \frac{X_{ij}}{X_j} \tag{3}$$

This matrix is made up of the elements defined in such a way. Its main advantage consists of every firm's row being comparable with the others, as the production scale elements have been corrected. Each column i represents the intensity of the specialisation of the different firms in product i.

Finally, the set of available data matrices x_{ij} is conditioned only by the existing observations in the analysed period t. For our purposes, we will employ eight balance sheet items (columns) (four asset items and four liability items), 127 firms[7] (rows) and 11 years (matrices).

8.3 Product mix measures

Taking the x_{ij} indicators as a starting point, it is possible to analyse the product mix from two different approaches:

- From the homogeneity between firms
- From the time evolution.

8.3.1 Homogeneity in specialisation

Let us consider now any of the column vectors in the matrix $x(x_{ij})$. Each of the elements of the vector i has a value which ranges from 0 to 1 and represents the intensity of the specialisation in one of the different firm's balance sheets. A homogeneous or heterogeneous product mix measure in a certain period of any of the balance sheet items will be given by the density function dispersion measures made up of the available observations: either the variation coefficient (ρ) or the standard deviation (σ) (depending on whether we want to take into account the mean values of x_{ij} for such an item or not).

The lowest values in the dispersion measures of the specialisation coefficients show the banking firms as being more homogeneous between them in the considered product line. As far as the variation coefficients are concerned, since they have been corrected by the mean we are able to check out the items where the relative homogeneity between firms is higher, regardless of their importance in the balance sheet.

Table 8.2 shows the variation coefficients' values corresponding to the most important assets and liabilities items[8] for each of the years of the sample. Table 8.1 shows in a decreasing order such coefficient values for the initial and final years and allows us to appreciate the highest relative inequality in issued securities, interbank deposits and

Table 8.1: Convergence in specialisation (relative dispersion): banking firms (1985 versus 1995)

	1985		1995
Issued securities	2.07	Issued securities	2.94
Interbank deposits	1.41	Interbank deposits	1.16
Interbank loans	0.84	Other deposits	1.07
Other deposits	0.72	Fixed-income securities	0.69
Savings deposits	0.53	Interbank loans	0.69
Cash and Bank of Spain	0.49	Cash and Bank of Spain	0.58
Fixed-income securities	0.39	Savings deposits	0.47
Credit to firms and households	0.36	Credit to firms and households	0.46

Table 8.2: Convergence in specialisation (relative dispersion): banking firms (1985–95)

	1985	1986	1987	1988	1989	1990	1991	1992	1993	1994	1995
Assets											
Cash and Bank of Spain	0.49	0.53	0.47	0.49	0.50	0.62	0.73	0.51	0.55	0.57	0.58
Fixed income securities	0.39	0.38	0.40	0.42	0.49	0.49	0.47	0.60	0.64	0.62	0.69
Interbank loans	0.84	0.71	0.94	0.94	0.89	0.81	0.83	0.72	0.62	0.67	0.69
Credit to firms and households	0.36	0.35	0.36	0.37	0.39	0.39	0.39	0.39	0.42	0.42	0.46
Liabilities											
Savings deposits	0.53	0.54	0.56	0.52	0.53	0.51	0.49	0.46	0.45	0.44	0.47
Other deposits	0.72	0.77	0.83	0.84	0.73	0.75	0.81	0.89	1.01	1.05	1.07
Interbank deposits	1.41	1.56	1.64	1.48	1.47	1.46	1.26	1.01	1.29	1.26	1.16
Issued securities	2.07	2.04	2.26	2.77	3.33	4.02	3.70	3.28	3.56	3.56	2.94

other deposits. In the same way, comparing the starting and final data, it is possible to notice how the dispersion has fallen in some cases but has increased in others, there being no *a priori* evident pattern towards homogeneity or diversity of the product mixes.

8.3.2   Evolution of specialisation: do tendencies exist?

Table 8.2 leads us in a natural way to wonder whether a steady tendency towards the homogeneity of product mixes exists or not. In order to identify such a tendency, we represent graphically the time evolution of certain x_{ij} item variation coefficients values.[9] Its decreasing evolution shows firms *converging* in the intensity of their specialisation in the item being analysed. We will discuss divergence in the opposite case.

Figure 8.1 shows the results for the four analysed assets items while Figure 8.2 does the same for the liability side. It is possible to notice a clear tendency towards convergence in interbank loans but, on the other hand, fixed income securities, other deposits, issued securities, and even (although to a lesser extent) credit to firms and households show a tendency towards diversity.

Another way to consider the tendency in the specialisation approach deals with analysing whether the intensity of the specialisation at the start influences the specialisation rate of change throughout the period being analysed. Thus, if a firm is more orientated towards a certain specialisation, does this lead it to experience smaller intensifications of such a specialisation in the future? On the other hand, if the initially less specialised firms grow faster in that way, we will notice an inverse relationship between the initial level $x_{ij,0}$ and the rate of variation of such a measure.[10] This behaviour leads to closer final x_{ij} values, so we will test in another way how product mixes converge.

In order to quantify if β-convergence exists, we must estimate for all the items the equation:

$$\frac{1}{T}\log\frac{x_{ij,t}}{x_{ij,t-T}} = a - \beta\log(x_{ij,t-T}) + u_{ij,t-T} \tag{4}$$

where T represents the length of the analysed period and $u_{ij,t-T}$ the error term.

Table 8.3 shows the estimates for equation (4) using least squares estimation for all of the contemplated balance sheet items of the considered Spanish banking enterprises. The results shown in the table allow us to assess the general sign of the tendency throughout the period. However, they do not allow us to notice the shocks which have taken place at any point in time. The value of the estimated β shows us

145

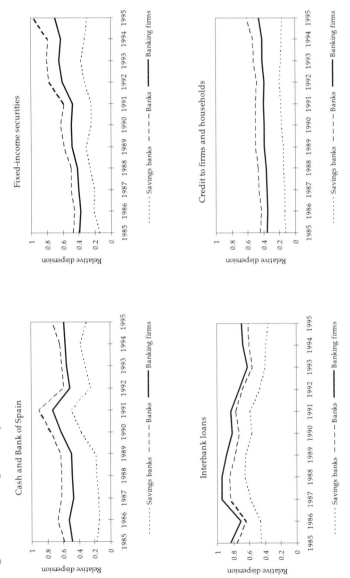

Figure 8.1: Convergence in specialisation: banks and savings banks (assets)

146

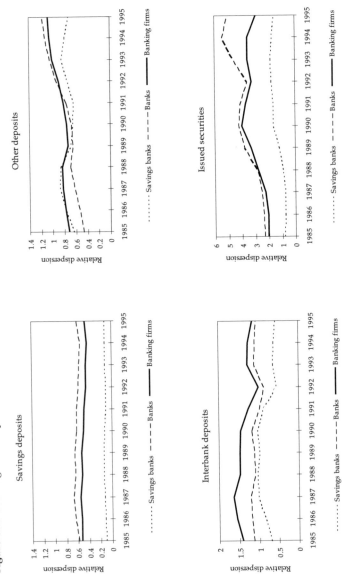

Figure 8.2: Convergence in specialisation: banks and savings banks (liabilities)

Table 8.3: Convergence in specialisation: banking firms (1985–95)

		Banks and savings banks
Cash and Bank of Spain	β	0.0575
	(t-Student)	(9.8222)
	R^2	0.4396
Fixed income securities	β	0.0341
	(t-Student)	(2.87)
	R^2	0.0647
Interbank loans	β	0.055
	(t-Student)	(7.5465)
	R^2	0.3147
Credit to firms and households	β	0.0315
	(t-Student)	(2.3081)
	R^2	0.0412
Savings deposits	β	0.0652
	(t-Student)	(11.7823)
	R^2	0.5405
Other deposits	β	0.0727
	(t-Student)	(6.9046)
	R^2	0.2777
Interbank deposits	β	0.0634
	(t-Student)	(10.0319)
	R^2	0.4711
Issued securities	β	0.0169
	(t-Student)	(0.8887)
	R^2	0.0248

Note: β values closer to zero suggest slower convergence.

the rate at which banking firms converge or diverge in a certain specialisation.

Excluding the issued securities case, we notice convergence in all product lines, although the fitness of the regression (R^2) is somewhat poor in the fixed income securities and credit to firms and households items. The β values, which show the rate at which firms are getting closer in their specialisation, suggests to us that the required time for the x_{ij} of the different firms relating to a certain column to be equalised is rather long. The rate is high in the case of savings deposits and other deposits, as well as cash and Bank of Spain and the interbank operations (both loans and deposits); in the remaining items, convergence takes place at a much slower rate.

The resulting conclusion of this analysis lies in a certain approach in the product mixes of the Spanish banking firms, although the speed differs substantially depending on the analysed item. These results are not confirmed when using σ-convergence: in this case neither generalised nor clear patterns emerge. However, if we interpret these results as a lack of relationship in the banks' selected product mixes, the prediction would not be consistent with the general idea of Spanish banks being increasingly sensitive to other firms' product mixes. Thus, it is possible that banks' and savings banks' concerns about other firms specialisations are focused only on their most immediate rivals. In such a case, in order to appreciate convergence it would be necessary to observe in a different way the conduct of Spanish banking firms, by trying to identify the groups of banks and savings banks which compete against each others.

8.4   Do competition clubs exist?

One of the possible choices is that, as Kolari and Zardkoohi (1987) pointed out, banking firms should not be treated as one homogeneous group, which used 'to cluster around specific market niches that are distinct from other markets'. Thus, it would be more interesting to study the evolution of the specialisation between groups of competitors instead of all banks. The regarded hypotheses to identify rival groups are multiple, but we will consider the following:

- *Type of institution*: in this case, the hypothesis lies in the difference between banks and savings banks being significant for specialisation due to their historical trajectory, as they currently face the same regulatory environment
- *Size*: we consider here large firms being rivals and imitating each other in their product mix. The same occurs with medium and small firms
- *Their own product mix*: in this case, the posed idea lies on firms' chosen specializations being the relevant issue to identify competitors and, therefore, to analyse the evolution of specialisation.[11]

The analysis in each of the different alternatives is focused as follows. First, depending on the selected criterion, groups on which the evolution of specialisation is going to be analysed must be identified. Second, it is necessary to check out if such a grouping influences firms' convergence in specialisation, both on its existence and its rate.

As far as the construction of the analysed groups is concerned, and with reference to the first hypothesis we have made, the institutional difference between banks and savings banks leads to an automatic clustering of firms. The size hypothesis forces us to decide on the selected steps, finally choosing four categories.[12] Finally, the chosen criterion to cluster firms by their product mix consists of identifying the specialisation patterns from the x_{ij} indicators and using the cluster analysis multivariate statistical technique. This analysis allows us to identify, through the application of a similarity or distance criteria to the different x_{ij}, how close firms' specialisations are. Once the distances have been computed, the following step deals with including in the same group (or cluster of firms) those which have an output mix similar to that of all other banks and savings banks in their group but unlike those firms in all other groups.[13] The Ward's method, which minimises the within groups variance, has been chosen to form the analysed clusters.[14]

From these criteria, and applying them to 1995 data, nine groups have been selected. Table 8.4 names the institutional nature (bank or savings bank) and each firm and groups' share of total banking sector assets indicated there.

Once banks and savings banks have been grouped according to the three described hypotheses, the σ and β convergence analysis has been replicated for each of the resultant banks' clusters: two in the first hypothesis, four in the second and nine in the third. As far as σ-convergence is concerned, it is difficult to define general behaviour guidelines because of the heterogeneity in the results, as shown before.[15] On the other hand, the β-convergence analysis does help us in assessing if the specialisation throughout the 1985 to 1995 period is influenced or conditioned in its significance or rate by the selected clusters of banks and savings banks. The expression of the β-convergence equation to be estimated is now:

$$\frac{1}{T} \log \frac{x_{ij,\,t}}{x_{ij,\,t-T}} = a - \beta \log(x_{ij,\,t-T}) + \phi z_{ij} + u_{ij,\,t-T} \qquad (6)$$

where z_{ij} is a vector of dummy variables which takes value 1 or 0 depending on the firm belonging to a certain cluster or not.

The results of the estimation with the first clustering (banks and savings banks) show a certain increase in the rate of convergence of some balance sheet items, specially between savings banks, although changes are not important (see Table 8.5, column 1). The second series

Table 8.4: Selected groups by product mix in the Spanish banking sector (1995)

	Assets*	% over total assets of the banking sector
Group 1		
Alicante, Banco de (B)	143 244	0.13
Altae, Banco (B)	94 512	0.08
Andalucía, Banco de (B)	401 118	0.36
Asturias, Banco de (B)	96 374	0.09
Exportación, Banco de la (B)	48 827	0.04
Mercantil de Tarragona, Banco (B)	12 119	0.01
Murcia, Banco de (B)	69 330	0.06
Vasconia, Banco de (B)	147 221	0.13
Asturias-Oviedo, C.A. (SB)	584 280	0.52
Baleares, C.A. y M.P. de las (SB)	407 684	0.36
Cajasur (SB)	616 205	0.55
Castilla-La Mancha, C.A. de (SB)	749 353	0.67
Guadalajara, C.A. Provincial (SB)	64 648	0.06
Huelva y Sevilla, M.P. y C.A. de (SB)	416 123	0.37
Ontinyent, C.A. y M.P. de (SB)	44 588	0.04
Pollença (Colonya), C.A. de (SB)	13 513	0.01
San Fernando de Sevilla y Jerez, Caja (SB)	473 507	0.42
Total	4 382 646	3.89
Group 2		
Popular Español, Banco (B)	2 145 877	1.91
Valencia, Banco de (B)	375 591	0.33
Avila, C.A. y M.P. de (SB)	218 217	0.19
Bancaja (SB)	1 497 478	1.33
CAI (SB)	463 868	0.41
CAM (SB)	1 493 227	1.33
España de Inversiones, C.A. y M.P. (SB)	1 068 146	0.95
Granada, Caja General de Ahorros (SB)	507 882	0.45
Ibercaja (SB)	1 278 974	1.14
La Rioja, C.A. de (SB)	143 273	0.13
Madrid, C.A. y M.P. de (SB)	4 886 000	4.34
Murcia, C.A. de (SB)	501 595	0.45

	Assets*	% over total assets of the banking sector
Group 5 *(continued)*		
Crédito Balear, Banco de (B)	107 133	0.10
Etcheverría, Banco (B)	19 156	0.02
Extremadura, Banco de (B)	53 930	0.05
Galicia, Banco de (B)	225 733	0.20
Granada Jerez, Banco de (B)	181 136	0.16
Pueyo, Banca (B)	23 378	0.02
Simeón, Banco (B)	114 286	0.10
Badajoz, M.P. y C.A. de (SB)	213 163	0.19
Canarias-Las Palmas, C. Insular de A. de (SB)	306 733	0.27
Canarias, Caja General de Ahorros de (SB)	313 144	0.28
Carlet, C.A. y Préstamos de (SB)	15 592	0.01
Extremadura, C.A. y M.P. de (SB)	335 028	0.30
Galicia-La Coruña, C.A. de (SB)	1 327 328	1.18
Jaén, Caja Provincial de Ahorros de (SB)	32 130	0.03
Orense, C.A. Provincial de (SB)	223 241	0.20
Tarragona, C.A. Provincial de (SB)	372 146	0.33
Total	4 199 406	3.73
Group 6		
Guipuzcoano, Banco (B)	447 465	0.40
Herrero, Banco (B)	418 288	0.37
Urquijo, Banco (B)	653 204	0.58
Vitoria, Banco de (B)	131 485	0.12
Barcelona, C.A. y Pensiones de (SB)	8 052 644	7.15
Bilbao Bizkaia Kutxa (SB)	1 495 606	1.33
Burgos, C.A. Municipal de (SB)	405 764	0.36
Catalunya-Barcelona, C.A. de (SB)	2 009 396	1.78
Girona, C.A. Provincial de (SB)	255 482	0.23
Guipúzcoa y San Sebastián, C.A. y M.P. de (SB)	1 033 117	0.92
Laietana-Mataró, C.A. (SB)	223 289	0.20
Manlleu, C.A. Comarcal de (SB)	107 244	0.10
Manresa, C.A. de (SB)	203 107	0.18

Table 8.4: Selected groups by product mix in the Spanish banking sector (1995) *(continued)*

	Assets*	% over total assets of the banking sector
Group 2 *(continued)*		
Pamplona, C.A. y M.P. Municipal de (SB)	153 061	0.14
Penedés – Vilafranca, C.A. del (SB)	523 252	0.46
Pontevedra, C.A. Provincial de (SB)	185 240	0.16
Sabadell, C.A. de (SB)	358 168	0.32
Santander y Cantabria, C.A. de (SB)	423 415	0.38
Segovia, C.A. y M.P. de (SB)	219 886	0.20
Unicaja. (SB)	1 202 636	1.07
Vigo, C.A. Municipal de (SB)	520 716	0.46
Total	18 166 502	16.13
Group 3		
Arabe Español, Banco (B)	75 654	0.07
B.N.P. España (B)	405 970	0.36
Catalana, Banca (B)	989 528	0.88
Citibank España, S.A. (B)	269 793	0.24
Deutsche Bank, SAE (B)	1 245 151	1.11
March, Banca (B)	337 034	0.30
Natwest España, Banco (B)	292 318	0.26
San Paolo, Banco (B)	231 462	0.21
Zaragozano, Banco (B)	711 497	0.63
Total	4 558 407	4.05
Group 4		
Atlántico, Banco (B)	1 060 115	0.94
Barclays Bank, S.A.E. (B)	636 606	0.57
Caixabank (B)	85 047	0.08
Condal, Banco (B)	4 827	0.00
Consolidado España, Banco (B)	1 496	0.00
Desarrollo Económico Español, Banco del (B)	71 886	0.06
Europa, Banco de (B)	57 153	0.05
Inversión, Banco de (B)	24 589	0.02

	Assets*	% over total assets of the banking sector
Group 6 *(continued)*		
Terrasa, C.A. de (SB)	322 728	0.29
Vital (SB)	414 586	0.37
Total	16 173 405	14.36
Group 7		
Bankinter (B)	1 665 501	1.48
Bankoa (B)	86 485	0.08
Comercio, Banco del (B)	1 084 226	0.96
Pequeña y Mediana Empresa, Banco de la (B)	112 524	0.10
Sindicatos de Banqueros de Barcelona.(B)	159 273	0.14
Navarra-Pamplona, C.A. de (SB)	572 685	0.51
Total	3 680 694	3.27
Group 8		
Bilbao Vizcaya, Banco (B)	10 578 312	9.39
Central Hispano, Banco (B)	9 659 867	8.58
Credit Lyonnais España (B)	393 533	0.35
Español de Credito, Banco (B)	4 911 180	4.36
Gallego, Banco (B)	153 408	0.14
Jover, Banca (B)	196 378	0.17
Pastor, Banco (B)	1 188 945	1.06
Santander, Banco de (B)	8 475 481	7.53
Burgos, C.A. y M.P. del C.C.O. de (SB)	294 938	0.26
Salamanca y Soria, C.A. de (SB)	804 292	0.71
Total	36 656 334	32.55
Group 9		
Espirito Santo, Banco (B)	99 411	0.09
Exterior de España, Banco (B)	6 263 135	5.56
Hispamer, Banco (B) Financiero	75 416	0.07
Huelva, Banco de (B)	2 006	0.00

Table 8.4: Selected groups by product mix in the Spanish banking sector (1995) *(continued)*

	Assets*	% over total assets of the banking sector		Assets*	% over total assets of the banking sector
Group 4 *(continued)*			**Group 9** *(continued)*		
Mapfre, Banco (B)	176 036	0.16	Industrial de Cataluña, Banco (B)	6 084	0.01
Sabadell, Banco de (B)	1 476 768	1.31	Luso Español, Banco (B)	349 634	0.31
Total	3 594 523	3.19	Santander de Negocios, Banco (B)	1 065 371	0.95
			Total	7 861 057	6.98
Group 5			**Total of groups**	99 272 974	88.16
Bancofar (B)	19 622	0.02	**Total of banking sector**	112 606 181	100.00
Castilla, Banco de (B)	316 527	0.28			

Notes:
* In millions of pesetas.
B: bank. SB: savings bank.

Table 8.5: Convergence in specialisation: banking firms (1985–95)

		Type of institution*	Size**	Product mix***
Cash and Bank of Spain	β	0.0662	0.0578	0.0727
	(t-Student)	(10.9484)	(9.6514)	(12.951)
	R^2	0.4964	0.4433	0.6831
Fixed income securities	β	0.0535	0.0068	0.0958
	(t-Student)	(4.3801)	(0.3772)	(13.6449)
	R^2	0.1758	0.0675	0.6974
Interbank loans	β	0.0659	0.056	0.0872
	(t-Student)	(8.4693)	(7.608)	(16.4191)
	R^2	0.369	0.3256	0.7594
Credit to firms and households	β	0.037	0.0393	0.0956
	(t-Student)	(2.7897)	(2.0132)	(9.3203)
	R^2	0.1161	0.0398	0.6356
Savings deposits	β	0.0722	0.0657	0.075
	(t-Student)	(11.6407)	(11.5175)	(29.1481)
	R^2	0.5609	0.542	0.9065
Other deposits	β	0.0499	0.0731	0.0974
	(t-Student)	(3.9002)	(6.8144)	(13.3681)
	R^2	0.3258	0.3234	0.7632
Interbank deposits	β	0.0721	0.0684	0.0814
	(t-Student)	(10.047)	(10.5029)	(15.6455)
	R^2	0.4968	0.5015	0.763
Issued securities	β	0.0174	0.0071	0.0194
	(t-Student)	(0.9675)	(0.285)	(0.0545)
	R^2	0.1606	0.0262	0.7169

Notes:
 * Includes type of institution dummies
 ** Includes size dummies
 *** Includes product mix dummies.

of estimations, related to the clustering by size, show dimension as a minor conditioning factor when analysing convergence in specialisation, except for certain items (see Table 8.5, column 2) for group 2 (medium banks).[16] Finally, the third clustering hypothesis does noticeably affect the results (see Table 8.5, column 3), leading to an important increase in the fitness of the regression (R^2) and the β values which represent the rate of convergence.

The way to interpret such results is the following: if banking firms are clustered by their current product mix similarity, and their last decade trajectory is analysed, we verify that, other things being equal, each of the clusters will have converged to a very similar product mix in a few years. In other words, if the current strategies in specialisation concerns are held, there will be groups of firms with almost homogeneous product bundles, depending on the level of detail that the available information permits.

8.5   Where is the banking sector diversity?

According to what we have seen, when all banking firms are considered, the different firms' product mixes do not show a clear pattern either towards homogeneity or towards diversity. If an aggregate indicator of the σ-convergence indicators is designed as a weighted mean of such indicators, a slight increase in heterogeneity is appreciated. This statement is justified by considering the weighted variance of the assets or liabilities specialisation indicators, or the whole balance sheet, computed in the following way:

$$\sigma_\omega = \sum_{i=1}^{n} \frac{X_i}{\sum_{i=1}^{p} X_i} \sigma_i^2 \qquad (7)$$

Figure 8.3: Convergence in specialisation, total balance sheet: banks and savings banks

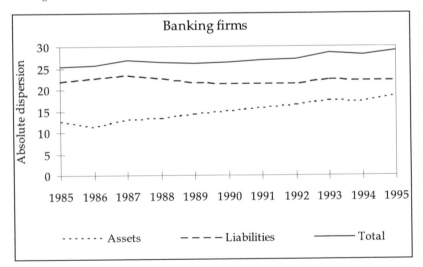

where, σ^2_i, $i = 1 \ldots n$, represents the sample variance of each of the variables considered in the balance sheet analysis of the banking firms, $n = 4,8$ (depending on whether we analyse a single balance sheet side or the total balance sheet) and $p = 4$.

Figure 8.3 shows an increase of the dispersion in the assets side of the balance sheet, although there are not clear tendencies in the liabilities side concerns. In the same way, it shows higher dispersion when the whole balance sheet is contemplated, along with an increasing heterogeneity. Despite all this, if the observed tendency to homogeneity in the conduct of the Spanish banking firms when the convergence between the members of a competitors club which face the same specialisation patterns is considered, we might wonder whether it is possible or not that a simultaneous increase in the diversity *between* groups together with a reduction of such diversity *within* groups is taking place.

In order to answer the above question, we might initially contemplate the same aggregate indicator for the product mix evolution, but compute it for each of the nine identified groups. The results are, according to Figure 8.4, very different from those presented in Figure 8.3. First, we observe that convergence in the whole balance sheet exists for the overwhelming majority of groups, especially during the 1990s. Second, a clear tendency towards convergence in the liabilities specialisation in eight of the nine groups is achieved, whereas no steady tendency is observed for the assets.

Thus results vary, depending on the contemplated grouping of banking firms. According to this, it is interesting to analyse their joint meaning, along with their compatibility. To this end we might employ a widely used instrument in the inequality studies: the Theil index. Such an index has the appealing feature of allowing a decomposition of the total inequality in terms of the observed inequality between different data groupings.

Our attempt is to differentiate the contribution to the total inequality evolution of the differences *between* groups and *within* groups. The Theil index is computed according to the expression:

$$TI = \sum_{i=1}^{I} x_i \log \frac{x_i}{y_i} + \sum_{i=1}^{I} x_i \sum_{j=1}^{J} \frac{x_{ij}}{x_i} \log \frac{\dfrac{x_{ij}}{x_i}}{\dfrac{y_{ij}}{y_i}} \qquad (8)$$

156

Figure 8.4: Convergence in specialisation, total balance sheet (product mix groups)

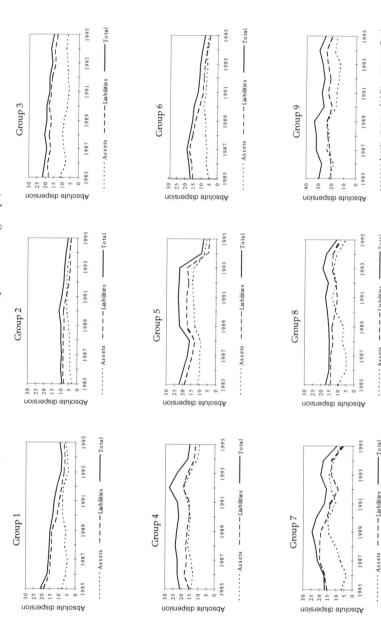

where:
TI: total inequality
$i = 1, ..., I$: cluster's subscript
I: number of clusters being considered
$j = 1, ..., J$: firm's subscript
J: number of firms in each cluster
x_i = total item amount of the ith cluster/total item amount of all *I* clusters
y_i = total assets of the ith cluster/total assets of all *I* clusters
x_{ij} = total item amount of the jth firm affiliated to cluster *i*/total item amount of ith cluster
y_{ij} = total assets of the jth firm/total assets of all *I* clusters

The first term on the right represents the contribution to the total inequality (for a certain item) of the between groups inequality. The second term is the weighted sum of the inequality (concerning the analysed item) between the firms within each of the clusters. Thus, we are considering separately the inequality *between* cluster and *within* cluster for the item being analysed.

The results of the Theil index computations applied to our data show that the index behaviour presents an increasing inequality for the total and between groups, but decreasing inequality within groups (see Figures 8.5 and 8.6). In the same way, the total existing inequality in each period is explained in an increasing percentage by the inequality between groups, which shows that the degree of the product line diversity is progressively being configured as a result of the different product bundles offered by the different clubs of firms (see Figures 8.7 and 8.8).

This joint assessment might be transferred to each of the contemplated product lines (the eight balance sheet items). For all of them, the within groups inequality is decreasing and hardly represents 20 per cent of the total (see Figures 8.5, 8.6, 8.7 and 8.8). The two exceptions are issued securities and fixed income securities, both of them related to the securitisation and, probably, to off-balance sheet activities.

8.6 Concluding comments

The developed analysis in the above sections has allowed us to approach the analysis of the product mix evolution of the banking firms, and its tendency towards convergence or divergence. The instruments used help us in detecting some features of such evolution. To be exact, we have found that the great freedom of banking firms in a less regulated

158

Figure 8.5: Evolution of product mix groups inequality, assets

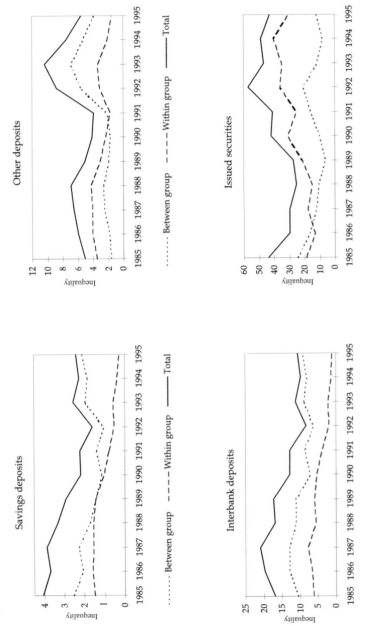

Figure 8.6: Evolution of product mix groups inequality: liabilities

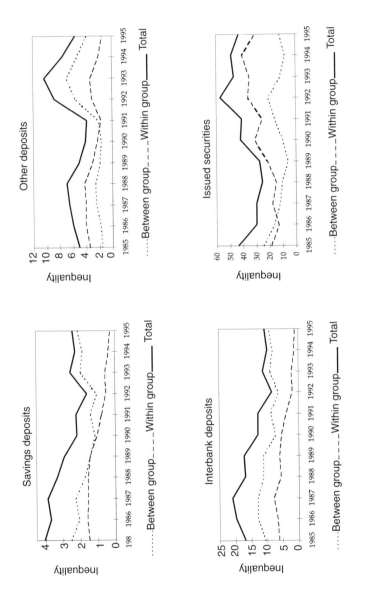

Figure 8.7: Evolution of inequality decomposition: assets

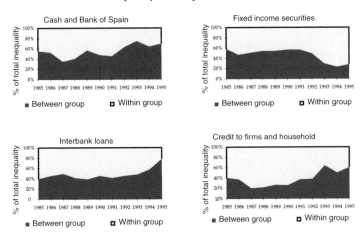

Figure 8.8: Evolution of inequality decomposition: liabilities

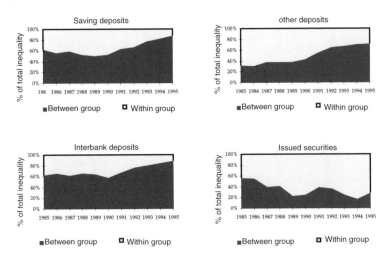

and more competitive context seems to produce a range of specialisations or combinations of the balance sheet items which makes banks more heterogeneous in their product mix. However, it can also be appreciated that a special kind of similar firms in their specialisations is being defined, and within each group we notice a fast and clear tendency towards more and more homogeneous product mixes.

As a consequence of the presented results, the heterogeneity of the specialisations is increasingly higher between the different clusters but lower within them. If this tendency is confirmed, we might reasonably expect more similar product conditions within these clubs of firms competing against each others with similar product mixes. In this case, the developed analysis on specialisation should be regarded as a starting point for the study of the differences in unit costs and scope economies. To be exact, it should help us in analysing if the different groups, as they produce different product ranges, employ significantly distinct cost functions and other production characteristics.

Notes

1. We are grateful to J. Maudos and J.M. Pastor for helpful comments. We also thank the Fundación Caja Madrid for financial support and the IVIE for providing data. The usual disclaimers apply. Correspondence to: Emili Tortosa-Ausina, Department of Economics, Universitat Jaume I, 12080 Castelló de la Plana, Spain. Telephone (34) 64-345700, or e-mail tortosa@uji.es

2. See, for instance, Kolari and Zardkoohi (1987).

3. However, some of the shortcomings, like the increasing importance of the off-balance sheet operations, have not been fully exploited in the literature on Spanish banking firms.

4. See, for instance, Freixas (1996), Gual and Hernández (1991) or Sánchez and Sastre (1995).

5. These are published by the Spanish Banking Association (AEB) and the Spanish Confederation of Savings Banks (CECA).

6. Nevertheless, as is shown in Tortosa-Ausina (1999), when the Pastor and Pérez (1999) analysis for the aggregate is replicated using AEB and CECA individual data, the results do not differ.

7. Although our original sample consisted of a larger number of banks and savings banks, the sample was reduced for two reasons. Firstly, as the considered period of analysis has witnessed a high number of mergers and acquisitions, we considered the firms involved in such actions as being the same firm since the beginning of the period. Secondly, we have dropped those firms which started up or ended their activity during the considered period. Although this could seem an important loss of data, the analysed banks and savings banks always represent around 90 per cent of total assets.

8. In the overwhelming majority of cases, they jointly represent around 90 per cent of all assets.

9. Such a representation has become usual in the empirical literature on economic growth in the nineties, following the Barro and Sala-i-Martin (1992) study, where the concept of σ-convergence is defined.

10. Again, this approach to convergence was proposed by Barro and Sala-i-Martin (1992) and has been widely used in the study of convergence in per capita incomes. It is known as β-convergence.
11. This approach has the shortcoming, pointed out by Dowrick and Nguyen (1989), of being an *a posteriori* study of convergence. Thus, it could be argued that there exists an *ex post* bias in favour of convergence as firms in each group show a similar product mix at the end of the analysed period.
12. Large banks and large savings banks (eight firms, which represent 49 per cent of the banking system's total assets in 1995), medium banks (seven firms and 7 per cent of total assets), medium savings banks (11 firms and 12 per cent), and the remaining entities (101 firms, which represent 21 per cent).
13. This approach has been used in other studies on banking product mix. See Freixas (1996), Gual and Hernández (1991), Kolari and Zardkoohi (1987), Korobow and Stuhr (1989) and Sánchez and Sastre (1995).
14. For a detailed exposition of the adopted method in the cluster formation and in the selection of those considered, see Tortosa-Ausina (1999). The chosen similarity measure to compute the distances has been the squared Euclidean distance, defined as:

$$d_{ij} = \sum_{k=1}^{p} (\chi_{ik} - \chi_{jk})^2 \tag{5}$$

where x_{ik} and x_{jk} are the observations values i and j for the x variable, and p is the number of variables (ratios) which characterise each observation (enterprise).
15. See Tortosa-Ausina (1999).
16. Again, further details of this analysis are thoroughly presented in Tortosa-Ausina (1999).

References

Barro, R.J. and X. Sala-i-Martin (1992), 'Convergence', *Journal of Political Economy*, 100, 2, pp. 223–51
Dowrick, S. and D.T. Nguyen (1989), 'OECD comparative economic growth 1950–85: catch-up and convergence', *American Economic Review*, 78, 5, pp. 1010–30
Freixas, X. (1996), *Los límites de la competencia en la banca española*, Bilbao: Fundación BBV
Gual, J. and A. Hernández (1991), 'Costes operativos, tamaño y especialización en las cajas de ahorro españolas', *Investigaciones Económicas*, 15, 3, pp. 701–26
Kolari, J. and A. Zardkoohi (1987), *Bank costs, structure and performance*, Lexington, Mass: Lexington Books
Korobow, L. and D.P. Stuhr (1989), 'A new look at US banking strategy and structure in the 1980s', Federal Reserve Bank of New York Research Paper 8917

Pastor, J.M. and F. Pérez, (1999) 'Specialisation and competitiveness of the Spanish savings banks: 1984–1995', *in* J. Falzon and E.P.M. Gardener (eds) *Strategic Challenges In European Banking*, Palgrave

Sánchez, J.M. and M.T. Sastre (1995), 'Es el tamaño un factor explicativo de las diferencias entre entidades bancarias?' Documento de Trabajo 9512, Banco de España, Servicio de Estudios

Tortosa-Ausina, E. (1999), 'Especialización productiva eficiencia y convergencia de las empresas bancarias españolas: evidencia empírica', Ph.D. thesis, Universitat Jaume I.

9
Institutional Investment Flows and the Regions of the UK: a Case for a New Financial Infrastructure?[1]

Jonathan Williams

9.1   Introduction and background

The UK financial system has evolved from a bank-oriented phase (circa 1930–1970) via a market-oriented era (circa 1970–1986) through to the present securitised system (from 1986) (Rybczynski 1988). One key feature of the post-1970 era is the emergence and eventual dominance of the industrial structure by institutional investors: first, through the separation of ownership and management functions; and second, as an institutional market for corporate control emerges in which economic power was further lodged in the hands of institutional investment managers (Gentle 1993). Since the bank-oriented era ended in 1970, the market share of institutional investors has virtually doubled. In fact, the UK capital markets are now dominated by institutional investors. The market value of the net total assets of institutional investors amounted to £1224 billion in 1995 (Office for National Statistics 1997a), a figure more than three times greater than it was at the start of the securitised phase in 1986 (Williams 1996).[2]

In the UK the financial sector dominates over the real sector of the economy. There has, however, been scant investigation into the spatial distribution of institutional funds and its relationship with regional development, even though the volume of respective funds being generated at regional level is substantial. Concurrent with the increasing power of institutional investors, the government began to alter its regional policy stance from the mid-1980s. Regional development is now considered a function of local business enterprise and innovation: regional policy aims to promote local indigenous business and entrepreneurial potential as opposed to diverting investment into structurally disadvantaged regions. The scope of regional policy has been broadened to include service industries whereas prior efforts were concentrated more towards manufacturing (Martin and Minns 1995).

A new awareness is beginning to emerge in regional economic theory which relates to the wider institutional dimensions of regional development. It is recognized that the regional problem centres on an unequal distribution of economic and political power: Martin and Minns (1995 p. 126) argue that 'the unequal cumulative concentration of wealth and production in particular regions is itself, of course, one source of regional imbalances in economic and political power. But it is the institutionalisation of those power inequalities, through the spatial configuration of corporate, financial and governmental structures, that plays such a decisive role in shaping and reproducing the pattern of uneven regional development.'

The institutional structure of the UK is characterised by a relative lack of regional autonomy, or decentralisation of economic and political power. Economic and political power is concentrated in London and the southeast of England. It is important to discover how the spatial polarisation of financial power impacts on regional economic development. Given that considerable sums of institutional investment funds are drawn from the regions by financial intermediaries, in the main to be managed and controlled from the national financial centre in London and the southeast of England, a relevant policy issue is whether and how could a portion of these funds be retained in the regions for development purposes. The remainder of the chapter is organised as follows.

Section 9.2 discusses the impact of financial liberalisation on the spatial economy. It contends that the benefits associated with liberalisation are primarily in the national financial centre in London and the southeast of England. The more remote regions became more peripheralised by the developments of the 1980s. The importance of the financial system in relation to the development and regulation of the national space economy is outlined with reference to the geography of the financial system and the issue of control.

Section 9.3 outlines the neo-classical theory of regional financial flows and the counter arguments of Dow (1992). It considers the concepts of integrated and segmented financial systems drawing on the earlier work of McKillop and Hutchinson (1990).

Section 9.4 provides an empirical assessment of the spatial distribution of, first, the annual contributions to institutional investment and, second, the value of assets owned by pension funds. It is found that expenditure on institutional investment is a function of distance from the financial centre. There are two exceptions, Scotland and Yorkshire and Humberside, which suggest that the presence of strong retail-oriented regional financial centres raises the level of household expenditure on institutional investment. The pension fund data support the *a priori* expectations that London and the southeast are dominant in terms of ownership of pension fund assets. Furthermore, Martin and Minns (1995) find that 95 per cent of assets are controlled from London and the southeast; they also estimate that around 66 per cent of pension fund equity investment is made in companies which are based or headquartered in London and the southeast.

Section 9.5 considers the policy implications of the spatial distribution of institutional investment and its implications for Wales and the regions. It is proposed that regional policy should seek to devolve institutional and economic power to the regions. In the continuing absence of a suitable institutional and financial framework at regional level, funds will continue to be drawn from the regions to be administered and controlled in the national financial centre. In order to ensure productive long-term investment in the regions it is claimed that financial regulation should be recast. The endorsement by Wales and Scotland of a regional assembly could prove to be the stimulus for a gradual dissolution of institutional power. In the absence of such an event, it is likely to prove difficult, though not impossible, to persuade fund managers of the viability of investing in (suggested) regional investment funds.

9.2   Financial liberalisation and the space economy

Beginning with the abolition of exchange controls in October 1979 and culminating with Big Bang and the Financial Services Act of 1986, the UK underwent a government-led process of financial liberalisation which included a number of once and for all acts of financial deregulation (Gentle 1993). The development of the Euromarkets during the 1960s and 1970s provided London with a unique position in the international financial system. In the face of international pressures and in order to maintain London's dominant position, the Thatcher government further liberalised (via Big Bang) the financial regulatory environment. While liberalisation sought to attract more international business into London, the domestic financial markets remained heavily controlled in order to maintain macroeconomic stability. Gentle (1993 p. 6) states that 'it is in this context that London acted as a conduit ... channelling the insurgent shockwaves from the international financial system into the British financial system resulting in the financial revolution.'

A major consequence of financial liberalisation has been the erosion of traditional barriers, or segmentation, between financial markets and institutions. The convergence and integration of financial markets facilitated a new round of innovation which led to the introduction of a whole array of financial products and services. Marshall *et al.* (1992 p. 465) explain that 'the Financial Services Act in 1986 polarised distribution channels, which encouraged a variety of institutions to "tie" themselves to insurance companies to sell contractual investment products, such as life assurance and pensions. In addition, companies have undertaken organic growth in such new products as PEPs (Personal Equity Plans).'

The transformation of the financial system turned it into an engine of economic growth for the regional economy of London and the southeast of England. Yet, the polarisation of financial power in one region meant that other regions were largely excluded from the benefits of financial liberalisation (Gentle and Marshall 1992). Whereas the economy boomed during the 1980s, it turned to bust during the recession of 1989 to 1992. The overheating of the economy has been attributed to the liberalisation of financial markets and the fact that liberalisation has made the financial system 'more open to the destabilising effects of shocks to the international financial system' (Marshall *et al.* 1992 p. 456). A unique feature of the 1989–1992 recession (compared with other earlier recessions) is that it centred on the regional economy of London and the southeast of England and hit hard both the housing and financial sectors (Audas and Mackay 1996); the relationship between the two sectors had deepened as a result of the 1986 legislation (Gentle and Marshall 1992).

The 1989–1992 recession, and the high costs of London relative to other towns and cities, helped to facilitate the decision by a number of financial intermediaries to relocate parts of their activities outside of London. A number of provincial towns and cities benefited from this move; although there was a flow of activity out of the centre, the areas which benefited the most lay in close proximity to London. Though this trend brought to a halt the growth in financial sector employment in London (and to a lesser extent the southeast), London and the southeast of England still account for around one-third of financial sector employment in the UK.

The financial system is important to the development and regulation of the national space economy. The collection and recycling of funds back across regional economies (and countries) creates a financial circuit. Martin and Minns (1995) have identified two main implications for the pattern of regional development which arise from the role of the financial system. First, the geography or locational structure of the financial system is such that the provision of retail financial services by banks and building societies is relatively evenly distributed throughout the regions. The more specialised financial services, such as fund management and capital markets activities, tend to be concentrated in and around the national financial centre in London. London is also the headquarters of many of the UK's major financial institutions.

The second implication relates to control. As the financial system evolves into new phases, a different relationship between the financial system and corporate restructuring emerges. In the case of the securitised era this relationship becomes increasingly determined by the markets for corporate control and venture capital. Corporate and economic restructuring affects the geography of the space economy as capital is divested out of loss-making concerns and reinvested into profitable areas across different regional locations. The role that institutional fund managers play in both markets should not be underestimated; the markets are driven by the price mechanism as a facilitator of the transfer of resources (see also Gentle 1993 and Rybczynski 1988). It is how these markets are continually moving and using money which exerts a profound influence on the geography of that investment (Martin and Minns 1995).

9.3   The financial system and regional development

There are a number of theories as to how the operation of the financial system 'intersects' with its spatial dimension. The traditional neoclassical theory of efficient capital markets and a nationally integrated financial system contended that interregional differences in rates of return on investments will be eliminated because there exist no regulatory barriers to the movement of money. If a region is in decline, local asset prices will fall as a result of declining demand. Declining asset prices and their associated factor costs imply higher potential returns which acts as a stimulus for capital inflows from other regions in search of higher yields. The neo-classical approach implies that financial institutions are efficiently and optimally located across space, while capital movements remove, or at least minimise, tendencies towards uneven regional development.

The relative liquidity preference theory of the relationship between the spatial evolution of a national banking system and uneven regional development developed by Dow (1992) is in contrast to the neo-classicists; liquidity in Dow's theory is relative to the perceived opportunities in the region. Dow argues that financial integration and the free movement of capital lead to the spatial centralisation of the financial system. Financial institutions adopt a tendency to centralise their operations as they accumulate capital through savings and profitable investments. This causes local depositors to lose faith in, and outlets for, local investment. Furthermore, external investors grow reluctant to invest in the region because of the outflow of finance and investment. Local investors and savers prefer to construct more liquid portfolios for their money rather than tie it up in local investments because of low confidence in asset values. Thus, 'this increases the pessimistic outlook for the declining region, increases local transaction costs which helps to re-emphasize the peripheral nature of poorer regions' (Mackay and Molyneux 1996 p. 758). As Martin and Minns (1995) note, the relatively more liquid financial assets are available from centre-based institutions which exacerbates poor regional performance.

The basis of Dow's argument is that financial integration, which is itself a feature of economic development, and the free movement of capital which accompanies integration, leads to a spatial concentration of the financial system, uneven development between the core and the periphery, and regional dependency. In contrast to the neo-classical theory, the integrated financial system encourages a net flow of capital from the periphery to the centre, and these flows fuel the process of uneven development. In Dow's view, this process is an inevitable outcome of capitalist economies where the motive of financial accumulation ensures an outcome whereby finance is allocated in such a way as to extract the highest expected financial returns.

An important issue arising from the debate is the question about whether local information costs in deregulated markets can create differential interest rates which could affect peripheral regions (Martin and Minns 1995); this area has been reviewed by McKillop and Hutchinson (1990). The neo-classical school approach claims that, if regional financial sectors are fully integrated into the national financial system, there will exist no rigidities which prevent the equalisation of rates of return on investments across regions. The possible existence of autonomous regional financial institutions does not lead to an exploitation of local monopoly power because such institutions will not be the sole providers of regional funds in a fully integrated financial system. In regionally integrated financial markets, national financial assets are predominant to regional financial assets. The trade in national assets takes place in the national financial centre: trade in such assets by the personal, corporate and public authority sectors of a regional economy can be carried out independently of regional financial institutions. Similarly, lending and borrowing can bypass the regional institutions and be undertaken at national rates of interest. This feature ensures that, even if regional financial institutions appear to operate in oligopolistic regional market structures, they are unable to exploit local monopoly power beyond the national level of exploitation.

If the central capital markets are not dominant and there exists some degree of financial institutional autonomy within the regional financial centre, it could be possible for the regional financial centre to raise its growth rate over and above that of the regional economy as a whole. In this scenario, the regional financial centre is said to be segmented from the national financial system. There are two types of segmentation: market segmentation and institutional segmentation. Market segmentation refers to the effects which information and transaction costs can have on regional development in terms of regional interest rate differentials (Roberts and Fishkind 1979). The regional financial market is segmented because of an opportunity cost in obtaining information on regional returns, which is a function of the distance or remoteness of the region from the central capital market. The distribution of risk, for example, may differ across regions, and there may be transaction cost premiums in buying and selling extra-regional assets which are positively related to regional remoteness.

Institutional segmentation occurs because there are different types of lenders available to supply regional finance (Moore and Hill 1982). The lenders are national financial institutions, which are headquartered in the national financial centre but typically run national branch networks, and autonomous but comparatively smaller, regional financial institutions. Information costs are again an important consideration: at the regional level the national financial institutions have relatively larger credit evaluation costs than the autonomous, regional financial institutions which generally have access to specialised local knowledge. This advantage of the regional institutions occurs mainly in the household and small and medium-sized enterprise (SME) customer segments; this class of borrowers is a major source of the demand for regional credit. Larger corporate customers generally have access to both national and regional financial institutions: because of reporting requirements there is greater information available on large companies relative to small and medium-sized companies. The financial requirements of large companies are more likely to be satisfied by national institutions (though some regional finance is also provided).

Both forms of segmentation can reduce interregional financial flows. In order to illustrate the differences between the two forms, consider the differences between unit bank structures and branch banking structures. Unit banking structures refer, in a regional context, to self-contained or autonomous regional banks which have a network of offices largely confined to a given region. The standard branch structure refers to an interregional branch banking system such as that operated by the London clearing banks throughout England and Wales. In the Moore and Hill (1982) and Dow (1992) models, it is the unit banking system which reinforces any tendency for there to be an unsatisfied regional demand for credit. Dow further recognizes that while a branch, relative to a unit banking system, eases the credit availability constraint on growing regions, it may increase the constraint on depressed regions (especially if lending is imposed on regional bank branches by central head offices). If lending limits can be imposed on regional bank branches, then the possibilities of non-uniform rate structures across regions are more than feasible.

McKillop and Hutchinson (1990) contend that the institutional segmentation approach of Moore and Hill (1982) mirrors more closely the present UK financial system.[3] The major financial institutions operate branch networks throughout the regions. If there are elements of regional financial market segmentation, the potential will exist for interregional differences in operations within a national branch network. This is because evidence shows that the major clearing banks have devolved authority to a series of regional headquarters. There are regions which show distinct evidence of institutional segmentation in the sense that independent financial institutions are based within the region. Scotland and Northern Ireland are prime examples. Yorkshire and Humberside is the regional headquarters of some national building societies, Manchester is headquarters to the Cooperative Bank, and Wales to the Principality Building Society.

9.4   The spatial distribution of institutional investment in the UK

Earlier in this chapter (in Section 9.1) the market value of the net total assets of institutional investors was reported to be £1224 billion in 1995. Institutional funds receive and pay out considerable sums each year. It is possible to derive estimates of the spatial distribution of contributions made to institutional investment using the regional household expenditure series contained in the Family Expenditure Survey (see Tables 9.1 and 9.2). At the regional level there are two items of household weekly expenditure that relate to institutional investment: expenditure on life assurance and pension funds,[4] and savings and investments.[5]

A number of points can be derived from Tables 9.1 and 9.2. First, regions in southern and eastern Britain (the southwest, southeast, and the east Midlands), and which are closer to the national financial centre, expend a greater proportion of household weekly expenditure on institutional investment relative to other regions. In the southern and eastern regions, households spend on average over 6 per cent of weekly expenditure on institutional investment. As one moves further from the national financial centre towards the more remote regions of western and northern Britain, the amounts spent on institutional investment lessen.[6]

Whereas households in the southeast spend the most (6.2 per cent) on institutional investment, households in the more remote areas spend on average, Wales (5.2 per cent), west Midlands (5.4 per cent), north (5.2 per cent), northwest (5.3 per cent) and Northern Ireland (4.3 per cent). Another feature of the data is that households in the more remote regions with a relatively strong rural nature, such as East Anglia (5.1 per cent) and Wales (5.2 per cent), are among those spending the least on institutional investment.

A case for supporting the development of regional financial centres can be made from Table 9.1. In both Scotland and Yorkshire and Humberside the average weekly amounts spent on institutional investment are higher than in other equally remote (from the national financial centre) regions. This feature is in spite of total weekly expenditure in the two regions being lower than in other remote regions. Yet, there are in Scotland and Yorkshire and Humberside relatively prosperous regional financial centres, notably at Edinburgh and in the Leeds/Bradford areas.

Table 9.1: Household expenditure on select investment items, by standard region, 1995–96

Region	Life assurance, pension funds £	Savings, investments £	Average weekly household exp. £	Investment as %age of household expenditure
East Midlands	19.05	5.34	403.04	6.1
East Anglia	15.26	2.73	351.19	5.1
Southeast	20.65	6.92	441.68	6.2
Southwest	18.15	4.35	376.65	6.0
West Midlands	15.91	3.30	353.75	5.4
North	14.10	2.88	329.01	5.2
Yorkshire & Humberside	16.64	3.36	356.07	5.6
Northwest	16.65	2.96	367.34	5.3
Wales	15.01	3.12	346.48	5.2
Scotland	18.26	1.83	344.97	5.8
N. Ireland	12.19	2.18	332.08	4.3
Total UK	17.82	4.35	383.41	5.8

Source: Office for National Statistics (1996a), *Family spending: a report on the 1995–96 Family Expenditure Survey*, Table 5.3, pp. 86–93.

Scotland is different from the other regions because of its history as a financial centre. The major financial activities in Scotland are banking, insurance and fund management. The autonomous Scottish clearing banks are headquartered in Edinburgh, which is the largest financial centre in the UK outside of London. Although Edinburgh is the main fund management centre, there is also a fund management presence in other Scottish towns and cities; the same is true for the insurance sector. Yorkshire, Leeds and Bradford house the headquarters of a number of major UK building societies with national branch networks, and Leeds is also the regional headquarters of the UK clearing banks.

The existence within the northwest of the Manchester regional financial centre does not appear to have the same effect as do centres in Scotland and Yorkshire and Humberside. Manchester is the third most important financial centre in the UK, after London and Edinburgh. Manchester has developed a regionally autonomous insurance sector capable of exporting services to other regions; it also hosts important regional operations for the UK clearing banks (McKillop and Hutchinson 1990). Merchant banking and venture capital have also developed in Manchester. A similar picture emerges in the West Midlands where Birmingham has developed as a financial centre specialising in the provision of financial services such as accounting and international banking. Yet the shares of expenditure on institutional investments by households in the two regions are among the lowest in the UK. A possible explanation for this feature is that the two centres predominantly serve the high value corporate customer segment within each region, whereas the Scottish and Yorkshire centres have a much stronger retail element. Indeed, the wave of management buyouts in the northwest during the late 1980s led to the establishment of Manchester-based managed funds (McKillop and Hutchinson 1990).

The bulk of regional household expenditure on institutional investment is spent on life assurance and pension funds. Households in the southeast record the greatest expenditure of £20.65 per week, while the lowest levels of spending occur in East Anglia (£15.26), Wales (£15.01), the north (£14.10) and Northern Ireland (£12.19). A similar pattern emerges with savings and investment. Once again, households in the southeast spend a greater share (£6.92), but Scottish households record the lowest expenditure (£1.83); the data capture the fact that Scottish households exhibit a particular household consumption preference for life assurance and pension funds (£18.26).

Table 9.2 shows the number of households in each region and their expenditure on institutional investment. The table also shows the regional shares of national spending on institutional investment and ranks each region accordingly. In 1995–96 over £27 billion was spent by households on institutional investment, with nearly 40 per cent of this total flowing from the southeast. With respect to Wales, our *a priori* expectation of the Welsh share of household expenditure on institutional investment is based on regional gross domestic product (GDP). The latest set of regional accounts (Office for National Statistics 1997b) show that in 1995 the GDP of Wales accounted for 4.1 per cent (or £24 billion) of total UK GDP. Wales is home to 5 per cent of the UK population whose personal income is equivalent to 4.2 per cent of national personal income in 1995. Table 9.2 shows that Welsh households expend just over £1 billion on institutional investment or 3.99 per cent of total national expenditure on such goods.

The final column of Table 9.2 shows an index of regional rank. This index has been constructed by scaling the regional shares of expenditure on institutional investment by regional shares of the UK population. The southeast (with an index of 125) outperforms all other

Table 9.2: Regional household expenditure on institutional investment, 1995–96

Region	Number of households 000s	Household expenditure £m	Regional Share of expenditure %	Index of regional rank UK = 100
East Midlands	1 636.5	2 076	7.66	109.1
East Anglia	849.5	795	2.93	81.4
Southeast	7 244.4	10 386	38.25	125.0
Southwest	1 947.3	2 278	8.39	102.1
West Midlands	2 081.2	2 079	7.66	84.5
North	1 265.0	1 117	4.11	77.4
Yorkshire & Humberside	2 032.9	2 114	7.79	90.5
Northwest	2 563.3	2 614	9.63	87.7
Wales	1 148.2	1 082	3.99	80.0
Scotland	2 089.1	2 182	8.04	91.5
Northern Ireland	572.6	428	1.58	56.2
UK	23 430.1	27 151	100.0	100.0

Source: derived from office for National Statistics (1996a), *Family spending: a report on the 1995–96 Family Expenditure Survey*, Table 5.3, pp. 86–93; Office for National Statistics (1996b), *Regional Trends*.

regions, many by a considerable margin. Wales, with an index of 80, seriously underperforms in comparison with the southeast. In the above we noted that both Scotland and Yorkshire and Humberside have relatively strong local retail financial centres. For these two regions the index records 91.5 in Scotland, and 90.5 in Yorkshire and Humberside, respectively. The poorest performance occurs in Northern Ireland (56.2); of the mainland regions Wales has the least impressive result.

The National Association of Pension Funds (NAPF) (1997) states that there are £600 billion worth of pension fund assets under management, generating an annual investment income of around £17 billion. Over time pension funds have accumulated a large pool of assets. In 1968, for example, the total assets amounted to £8.1 billion, or £45.4 billion at 1992 prices: in comparison, the actual value of pension fund assets in 1992 was over £400 billion (Martin and Minns 1995). There are four main types of pension scheme available in the UK: the basic State pension, the State Earnings-Related Payments Scheme, occupational pension schemes, and personal pension schemes. Occupational pension schemes are organised, or sponsored, by employers on behalf of their employees or members of the scheme. Around 28 000 employers run occupational pension schemes of which there are roughly 11 000 members, less than 50 per cent of the working population (NAPF 1997).

The *National Association of Pension Funds Yearbook* 1997 reports that the annual contributions to occupational pension schemes is in the region of £11 billion. Between 1984 and 1991 the equivalent figure averaged around £9–10 billion (Martin and Minns 1995). Investment incomes accruing to pension funds ranged from £7.7 billion (in 1984) to over £17 billion (Martin and Minns 1995; NAPF 1997). Concomitant with rising investment income has been the increasing maturity of pension schemes: that is, the ratio of pensioners to contributors has risen. An occupational pension scheme is organised as follows: employers collect the contributions made by employees to a pension scheme and add on their contributions. The maximum total contribution allowed is 17.5 per cent of the employee's net relevant earnings: this is because of the availability of income tax relief for the employee and corporation tax relief for the employer on their contributions.

Martin and Minns (1995) explain how all this money is managed and invested. The administration of the pension scheme is the responsibility of the employer who sets up a Board of Trustees for this purpose. The Board of Trustees is responsible for drawing up an investment strategy which is designed to achieve the best returns for its members; the Board of Trustees may comprise employer and employee representatives. In order to ensure the professional management of the trust fund, the Board of Trustees appoints a fund manager to invest the money on their behalf, subject to the objectives and constraints of the trustees' investment strategy. The fund manager may be an in-house employee or department, which is typically the case for a large pension fund. Alternatively, the assets of the fund may be managed by a specialist institution like an insurance company or the investment section of a merchant bank. The latter service is subject to management fees. It is also quite common for more than one fund manager to be appointed in order to manage a single pension fund. Fund managers invest the pension fund in a variety of assets. The most common are UK equities. In 1996 pension funds invested 53.5 per cent of their total investments in UK equities, a further 20.1 per cent in overseas securities, with the remainder in fixed interest securities, property and cash (AP Information Services 1996). Returns on investments accrue to the fund, and are either reinvested or paid out to pensioners.

The spatial distribution of UK occupational pension funds has been sourced from statistical tables provided by AP Information Services. These data analyse the geographical distribution of pension funds by size and assets of pension funds, and by region. The data cover 1976 pension funds with a total asset value of nearly £400 billion, including all funds with an asset market value above £10 million. Those funds which have been excluded are typically smaller funds which have been contracted out with an insurance company.

On a spatial basis the data emphasize the concentration of the pensions business in London and the southeast, the main financial centre of the UK. Over 45 per cent of the number of funds, with an accumulated asset value of nearly 56 per cent of the total, that is, £222 billion, are owned by organisations and companies with their headquarters situated in the southeast of England. One of the reasons for this regional bias is that a large number of national organisations and companies are headquartered in London and the southeast of England. The institutions which undertake multiregional activities draw pension fund contributions from all over the UK and administer the funds in one region. It is the larger national organisations and companies that have the largest pension funds under management and also the highest degrees of pension fund membership. British Telecommunications plc, for example, owns the largest pension fund in the UK (£18.5 billion); its employees are distributed across the regions but the registered address and the administration of its pension fund is in London. Thus, while London and the southeast account for around 32 per cent of national employment, the region administers around 56 per cent of national pension fund assets.

The more remote regions of Britain (northwest, northeast, Wales, Scotland and Northern Ireland) account for just under 29 per cent of the total number of pension funds. The market value of the assets of these funds is around 26 per cent of the total. This feature of the spatial distribution of pension funds is in spite of the fact that there is a tradition of fund management in Scotland, while in Yorkshire there is an emerging fund management presence. Wales's share of the number of pension funds is nearly 2 per cent but the value of these funds is just over 1 per cent at nearly £4.5 billion. Of all the regions the number and value of Welsh registered pension funds are the lowest. This feature of the spatial distribution reflects the likelihood that the majority of contributions made by both employers and employees in Wales is being administered outside of Wales, and probably in London.

Table 9.3 shows that just over 30 per cent of UK pension funds are relatively small, that is between £0 and £4.9 million. There are few extremely large pension funds (only 3.5 per cent of funds own over £1 billion of assets), but they account for around 58 per cent of total funds under management: about half of these funds are registered in London and the southeast and they own just under 60 per cent of the assets of this size class. The concentration of the market value of pension fund assets increases to 84.6 per cent if funds with assets greater than £250 million are counted; that is, 289 pension funds (or just under 15 per cent of the total number of funds) account for 86 per cent (or £338 billion) of the total market value of pension fund assets.

There are ten pension funds registered in Wales within the size band £250 million to £1000 million. Approximately 86 per cent of the value of the pension funds registered in Wales is accounted for by the ten funds in the size band £250 million to £1000 million; the market value of the assets of the ten funds is £3752.2 million. There are no pension funds registered in Wales with over £1 billion of assets at market value (see Table 9.4). The data refer to pension schemes registered by region. Thus, both the level and amount of contributions made by, and on behalf of, employees in Wales are understated. The main reason for this is the drawing of contributions from Wales by national organisations and companies.

The index in the final column of Table 9.4 has been constructed by scaling regional shares of the value of pension funds by the regional

Table 9.3: Number of pension funds with capital values: by region and size

Region	Size of fund £ million								
	0–4.9	5–9.9	10–19.9	20–49.9	50–99.9	100–249.9	250–1000	1000+	Total
London	102	20	44	60	58	53	51	20	408
Southeast	115	25	59	90	60	73	57	14	493
East Anglia	29	11	13	16	9	8	13	2	101
Midlands	126	17	30	48	27	12	26	8	294
Southwest	32	12	6	16	14	12	17	5	114
Northeast	94	7	19	37	18	11	13	8	207
Northwest	53	12	24	25	18	11	16	6	165
Wales	10	2	6	6	3	1	10	0	38
Scotland/Northern Ireland	55	10	19	23	12	14	17	6	156
Total	616	116	220	321	219	195	220	69	1976

Source: AP Information Services (1996), *Pension Funds and their Advisors*, p. 516.

Table 9.4: Value of total pension fund assets: by region and size

Region	Size of fund £ million								Total	Index UK = 100
	0–4.9	5–9.9	10–19.9	20–49.9	50–99.9	100–249.9	250–1000	1000+		
London	25.5	143.9	608.0	1 852.1	3 963.2	9 260.9	23 892.9	94 344.4	134 090.9	281.6
S. East	50.0	174.9	845.5	2 900.1	4 029.2	1 1830.8	28 714.2	39 815.9	88 360.6	118.6
E. Anglia	20.5	76.6	187.9	530.3	556.9	1 358.9	6 195.5	2 127.4	11 054.0	76.9
Midlands	47.0	121.6	440.6	1 492.6	1 825.2	1 786.9	13 389.9	16 549.0	35 652.8	172.1
S. West	25.8	93.8	80.0	487.3	936.8	1 886.0	7 420.0	15 802.4	26 732.1	81.5
N. East	48.0	45.3	254.3	1 315.6	1 286.3	2 024.9	6 222.9	28 777.8	39 975.1	72.0
N. West	23.4	90.6	343.0	836.8	1 342.9	1 496.0	9 038.5	18 610.7	31 781.9	72.5
Wales	3.6	15.0	88.8	187.3	220.0	1 69.8	3 752.2	0.0	4 436.7	22.2
Scot/NI	34.6	72.8	285.4	726.0	828.6	2 185.4	9 141.1	13 800.8	27 074.7	58.4
Total	278.4	834.5	3 133.5	10 328.1	14 989.1	31 999.6	107 767.2	229 828.4	399 158.8	100.0

Note: The percentage share of the population of the Midlands comprises the populations of the West and East Midlands; the northeast that of the North and Yorkshire and Humberside; and Scotland/Northern Ireland that of the two countries, respectively.

Source: AP Information Services (1996), *Pension Funds and their Advisors*, p. 517; Office for National Statistics (1996b), *Regional Trends*.

shares of population. London, as expected, outperforms the national index by nearly threefold. The remainder of the Southeast (118.6) and the Midlands (172.1) also perform strongly. The more remote regions like Wales (22.2) and Scotland/Northern Ireland (58.4) are seriously underrepresented in terms of the regional values of pension funds relative to population. These data illustrate the power of London and the southeast of England in terms of drawing, managing, and controlling regional financial flows in the UK.

In their study, Martin and Minns (1995) examined the extent of inhouse and external fund management. Their aim was to determine to whom the role of fund manager is delegated, regardless of where the organisation or company is located and the fund administered. The large funds, such as British Petroleum and ICI, typically employ inhouse fund managers and management is centred on London and the southeast. In 77 per cent of cases the fund management function is delegated to an external manager, a small percentage of which are based in Scotland. Martin and Minns (1995 p. 135) calculate '... that 95 per cent of all pension fund assets, regardless of the employer's location and geographical source of contributions, are *controlled* from the southeast of England, first by large companies and corporations with inhouse investment departments and, second, by the investment departments of banks and insurance companies, along with a few small independents' (emphasis added by the author).

Martin and Minns (1995) also examine the spatial implications of the investment of pension fund assets. Pension funds invest over 50 per cent of assets in UK. Around 70 per cent of the total market capitalisation of all equities listed on the Stock Exchange are headquartered in the southeast. Thus, it is reasonable to assume that there is a significant bias towards investment in companies headquartered in the southeast, the same companies from which contributions are drawn nationally and centralised. Furthermore, Martin and Minns (1995 p. 136) estimate that around 'two-thirds of all pension fund equity investment is invested in the shares of the top 90 companies based or headquartered in the Southeast.'

9.5   Policy implications for Wales and the regions

There is relatively little known about actual regional money flows in the UK and of the role of financial institutions in this process. This chapter has attempted to rectify this situation by quantifying the spatial flow of contributions to institutional investment and secondary reporting of the value of the assets held by pension funds across regions. The research has identified an institutional funds expenditure of £1 billion by Welsh households in 1995–96. The value of pension fund assets owned by Welsh registered pension schemes is just under £4.5 billion, but this figure seriously underestimates the 'true' value of pension fund assets owned by persons living in Wales whose funds are drawn from Wales to be administered and controlled in London and the southeast of England. In contrast, the value of regional selective assistance received by Welsh firms in 1993–94 amounted to £95 million (Welsh Office 1996).

Mackay and Molyneux (1996 p. 760–1) illustrate the relationship between the spatial distribution of the financial system and national economic prosperity: 'the location of financial institutions has implications which reach well beyond direct employment. Their reach, their regional operation and spread of funds may be important to national competitive advantage as well as regional equality.' This line of argument is supported by various authors including Dow (1992, 1996), Gentle (1993), Gentle and Marshall (1992), and Martin and Minns (1995).

Gentle and Marshall (1992) argue that the financial liberalisation of the 1980s has caused recession and a short-term or myopic outlook on investment that is detrimental to regional economic development. They question whether free markets in finance and takeover produce a healthier economy than in situations where stricter regulation and control limit the separation of ownership and management.[7] The crux of Gentle and Marshall's argument is that competition should be encouraged wherever possible, but regulation must be endorsed wherever necessary.

Dow (1992) argues that integrated financial systems, like in the UK, encourage the net flow of funds from peripheral regions to the centre. Furthermore, this tendency is considered by Dow to be an inevitable outcome of capitalist systems. Dow bases her model on the dependency theory developed by Prebisch (1962) and uses Scotland as a case study. In the more depressed remote economies, Dow (1992, 1996) argues that economic vulnerability conditions household preferences; householders opt for conservative or defensive financial strategies and construct relatively more liquid portfolios consisting of financial assets which are centrally available. This behaviour denies local entrepreneurs both investment capital and long-term investment opportunities.

In response to Dow (1992), Martin and Minns (1995) contend that it is the market in general which has become more liquid.[8] This has led to a preference for liquid short-term investment rather than long-term productive investment: stock market investment provides a mechanism for maximising liquidity rather than the rate of return. Furthermore, short-term investment strategies which are a function of the demand for liquidity operate against maximising the long-term rate of return. This is likely to have an adverse effect on regional development, especially as 'the internationalisation of financial management and the securitisation of markets itself promotes greater liquidity because of the fees which can be generated from trading and increased turnover. In addition, cost minimisation and fee maximisation mean that decisionmaking becomes increasingly concentrated and centralised ... . This has led to the global shifting of money by international financial institutions and corporations in what [is] characterised as "spatial arbitrage".' (see Martin and Minns 1995 p. 140)

An important aspect of the spatial distribution of financial flows is how they impact on the availability of investment finance for new and small to medium-sized companies: that is, those companies which are advocates of the new regional policy of local indigenous development are considered to play a pivotal role in regional regeneration. A feature of the remoteness argument is that national financial intermediaries may not be as well placed as autonomous regional institutions to ascertain and monitor risks associated with regional economies because they have incomplete local knowledge. Dow (1996 p. 6), in her analysis of the benefits to Scotland of a Scottish assembly, contends 'the closer the banks are to potential borrowers, the better their knowledge and thus the better their capacity to assess risk. Thus, even if their lending behaviour is conservative, the Scottish banks can more effectively promote economic development in Scotland because of their superior knowledge base.'

Information and transaction costs are particularly important when considering the role that financial institutions play in regional development. The new institutional economics school of thought believes information to be rarely complete: transaction costs are defined as the prices of negotiating and of concluding contracts, and then of enforcing them. Institutions are formed to reduce the uncertainty associated with human exchange; that is, institutions (if they are efficiently organised) reduce transaction and information costs (see Harriss *et al.* 1997). Economic development depends upon the existence of a favourable institutional environment: institutions that are carefully and properly developed are crucial determinants of the efficiency of markets (North 1997).

It is being suggested that a segmented financial structure would be more likely to enable autonomous regional financial intermediaries to compete with relatively larger national institutions. In this context Martin and Minns (1995), Dow (1992) and Gentle and Marshall (1992) stress the need to reform the national financial system and develop the regional financial infrastructure. To Martin and Minns' regional policy should be about decentralising political and economic power to the regions. Martin and Minns (1995 p. 139) consider whether a more segmented banking structure, in which local institutions have a greater chance of competing, either constitutes 'a social measure to fund local investment and help regional development, or an economic measure designed to promote the national economic interest. Is it a matter of ensuring investment in profitable investment opportunities which a centralised system cannot identify because of negative perceptions and inadequate local information?'. Gentle and Marshall (1992 p. 585) emphasize the need to recast financial regulation: '... the rehabilitation of the macro-institutional structures of economic financial management, rather than regional policy *per se*, will provide a more immediate and effective response to regional problems.'

The present UK financial system may be described as a branch banking system. It is an integrated structure in which the major financial institutions' head offices are concentrated in the central capital markets, yet there is a growing tendency for certain activities to be relocated, mostly in other provincial towns and cities. Thus, regional financial sector growth opportunities, above those facilitated by the overall growth of a regional economy, largely depend on the willingness of the central capital markets to devolve their activities to the regions. The evidence on relocation shows that there is a proximate relationship between relocation to regional financial sectors and the central markets (McKillop and Hutchinson 1990).

The clearing banks and the building societies have redefined their organisational structures. The larger building societies are considered to be locally administered but centrally driven; they have created market-orientated quasi-divisional structures which are reminiscent of retail bank structures during the 1970s (Marshall *et al.* 1992). For the banks, the merging of organisational and spatial decentralisation has been a feature of corporate change. For example, individual operating divisions set up to contain new businesses have developed into profit centres, corporate and personal business have been separated, and international and institutional business have been combined to form investment houses. The headquarters of the new operations are to be found outside, but within a 60–100 mile radius, of London (Marshall *et al.* 1992). Other activities, such as the decisionmaking responsibilities for marketing and lending, have been devolved to regional offices based mostly in provincial cities. McKillop and Hutchinson (1990) and Gentle (1993) claim that regional divisions are better suited to appraise the degree of risk associated with regional lending. These trends have benefited localities close to the financial centre notably in the south and east of England. In contrast, a recent feature is that the brunt of retail branch closures has been borne by the remote regions in the north and west (Marshall *et al.* 1992).

Wales satisfies many of the conditions Dow (1992) uses to classify Scotland as a peripheral economy.[9] Unlike Scotland, however, Wales does not have its own independent banking and financial sector. Indeed, there is little tradition of financial activity in Wales despite the existence of a previously strong export base. Since 1979 the Welsh economy has been subject to major changes to the industrial base. The traditional heavy industries have all but gone and are being replaced by lighter manufacturing activities and a growth in services. One consequence of industrial change has been the loss of skilled and relatively well-paid male employment opportunities. Average weekly earnings in Wales are the lowest in Britain (Central Statistical Office, 1995b). While there is an industrial base in southeast and northeast Wales, the west of Wales is largely agricultural.

As demand for more innovative financial products and services increased throughout the 1980s, regional financial centres and their institutions responded by expanding and broadening the range of financial services on offer. This trend was aided by three significant factors: the tendency of the government sector, the manufacturing sector, and the traditional services sector to outsource specific activities which had previously been performed on an inhouse basis; the advent of information technology, and the instantaneous information flows, led to regionally-based financial institutions competing on an almost equal footing with their counterparts in national financial centres; and the demand for financial products from regionally-based financial intermediaries is directly linked to the take-off of financial services nationally (McKillop and Hutchinson 1990).

As financial institutions sought to relocate parts of their activities out of London during the 1980s, south Wales was well placed to benefit from such moves. Cardiff is only two hours travel from London and though information technology allows the separation of front and back office tasks, it is considered important that regular personal contact is maintained if operations are to be managed efficiently. The fact that Cardiff and other cities in south Wales offered lower establishment costs, good telecommunications links, and a plentiful supply of relatively cheap labour made these areas particularly attractive (McKillop and Hutchinson 1990).

The first relocation to Cardiff occurred in 1983 when Chemical Bank, one of the major dealers in global market activities, relocated its processing operations out of central London. The major wave of relocation to southeast Wales began around 1988 when the TSB Group relocated the processing side of its general insurance business to Newport. In October 1988, the National Provident Institution transferred its group pension activities from Tunbridge Wells to Cardiff; the company cited worsening demographic trends in the southeast and the increasing cost of labour in the Tunbridge Wells area as the reason for the move. At the end of the 1980s, the mortgage processing arm of the French commercial bank, Banque Nationale de Paris, purchased Chemical Bank Home Loans (McKillop and Hutchinson 1990). More recently, Lloyds TSB has established its telephone banking operation in Swansea. Cardiff has also benefited from the regional diversification in brokerage activities while its traditional stockbroking presence has increased. A capability in merchant banking and venture capital has also developed: a joint venture between the Welsh Venture Capital Fund and English Development Capital was reported to be particularly successful (McKillop and Hutchinson 1990).

There are 38 Welsh registered pension funds which account for just over 1 per cent of the total value of pension fund assets in the UK (see Table 9.3). The majority of these funds are small: there are no pension funds registered in Wales with over £1 billion of assets (see Table 9.4). The outflow of institutional funds from Wales reflects the lack of a sufficient financial infrastructure to retain such funds within Wales. The recent developments in Cardiff and other parts of south Wales are attributable in the main to relocation. Dow (1996) has outlined the potential benefits to the Scottish financial sector from the creation of a Scottish assembly. While Scotland has a much stronger financial tradition than Wales, the possibility of a Welsh Assembly may provide a stimulus for developing further the necessary financial and institutional infrastructure to aid economic development in Wales.

In the absence of an Assembly induced reform of institutional practices in Wales there remains the task of convincing fund managers to invest part of their funds in Welsh assets. Fund managers are subject to the constraints and objectives of the pension fund trustees. While it is the legal objective of trustees to maximise the returns to fund members and/or minimise the risk, the trustees (which generally include both employer and employee representatives) can specify areas of investment and non-investment. The greater awareness of environmental and health issues is having an effect on the investment strategies of trustees: for example, during the summer of 1996 it was reported that around six UK local authorities had recently adopted an ethical/environmental element in their investment portfolios (Thornton 1996).

Pension fund managers invested 53.5 per cent of their funds in UK equities in 1996 (AP Information Services 1996); the return on UK equities earned by pension funds was 17.2 per cent in 1996 (*Investment Management* 1997). In 1997 there were only 26 Welsh based quoted plc companies. Despite a shift away by pension fund managers from investments in fixed-interest securities and property between 1986 and 1996 there are the beginnings of a rebalancing of pension fund assets which suggests that bonds and property will become more attractive to fund managers (Riley 1997). Local authority bonds and property are possible Welsh based assets in which fund managers may invest. An emerging trend has been the development of index funds. In the UK, Virgin Direct which sells index funds managed for it by Norwich Union, amassed a £500 million inflow during the three months up to the end of the 1996 tax year.

The impressive performance of ethical investment funds and the continuing attraction of the small company sector are aspects which the instigators of the concept of a Welsh based investment fund should consider further. Thornton (1996) has shown that ethical investments can more than provide the required risk–return performance sought by fund managers. A number of institutional fund managers offer regional based investment funds. The M&G Midland and General Trust Fund, for example, invests in small companies located in the Midlands and other regional centres; since its constitution in 1956 the fund has realized an annual growth of 14.8 per cent compared with an inflation rate of 7.1 per cent (*The M&G Handbook* 1993).

A different approach to regional development has taken place in North Dakota. Here, regional development funds are created through the imposition of a 1 per cent retail sales tax. Bangsund and Leistritz (1997) report that 35 cities and 23 counties in North Dakota have thus far created economic regional development funds and job development authorities. Between 1988 and 1995 these funds have supported 4485 jobs at a cost of $4878 per job. In the UK the taxation raising powers lie with the Westminster government; the Welsh Assembly is devoid of such powers. Yet, in North Dakota regional development funds part of a *long-term* initiative intended to transform the industrial base from an overreliance on traditional primary industry to a more diversified and self-sustaining regional economy.

There is a much stronger tradition of regional and local banking in continental Europe. A large proportion of these operations have been carried out by the savings and co-operative banking sectors. Although many of these institutions are small in terms of asset size they nevertheless provide a vital service, especially to the household and SME customer segments. In a strongly market-oriented (or securitised) financial system like that of the UK, the future of mutual institutions is coming under threat. There are fears that, under a fully competitive financial market, certain customer segments could be disenfranchised (European Commission 1997). The case for local and regional banking has been advocated at EU level. A recent study finds support among bankers and policymakers for such a system in which local and regional banks would lower information costs and provide necessary risk assessment and credit for households and the SME sector (EC 1997).

Further moves towards European convergence are likely to increase concentration in the main sources of capital and credit. In turn, this is likely to increase the dependency of the remote regions on the financial centre for support and further stimulate capital outflows from the periphery to the centre (Martin and Minns 1995). The depressed regions may find themselves increasingly peripheralised with respect to flows of savings, investment funds, and credit. In contrast to countries such as France and Belgium, there do not exist any specialist regional financial institutions in the UK. In both France and Belgium central government has deliberately sought to decentralise the decisionmaking and investment processes in an attempt to raise substantial private capital for local investment. Martin and Minns (1995) highlight another difference between the UK financial system and those in continental Europe by citing the fact that German regional and local savings banks, the Landesbanken and Sparkassen, are legally bound to service and invest in their respective territories.

In conclusion, the vast sums of institutional investments which are drawn from the regions, to be administered and controlled in London and the southeast, are likely to remain untapped at a regional level if present trends and policies continue, that is unless there is the recognition that, in order to support regional economic development at national and EU level, a suitable and efficient financial infrastructure is created which will retain locally a sizeable portion of regional funds. In a large number of European countries, such as Germany, France, Spain, Belgium and Italy, national financial institutions, which provide a full range of financial services, operate alongside regional and local financial institutions whose task is to supply credit to the local economy. An evolving opinion among bankers and policymakers is that the UK could benefit from a local/regional banking capability in conjunction with the national financial system.

Notes

1. The chapter has its genesis in an Institute of European Finance research project (sponsored by the Welsh Development Agency) which is attempting *inter alia* to quantify the amount of institutional investment funds emanating from Wales.
2. There are four main types of institutional investor: the two largest are insurance companies and pension funds which accounted for 46.5 per cent and 41.5 per cent, respectively, of the market value of assets owned by institutional investors in 1995. The two other groups are investment trusts and units trusts. Since 1986, the market value of the assets held by insurance companies has risen by around 212 per cent, pension funds by over 166 per cent and investment and unit trusts (combined) by about 180 per cent.
3. Martin and Minns (1995) report that the neo-classical approach has tended to figure prominently in the recent discussions of the liberalisation of financial markets and regional development in both the UK and the EU. Dow (1992) also emphasizes the adoption of neo-classical principles at UK and EU levels when she states that in the wider European context it is anticipated that the integrated capital market will improve the availability of credit to all regions, in the sense of a more efficient allocation at lower cost. Commentators such as Goodhart (1987) and Branson (1990), however, believe that a two-tier financial market will emerge in Europe like the unit banking and branch banking system in the USA. Dow (1992) concludes that, whichever system prevails, integration means that peripheral regions will face financial constraints.
4. The pension fund data comprise contributions to pensions and superannuation funds deducted by employers and personal pension funds.
5. Including additional voluntary contributions.
6. The northern and western regions were subject to a major restructuring of the industrial base during the early 1980s. One significant repercussion has been the loss of a high proportion of skilled and relatively well-paid male employment opportunities. It is not possible in this study to say whether this has had an effect on the levels of contributions in those regions.
7. The question whether free markets in finance produce a healthier economy centres on the alleged short-term or myopic outlook of financial markets. Gentle and Marshall (1992) argue that this outlook has occurred because of financial liberalisation. In support of their argument they quote Porter, as cited in G. Brown and G. Mulgar (1990) 'Britain takes the biscuit', *London Review of Books*, 25 October, pp. 10–11, who claims that the structure of the

UK capital markets has affected corporate goals which are not supportive of investment and innovation. Thus, events such as the Basle Capital Convergence Accord and further moves towards European convergence offer the UK authorities opportunities to reform and reorientate the UK financial system towards a more supervised and regulated regime (Gentle and Marshall 1992). Reorientation must encourage financial innovation while at the same time it negates the crisis tendencies of the financial system. Gentle and Marshall (1992) advocate the introduction of an inter-bank interest rate modelled on the German Lombard system in which the cost of interbank funds modulates and controls the cost of credit.

8. The Martin and Minns (1995) theory of liquidity is more general than that of Dow (1992). Martin and Minns argue that the industrial structure of finance has changed which restricts choice and offers limited long-term and profitable investment opportunities in the regions. For Martin and Minns the plausible solution would be to improve local/regional financial infra-structures and change the corporate structure of companies to a model more in line with the German stakeholder concept.

9. Dow (1992) bases her classification on the dependency theory developed by Prebisch (1962). Peripheral economies are dependent on the centre for trade and investment; production is concentrated in primary industry activities usually with the headquarters situated in the centre; export income is sensitive to economic conditions in the centre and the terms of trade may be unfavourable. Expansion is financed typically by capital inflows but such flows are erratic, which leads to the instability of primary export earnings. Foreign (non-regional) ownership is high in peripheral regions. Peripheral regions are also characterised by 'endemic' liquidity preference, that is 'financial behaviour is conservative or defensive given the long experience of economic vulnerability' (Dow 1992 p. 627).

References

AP Information Services (1996), *Pension Funds and their Advisors*, London: AP Information Services

Audas, R.P. and R.R. MacKay (1996), *A Tale of Two Recessions*, Bangor: School of Accounting, Banking and Economics Research Paper Series, RP 96/21

Bangsund, D. and F.L. Leistritz (1997), 'Regional development funds in North Dakota', *Agricultural Economics Report No. 369*, North Dakota State University, February

Branson, W.H. (1990), 'Financial market integration, macroeconomic policy and the EMS', in J. Brago de Macedo, and C. Bliss (eds) *Unity with diversity within the European economy: the Community's southern frontier*, Cambridge: Cambridge University Press

Central Statistical Office (1995a), *Regional Trends*, London: HMSO

Central Statistical Office (1995b), *New Earnings Survey 1995, Part E*, London: HMSO

Curry, S. (1995), 'Institutional investment: theory and practice', in B. Anderton (ed.) *Current issues in financial services* Basingstoke, Hampshire: Macmillan Business

Dow, S.C. (1990), *Financial markets and regional economic development: the Canadian experience* London: Gower

Dow, S.C. (1992), *The regional financial sector: a Scottish case study, Regional Studies*, 26, pp. 619–31

Dow, S.C. (1996), *Scottish devolution and the financial sector*, paper presented to the Regional Science Association, British and Irish Section, Annual Conference, Edinburgh, September

European Commission (1997), *Credit Institutions and Banking*, Volume 3, sub-series II: Impact on services, *The Single Market Review*, Kogan

Financial Times (1997), 'Survey: pension fund investment', 9 May

Gentle, C.J.S. (1993), *The Financial Services Industry*, Aldershot: Avebury

Gentle, C. and N. Marshall (1992), 'The deregulation of the financial services industry and the polarisation of regional economic prosperity', *Regional Studies*, 26, 6, pp. 581–6

Goodhart, C.A.E. (1987), 'Structural change in the British capital markets', in C.A.E. Goodhart, D. Currie and D.T. Llewellyn (eds), *The operation and regulation of financial markets* London and Basingstoke: Macmillan – now Palgrave

Harriss, J., J. Hunter and C. Lewis (eds) (1997), *The new institutional economics and Third World Development*, London: Routledge

Investment Management (1997), January/February

The M&G Handbook 1993, London: M&G

Mackay, R.R. and P. Molyneux (1996), 'Bank credit and the regions: a comparison within Europe', *Regional Studies*, 30, 8, pp. 757–63

McKillop, D.G. and R.W. Hutchinson (1990), *Regional Financial Sectors in the British Isles*, Aldershot: Gower

Marshall, J.N., C.J.S. Gentle, S. Raybould and M. Coombes (1992), 'Regulatory change, corporate restructuring and the spatial development of the British financial sector', *Regional Studies*, 26, 5, pp. 453–67

Martin, R. and R. Minns (1995), 'Undermining the financial basis of regions: the spatial structure and implications of the UK pension fund system', *Regional Studies*, 29, 2, pp. 125–44

Moore, D.L. and J.M. Hill (1982), 'Interregional arbitrage and the supply of loanable funds', *Journal of Regional Science*, 22, 4, pp. 499–512

National Association of Pension Funds (1997), *NAPF Yearbook 1997*, London: Edmund Kirby

North, D.C. (1997), 'The new institutional economics and third world development', in J. Harriss, *et al.* (eds) (1997), *The new institutional economics and Third World development*, London: Routledge:, pp. 17–26

Office for National Statistics (1996a), *Family spending: a report on the 1995–96 Family Expenditure Survey*, London: The Stationery Office

Office for National Statistics (1996b), *Regional Trends*, 31, London: The Stationery Office

Office for National Statistics (1997a), *Financial Statistics*, no. 421, May London: The Stationery Office

Office for National Statistics (1997b), *Economic Trends*, no. 523, June London: The Stationery Office

Porteous, D.J. (1995), *The Geography of finance*, Aldershot: Avebury

Prebisch, R. (1962), 'The economic development of Latin America and its principal problems', *Economic Bulletin for Latin America*, 1, pp. 1–22

Riley, B. (1997), 'Rebalancing comes next', Pension Fund Investment Survey, *Financial Times*, 9 May, p. 3.

Roberts, R.B. and H.H. Fishkind (1979), 'The role of monetary forces in regional economic activity: an econometric simulation analysis', *Journal of Regional Science*, 19, 1, pp. 15–28

Rybczynski, T. (1988), 'Financial systems and industrial restructuring', *National Westminster Bank Quarterly Review*, November, pp. 3–13

Sarchett, D. (1995/96), 'Small emerging pension funds', *Investment Management*, December/January, pp. 29–31

Thornton, J. (1996), 'Being ethical does work', *Investment Management*, Summer, pp. 15–16

Tidbury, K. (1995), 'Picking the right smaller companies', *Investment Management*, February/March, pp. 6–8

Welsh Office (1996), *Digest of Welsh Statistics*, Government Statistical Service

Williams, J.M. (1996), 'Primary market intermediaries', in E.P.M. Gardener and P. Molyneux (eds) *Investment Banking: Theory and Practice*, 2nd edn, London: Euromoney Books, pp. 91–107

10
Characteristics of International Financial Centres

Joe Falzon

International financial centres have become increasingly more important in the world financial system because they have contributed to the explosive growth in the volume of international financial transactions witnessed in the 1980s and 1990s. They can be classified and distinguished in terms of historical growth, regional influence, number of international banks located and volume of international transactions generated. However, in spite of these apparent differences, there seem to be underlying common characteristics that can help explain the growth and development of these international financial centres.

This short chapter traces the main underlying forces that are shaping and driving international financial centres. Section 10.1 distinguishes the different types of international financial centres and the important factors of external economies of scale, economies of agglomeration and increasing returns to scale, that play such a crucial role in the competitive advantage of financial centres. Section 10.2 shows that economies of scale and centralisation are again the powerful forces behind the historical development of the leading international financial centres, culminating in globalisation, deregulation and financial innovation as strong unifying processes in the 1980s and 1990s. Section 10.3 concludes with the effects on international financial centres of the advances of telecommunication and computer technology, and the subsequent complete elimination of spatial barriers in the conduct of international financial transactions.

10.1   Concepts and characteristics

10.1.1   Types of international financial centres

International financial centres can be classified into different categories. Roberts (1994), for example, distinguishes four different types: domestic, global, regional, and offshore. Domestic financial centres pertain to a particular country and serve a specific national clientele, while global financial centres like London and New York, are truly international centres serving a worldwide clientele. Regional financial centres serve a regional clientele where a region is defined as a supranational rather than as a subnational entity. Finally, offshore financial centres serve as financial entrepots and conduct international activities outside of the financial system of the host country.

Global financial centres that are international hubs of great financial activity are distinguished, according to Dufey and Giddy (1978), by four main characteristics: economic and political stability; an efficient and experienced financial community; good communications and supportive services; and an official regulatory climate favourable to the financial industry, whereby it protects investors without excessive restrictions.

Moreover, Dufey and Giddy (1978) define offshore financial centres as that particular sub-group among the providers of entrepot financial services that offer the much narrower service of intermediation for non-resident borrowers and residents. The principal attraction for banks of location in offshore banking centres remains the absence of intrusive and expensive official regulation and taxation.

10.1.2   A three-tier classification

An alternative three-tier classification of international financial centres is suggested by Reed (1983) who studies a data set of 16 variables measuring international clearing operations, global portfolio management and communications links covering the 36 leading world centres in 1980. Reed classifies financial centres into three main types: supranational, international and host international.

Supranational financial centres are managers of large amounts of foreign financial assets and liabilities and are consequently net suppliers of foreign direct investment capital to the rest of the world. They are located close to a large number of large industrial corporations and are active users of global communications facilities. Supranational financial centres also become management centres that foster and create ideas and information regarding the future operating procedures of international corporations. New York and London are examples of 'first order' supranational financial centres, while Tokyo, Amsterdam, Frankfurt, Paris and Zurich are examples of 'second order' financial centres.

International financial centres are those centres that become headquarters for large internationally active banks which influence events that pertain to global asset and liability management. Examples of cities include Basle, Brussels, Dusseldorf, Hamburg, Madrid, Rome and Vienna in Europe; Chicago, Mexico City, Rio de Janeiro, São Paulo, San Francisco and Toronto in North and South America; and Bombay, Hong Kong, Singapore, Melbourne and Sydney in Asia and Australia.

Host international financial centres enhance their own financial infrastructures and capabilities by attracting relatively large numbers of foreign financial institutions from a large number of countries. Examples of host international financial centres include Luxembourg, Milan, Bahrain, Buenos Aires, Los Angeles, Montreal, Panama City, Osaka, Seoul and Taipei.

10.1.3   The location decision

The reasons that influence the location decision of banks and other financial institutions are of crucial importance for the existing and evolving international financial centres. Davis (1990), for example, identifies three crucial factors that influence location selection: supply of factors of production; demand for output; and external economies of scale and economies of agglomeration.

The supply of factors of production include the availability of suitable personnel, the cost of funds, the efficiency of settlement systems, and the type of regulation. Financial firms already established in a particular location need to consider the unrecoverable 'sunk costs' which may be substantial before moving to another location.

The demand for output of financial firms can originate from both retail activities which still require face-to-face access with clients, and from wholesale activities which, with today's modern communications technology can be undertaken from almost anywhere. Moreover, the time zone location remains an important factor in generating demand.

External economies of scale and economies of agglomeration are the third set of critical important factors that determine location decision. Many of the external economies are related to superior information flows which provide the basis for more accurate and more competitive pricing of financial services and financial instruments. The increased volume of financial activity generates further economies of scale because, other things being equal the larger the financial market, the greater its efficiency and liquidity. Moreover, financial markets are closely interrelated and reinforce each other when located together. Agglomeration also fosters the growth of related professionals, such as lawyers, accountants, bankers, and computer specialists, providing a richer and more specialised menu of services for financial firms.

10.1.4   Competitive advantage

McGahey *et al.* (1990) identify and examine four dimensions of competitiveness. These include location costs and location advantages; the labour force and human resources; telecommunications and technology; and regulation and taxation. A crucial factor that determines competitiveness appears to be the belief that the financial services industry exhibits increasing returns to scale at all levels of activity (Davis 1990). This implies that major financial centres have a competitive advantage over smaller centres, and their growth may be at the expense of smaller centres. It also means that concentration of financial services in major centres offers a global gain in terms of improved economic efficiency. Once established, the growth of major financial centres is likely to be self-sustaining and may prove to be cumulative, given the nature and importance of external economies.

The variation in size of financial sectors between countries, regions and cities is analysed by Goldberg *et al.* (1988) who identify four principal factors: the level of overall economic development; the level of international trade; the extent of financial intermediation; and the stringency of financial regulation. The authors use regression analysis to investigate financial centres at three levels using 1984 data: the international level (assessing the determinants of the level of international banking and financial activity in 42 countries); the interregional level (examining the determinants of the level of financial activity across the regions of the USA); and the interurban level (investigating the determinants of the size of the banking sector across 31 cities containing the world's 750 largest banks).

The researchers find that the following independent variables are statistically significant in explaining the variation in size of financial sectors: income levels, hosting of corporate headquarters, the occupational and industrial structure of centres, importance within a country or time zone, and international trade. Their results suggest that the same basic economic forces underlie the development of the financial services industry across countries, regions and cities, that is, at each of the three levels analysed – international, interregional and interurban.

10.2   Historical development

10.2.1   Forces of economies of scale and centralisation

Powerful economies of scale and centralisation in financial markets are identified by Kindleberger's (1974) pioneering study on the forces leading to a single pre-eminent domestic financial centre in each country. These same forces led to the development of a hierarchy of international financial centres that culminated in a sequence of pre-eminent world centres: London prior to 1914, then New York and, since the 1960s, the international euromarket. Kindleberger derived his conclusions from a series of comparative historical case studies on London, Paris, Berlin, Frankfurt, Italy, Switzerland, Canada and New York. Amsterdam was the leading international financial centre of the 17th and 18th centuries (Smith 1984) but it was omitted in Kindleberger's historical survey. Amsterdam enjoyed a pre-eminent position as the hub of several regional and intercontinental trading systems and became the focal point for information flows and Europe's leading 'information exchange'.

Smith (1984) proposes six characteristics of the functions of an information exchange: acquisition of information, transfer, short-term analysis, dissemination, long-term accumulation, and long-term analysis. An innovation pioneered by Dutch institutions, especially the Dutch East India Company, was the systematic filing of quantitative commercial information and the specific use of information as the basis for innovative market analysis. As early as 1692, elaborate time-series data were used to identify inventory cycles and to plot a marketing strategy. Amsterdam's competitive edge in the sources and uses of information explains its continued importance as an international financial centre, even when surpassed as a port by London and Rotterdam.

10.2.2   Growth and decline

Jones (1992) traces the growth and decline of international financial centres in Asia and the Middle East. In the interwar years, Shanghai, Hong Kong and Singapore functioned as subregional (mainly domestic) financial centres. Then, during the two decades after the Second World War, Beirut emerged as a dynamic regional financial centre while Hong Kong and Singapore continued as subregional financial centres. Shanghai's function dwindled due to the Communist Revolution in China.

In the years 1965–75, the rapid growth of the eurocurrency markets helped Singapore and Hong Kong to become regional financial centres.

In 1975, the Lebanese Civil War destroyed Beirut as an international financial centre. Thereafter, in the late 1970s, Bahrain emerged as a regional financial centre, filling the vacuum created by Beirut.

According to Jones (1992), the emergence of regional and sub-regional financial centres depends on the achievement of reputations for stability, integrity, impartiality and confidentiality, their 'haven' status, and accessibility. Once established, further growth of financial centres is encouraged by external economies, economies of scale and agglomeration. Beirut and Shanghai were removed from the international financial scene by political and military developments and not by loss of competitiveness and/or economic decline.

10.2.3   International financial centres in the 1980s and 1990s

An explosive growth in the volume of international financial transactions was witnessed in the 1980s and 1990s (Roberts 1994). Globalisation is acting as a strong unifying process by which the world's various national financial marketplaces are beginning to act as if they were one single, integrated market. Moreover globalisation is causing strong price linkages (Bleeke and Bryan 1988) between all types of financial assets in the international foreign exchange markets, bond markets and equity markets. Examples of these strong price linkages are the international stock market crashes of October 1987 and October 1997, which witnessed simultaneous large price declines across the world's capital markets.

Other important competitive forces have been: deregulation or the removal or restrictions on financial markets, allowing them to become more competitive and efficient; securitisation or the substitution of various kinds of negotiable instruments for bank lending and; innovation in financial products, derivative hedging tools and institutional arrangements. These developments continue to make the international financial marketplace even more competitive, unified and efficient.

10.3   Communications and financial centres

10.3.1   Elimination of spatial barriers

The 'end-of-geography' is proposed by O'Brien (1992) in order to describe the complete elimination of spatial barriers in the conduct of financial transactions through advances in telecommunications and computer technology. The author suggests two opposing propositions concerning the impact of communications technology on the development of international financial centres.

The first proposition regards communications improvements as the process that undermines local monopolies and broadens financial markets. These improvements in communications technology facilitate the operation of economies of scale and strengthen the position of the leading world centres like London, New York and Tokyo.

The second proposition sees financial markets as being now electronic and no longer confined to a physical space. Hence, electronic linkages make it no longer necessary to have the traditional concentrations of firms and practitioners in the same physical financial centre.

O'Brien concludes that both processes are operating simultaneously, but at different levels. In wholesale markets, global centres will continue to be increasingly dominant and to enjoy comparative advantages in specialist services requiring high levels of expertise like corporate finance and exotic derivatives. In retail activities, however, new technology should strengthen the position of regional and domestic financial centres. Both wholesale and retail centres will continue to grow with the dynamic and continual increase in the aggregate demand for the services offered by both types of international financial centres.

10.4 Conclusions

International financial centres are facing great competitive forces with the increasingly stronger unifying processes of globalisation, deregulation and communications technology. The important question remains as to what can be considered to be the competitive advantage of each international financial centre. Several survey studies conducted in the last five years including Gardener and Molyneux (1998), Maude and Molyneux (1996) and Price Waterhouse (1996), emphasize the increasing importance of the following three variables in determining competitiveness: comparative costs and competitive prices; operating and producer efficiency; and return on equity and value added. As international financial centres become more closely linked through the strong underlying forces of communications, deregulation and globalisation, they will constantly have to seek new ways of maintaining and improving their competitive advantage *vis-à-vis* competitor financial centres. In this regard, comparative costs and prices, producer operating efficiency, and value added will become increasingly more important in developing and shaping the competitive position of international financial centres in the 21st century.

References

Bleeke, J.A. and L.L. Bryan (1988), 'The globalisation of financial markets', *The McKinsey Quarterly*, Winter, pp. 17–38

Davis, E.P. (1990), *International financial centres: an industrial analysis*, Bank of England Discussion Paper, No. 51, September, pp. 1–23

Dufey, G. and I.H. Giddy (1978), 'Financial centres and external financial markets', Appendix 2 of *The International money market*, Englewood Cliffs, NJ: Prentice-Hall, pp. 35–47

European Commission (1997), *Credit institutions and banking, The single market review*, subseries II: vol. 3, London: Kogan Page

Gardener, E.P.M. and P. Molyneux (1998), *Deregulation of foreign bank entry: a study of Bermuda*, Commissioned report, Bangor: Institute of European Finance

Goldberg, M.A., R.W. Helsey and M.D. Levi (1988), 'On the development of international financial centres', *Annals of Regional Science*, **XXII**, February, pp. 81–94

Jones, G. (1992), 'International financial centres in Asia, the Middle East and Australia: a historical perspective', in C. Youssef, (ed.), *Finance and financiers in European history, 1880–1960*, Cambridge: Cambridge University Press, pp. 405–28

Kindleberger, C.P. (1974), *The Formation of financial centres: a study in comparative economic history*, Princeton Studies in International Finance no. 36, Princeton, NJ: Princeton University

Maude, D. and P. Molyneux (1996), *Private banking: maximising performance in a competitive market*, London: Euromoney Publications

McGahey, R., M. Malloy, K. Kazanas and M.P. Jacobs (1990), 'What makes a financial center?', in *Financial services, financial centres: public policy and the competition for markets, firms, and jobs*, Boulder, Colorado: Westview Press, pp. 15–76

O'Brien, R. (1992), 'Everybody has to be somewhere: the new determinants of location', in *Global financial integration: the end of geography*, London: The Royal Institute of International Affairs/Pinter Publishers, pp. 73–82

Price Waterhouse (1996), *Corporate taxes: a worldwide summary*, London: Price Waterhouse

Reed, H.C. (1983), 'Appraising corporate investment policy: a financial center theory of foreign direct investment', in C.P. Kindleberger, and D.B. Audretsch (eds), *The Multinational corporation in the 1980s*, Cambridge Mass: MIT Press, pp. 219–44

Roberts, R. (1994), 'Introduction', in *R. Roberts (ed.), International financial centres: concepts, development and dynamics*, Aldershot, Hanphire: Edward Elgar Publishing Limited

Smith, W.D. (1984), 'The function of commercial centres in the modernisation of European capitalism: Amsterdam as an information exchange in the seventeenth century', *Journal of Economic History*, **XLIV**, 4, pp. 985–1005

11
Globalisation, Cross-border Trade in Financial Services and Offshore Banking: the Case of Ireland

Philip Bourke and Ray Kinsella

Introduction

The International Financial Services Centre (IFSC), located in the dockland region of Dublin, was established in 1987. In the intervening years it has emerged as one of the most significant offshore centres in the EU and is, in certain niches, a truly global player. To take one example, nine of the top 15 reinsurance companies have located in Dublin. Well over 400 companies, including many blue-chip global multinational companies (MNCs), now employ in excess of 4000 people within the IFSC. This chapter examines the development of the IFSC against the background of the cross-border trade in financial services.

An analysis of financial centres operating in a diversity of environments highlights the importance of certain predisposing 'success factors': notably among these is the taxation regime. This is also evident in the case of the IFSC where a 10 per cent corporation tax rate provided an important initial attraction to internationally mobile financial service providers. In strategic terms, however, factors such as taxation are easily emulated. What is more important is the *combination* of 'success factors' and the ability of national authorities to manage these. This is the essential basis of *sustainable competitive advantage*.

In this regard, it is possible to identify certain features which differentiate the IFSC from its peers. The extent to which the Irish authorities have, in fact, succeeded in differentiating the IFSC makes it a particularly interesting and relevant case study. More generally, we argue in this chapter that sustainable competitive advantage is based on what we term 'rolling innovation' in relation to taxation, human resources, product development and, perhaps most important of all, marketing. It is this combination of factors which has generated a self-sustaining critical mass of information intensive internationally traded financial service activity in the IFSC.

The first section of this chapter contextualises our argument by examining, *inter alia*, the basis for cross-border trade in financial services. Section 11.2 outlines the background to the IFSC and the predisposing 'success factors' which underpin its development. Section 11.3 examines the composition of cross-border activity within the Centre. Finally, the chapter outlines some of the implications of the success of the IFSC for the wider process of cross-border activities in financial services.

11.1 Background

The basis for cross-border trade in financial services is not, *a priori*, obvious.[1] There are, to begin with, start-up costs which, whatever the market entry strategy, are considerable. Domestically-based firms have informational advantages. Moreover, the markets within which the firm is seeking to establish may already be competitive. Equally there may well be regulatory constraints which, indeed, frequently take the form of discriminatory non-tariff borders.

International trade in financial services, and more specifically cross-border activity, is generally rationalised in terms of the standard theory of comparative advantage. In this regard it can be argued that institutions may have transferable core competencies, economies of scale or reputational advantages which may offset entry and other costs.

The growth in foreign direct investment also provides a robust explanatory platform for examining the parallel cross-border expansion of financial institutions. It is certainly the case in Ireland that the growth of direct foreign investment post-1960 was accompanied by the establishment of USA and EU banks to service the needs of such companies. Such banks had, as noted, informational advantages in regard to inward investment which allowed them to price risk for MNCs more effectively than could domestic institutions. Equally, they had a vested interest in monitoring the foreign investment of their own clients: these arguments still hold.

The operation of these has been facilitated over the last 20 years or so by the progressive removal of restrictions on capital as well as on current payment arrangements. There has been rapid growth in the volume of international capital flows reflecting, in part, increased openness, or trade dependence, of nations (see Figure 11.1). The

Figure 11.1: Globalisation and emerging risk management needs

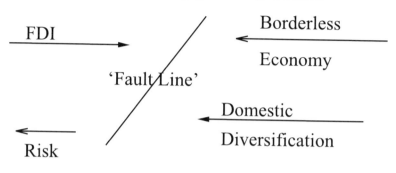

growth in global capital flows has been greatly reinforced by the expo-
nential growth in financial derivatives and in other new forms of
financial instruments. Given the increased scope for global capital
mobility, financial institutions have an incentive to diversify risk
through cross-border expansion.

The inclusion, for the first time, of financial services within the trade
liberalisation programme of the General Agreement on Tariffs and
Trade (GATT), now the World Trade Organisation (WTO), has greatly
facilitated cross-border activity in financial services. In the EU, the
single financial market provides an environment which is *specifically
intended* to facilitate cross-border trade within, and also without, estab-
lishment/localisation. This factor alone is likely to lead to a significant
rise in cross-border activity. Insurance providers within the EU, to take
an example, still operate primarily within the framework of historically
shaped structures. By contrast, non-EU providers seeking to enter the
EU market can develop a market presence unconstrained by historical
baggage and inertia and which exploits the full possibilities of the
Third Directive. When this is leveraged by the increasing scope for IT-
based distance/direct selling of products from one EU location (the EU
directive, Undertakings for Collective Investment in Transferable
Securities (UCITS) is a good example) the basis for offshore centres specialising in and supporting such activities becomes apparent.

All of this provides a necessary first step. It helps to explain the basis
for the expansion of financial institutions across different countries.
But it does not provide a sufficiently robust explanation for offshore
banking *per se*, including the establishment of financial centres such as
the IFSC.

11.1.1 Globalisation of business and offshore banking

The *globalisation* of business encompassing new forms of economic activity, shaped by global economic and political co-operation, has created a fundamentally new environment within which to examine the rationale for, and the role of, offshore financial centres. It helps to place the rapid growth of offshore banking, including such activities as insurance and reinsurance (both of which are core activities of the IFSC), in the broader context. Large MNCs now operate in a borderless economy. Developments in systems logistics and telecommunications mean that the activities of such companies are distance-independent. Activities may be delegated or outsourced. This process is operating alongside a technologically driven transformation in indigenous industry within economies. What is evident here is a new 'fault line' (Figure 11.1) between these two developments, generating both new production/servicing possibilities and new forms of risk. Risk, and this process of 'corporate deconstruction' in the global economy, is spontaneously generating a process of agglomeration, whereby such activities as risk management in all its forms, together with activities such as treasury management, are attracted to locations which provide optimum conditions for servicing these new core needs, efficiently and at a minimum cost. Equally, *precisely because* IT support services are now distance-independent, they tend to coalesce in such centres to provide the necessary 'back office' facilities for such activities.

All of this points to the development, for the first, of a truly global economy which transcends the national market. The important point is that within this new economy the theory of competitive advantage, and specialisation to which it leads, still holds. *International financial activity will coalesce around 'nodes' or environments in which competitive advantage is engineered around the financial, insurance and risk management needs, and possibilities, of information intensive globalised companies.*

Recent global macroeconomic trends have provided further impetus to cross-border activity. Economic growth, in particular, a shift in the global economic centre of gravity toward the 'Pacific rim', has generated significant M&A activity.[2]

At a yet deeper level, the last ten years have seen the emergence of the 'knowledge economy' as a source of innovation and the major catalyst of indigenous growth. It is clear, for example, that fundamental advances in biotechnology will reshape global trade and corporate activity, forcing demand and requiring that global financial markets (including insurance markets) provide specialised risk services management.

Consonant with these developments, there is an accelerated process of conglomeration among major financial services providers. This is, in part, based on the imperative of scale in facilitating 'global reach' within a global economy. More fundamentally, there is a fusion in financial markets themselves, notably, for example, in relation to risk management products in insurance and in capital markets. Increasingly for these companies, the concept of national markets is becoming redundant: a new global supervisory structure is needed to accommodate this development.

What all of this points to is a fundamentally new type of global economy and a paradigm shift in the structure of credit, capital and insurance markets servicing this economy. The opposing forces of, on the one hand, deconstruction of activities throughout the global economy and, on the other hand, the process of agglomeration are spontaneously creating the conditions for offshore banking. In such centres, the authorities can engineer comparative advantage based not on factor endowment but, rather, on the provision of knowledge intensive services supported by regulatory, taxation and infrastructure facilities.

11.2   The IFSC

The development of the IFSC differs in a number of important respects from other offshore centres. First, it was conceived as a means to an end rather than an end itself. That is, the overriding impetus came from a decision by the Irish government to redevelop a derelict site in the heart of the city. The IFSC was conceived as the anchor project for this wider developmental objective.

Moreover, the development was to be accomplished by a public/ private sector partnership operating within strict financial parameters. Basically, the government provided the land and facilitated the physical planning system within this environment. It also provided a highly favourable taxation regime, approved by the EU Commission on the basis of Ireland's Objective One status. It did not provide direct financial assistance. Indeed it stipulated that in the event (and to the extent) that the project was successful, the full value of the land should be repaid. In effect, the public/private partnership insulated the State against any downside risk while it captured at least some of the upside.

The difficulties confronting the IFSC Development Group in establishing a solid offshore financial centre, were formidable. Ireland's indigenous financial system, while well established and including a substantive foreign presence, is small in scale. To establish a robust and *sustainable* offshore banking centre on a green field site, in the shadow of the London markets and in the face of competition from established offshore banking centres, posed formidable management and strategic difficulties.

11.2.1 'Success factors'

The three distinctive features underpinning the success to date of the IFSC and which, at least in part, differentiated it from other competitors can be characteristised as vision, leadership and strategy. Significantly it is precisely these same characteristics that underpin *successful* cross-border expansion.

The decision to establish the IFSC, and to establish it as part of a wider urban regeneration programme, was visionary in conceptual terms as well as in terms of its scale and the projected scope of activities. Such an initiative had not previously been conceived: significantly, the initial concept was proposed by an innovative market practitioner who had earlier established the first interbank money market. The fact that the genesis of the project was rooted within the market enhanced its credibility and facilitated 'selling' the concept to domestically based institutions.

In terms of leadership what was important was the *reality* of direct 'ownership' of the IFSC project by the government. In particular, the project was championed by the then prime minister and the IFSC Development Group was chaired by the Secretary of the Prime Minister's department. This leadership at the highest level meant that the committee could orchestrate and co-ordinate across separate government departments and, where necessary, override constraints. We see in all of this the classic elements of effective project planning.

The major element of the third feature – strategy – aimed at attracting a critical mass of international mobile cross-border activities to Dublin and included the following:

- a favourable taxation regime including, in particular, a 10 per cent corporation tax rate as well as a highly competitive set of capital and other allowances. At least as important is the existence of an extensive network of double taxation agreements
- a physical and telecommunications structure, creating for companies attracted to the Centre a state-of-the-art working environment
- an integrated, and practitioner focused, certification and licensing procedure. This eschewed the 'brassplate' syndrome of some off-

shore centres by ensuring that the supervisory process was rigorous without being overly interventionist.

- human resources, specifically a young and highly skilled work force. The quality of the workforce, especially at graduate and postgraduate level, provided the 'knowledge equity'. Essential to the creditability of the Centre was the willingness of the universities and professional industry representative bodies to develop courses attractive to companies. This had two effects: it meant, for the overseas companies, a minimum level of enforced migration on the part of their executives; it also minimised inflationary remuneration packages, which would have been generated by skill shortages. As it was, the availability of such skills facilitated a spontaneous and self-fulfilling development cycle within the IFSC

- perhaps most important of all in terms of strategy was a distinctive marketing strategy. The Irish Development Agency (IDA), which had had some 25 years expertise in attracting foreign direct investment to Ireland and which enjoyed a high reputation internationally, was deployed *alongside* a high level group of financial services practitioners headed by the former governor of the Central Bank and the Secretary to the Department of Finance. This lent depth and credibility to the marketing of the IFSC to major internationally mobile clients.

11.2.2   Nature of activities

The essence of the activities carried on in the IFSC is that they are, by their nature, internationally mobile and cross-border in nature. Equally, for taxation and administrative purposes, they are 'ring fenced' from the domestic economy and markets. The activities include asset financing, mutual funds, treasury, securities trading, international banking activities, as well as insurance and reinsurance. Tables 11.1a, 11.1b and 11.1c show the composition of activities, by sector and broken down by geographical composition.

The insurance sector, comprising life, non-life and international reinsurance and captive components, within the IFSC exemplifies the manner in which greatly increased cross-border activity by MNCs has generated new opportunities for risk management.

One such decision relates to whether to transfer risk to an insurance carrier or, alternatively, to 'internalise' the risk in a 'capture'. Central to the decision of retention or outsourcing, is the risk culture of the organisation and the relative cost of the two options. The 'capture' option may be used where, for example, risk is characterised in terms

Table 11.1a: Stand alone activities in the IFSC: by sector and geographical distribution (December 1996)

Country	Total	Banking and asset financing	Mutual funds	Treasury	Insurance	Securities trading and other
USA	66	11	19	7	14	15
Ireland	64	18	2	10	7	27
UK	33	3	15	4	10	1
Germany	33	18	3	4	5	3
Japan	13	12	–	–	1	–
Denmark	9	5	2	1	1	–
Sweden	8	–	–	3	5	–
Netherlands	8	3	1	3	1	–
Canada	8	3	2	–	2	1
Italy	8	6	–	–	–	2
Switzerland	6	–	–	1	5	–
Belgium	6	6	–	–	–	–
Others	27	11	5	6	3	2
Total	289	96	49	39	54	51

Source: IDA Ireland.

Table 11.1b: Agency activities in the IFSC: by sector and geographical distribution (December 1996)

Country	Total	Treasury	Insurance
USA	62	56	6
Germany	23	11	12
Canada	15	15	–
Sweden	14	14	–
UK	14	12	2
Netherlands	19	7	2
Others	25	21	4
Total	162	136	26

Source: IDA Ireland.

of low severity and high frequency and, also, where the cost impact is predictable. In practice, many of the largest MNCs, whose activities are truly global in scope and scale (Heinz, IBM, Coca Cola) have established 'captures' and in these and other instances have located them within the environment created within the IFSC.

Dublin, unlike other major offshore locations, has not legislated specifically for captives but, rather, has accrued strategic advantages attracting major corporations in all captive sectors (single parent, group

Table 11.1c: Captive insurance activities in the IFSC: by sector and geographical distribution (December 1996)

Country	Total	Treasury	Insurance
USA	58	24	34
Sweden	28	4	24
Canada	17	15	2
Belgium	14	1	13
Germany	13	3	10
Netherlands	16	2	14
UK	9	4	5
France	8	2	6
Others	34	12	22
Total	197	67	130

Source: IDA Ireland.

Figure 11.2: MNCs: risk management options

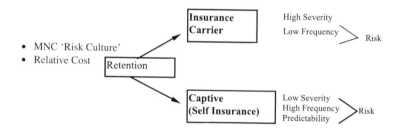

captives and third party) which provide cover over the entire risk/benefit spectrum. Having generated a 'critical mass' in terms of activity, the authorities have facilitated 'rolling innovation' by, for example, tax legislation permitting deferment and by facilitating product development within the sector. All of this complements the needs of MNCs for increasingly sophisticated risk management services.

11.2.3   Impact of the IFSC

A comparative analysis of the IFSC can be undertaken at three levels.

First, there is the direct *economic* impact. This is relatively easy to quantify and encompasses such measures as:

- growth of employment arising directly from the activities carried on in the centre, net of any diversion of hitherto domestic activities into the centre
- the *quality* of such employment

- the fiscal impact including, on the one hand, fiscal expenditures in the form of tax breaks and, on the other hand, direct and indirect taxes generated by activities carried on in the Centre.

Second, there is the *developmental* impact. This can be measured in terms of, for example, occupancy rates, as well as house prices and rental incomes generated in the immediate hinterland of the IFSC. Perhaps more significant in terms of the initial mandate of the initiative, has been the *societal* impact within the area and its environs in the form of community building, education participation ratios (which were very much below the national average), and so on. These are of pivotal importance but are not within the remit of this chapter.

Third, and more directly relevant to this analysis, has been the impact on cross-border financial activity in Ireland as well as the corporate structure of financial institutions. These are of particular interest and, indeed, have a wider relevance. Politically, the island of Ireland, with a total population of just under 6 million, is divided into two parts: the Republic of Ireland comprising 26 of the 32 counties and Northern Ireland, which comprises six of the Northern Counties. Northern Ireland is part of the UK and its financial institutions are supervised by the UK authorities.

Notwithstanding this division, there are close historical and institutional linkages between financial institutions and markets on the island as a whole. These linkages are reinforced by the work of the main representative bodies, such as the Irish Bankers' Federation (IBF). Strategic planning in areas such as payments systems and, a more immediate example, planning for EMU, is co-ordinated through the IBF, with individual banks free to pursue their own specific agendas within this framework.

At one level, cross-border trade in financial services in Ireland has been generated by the existence of risk, created by the existence of the two systems. The prospective entry of the Republic into the Single Currency Zone, with the UK, including Northern Ireland, remaining outside, at least initially, is an example.

In this environment, the development of the IFSC has effectively precluded a similar initiative in Northern Ireland. In effect, Dublin as a national market has 'captured' the benefits of proximity to the London markets, in terms of location, time zone and language, advantages which may be leveraged by Ireland's participation in EMU, so long as the UK remains outside. Northern Ireland, by contrast, is a small regional market servicing a distinctive, but increasingly contestable, market.

This macro impact on cross-border activity in Ireland has been reinforced by the reshaping, at the micro level, of the *organisational structures* of financial institutions, especially in respect of Treasury leasing and international services. In effect, this new *international* domain, shaped around the IFSC, has re-engineered the domestic organisational/functional activities of institutions operating in Ireland: certain core activities have simply migrated to the IFSC.

It should, of course, be noted that the IFSC relates specifically to international activities, 'ring fenced' from the domestic markets. But the small size of the domestic market has enforced an international orientation: the major clearing banks, AIB and Bank of Ireland, now have a substantial foreign presence which generates over 40 per cent of their total income. AIB, in particular, has pursued an aggressive geographical and functional diversification programme in the EU, the USA and the Far East. The IFSC has reinforced and facilitated this international perspective, within the domestic system.

Conclusion

The three 'success factors' of vision, leadership and strategy, which we have identified within the IFSC have been meshed within an organisational structure that is continually interrogated and reshaped in the light of global market trends. Importantly, the government has retained 'ownership' of the project which has, for example, facilitated securing from the EU Commission an extension of the 10 per cent corporation tax rate. In 1997, the Customs House Docks Development Authority (which was responsible from the outset for the whole physical development of the area, including the IFSC, and for training and education) was transformed into the Dublin Docks Development Authority. This reflected a perceived need to build on the success to date and, more specifically, to extend the development remit to a much wider (127 acre) area in the city centre.

At another level, successive Finance Acts have modified the fiscal incentives in a conscious strategy to attract and anchor existing, as well as emerging, products and services. Equally, both through the representative bodies which have emerged, and which have been subsumed into the policy structure which guides the IFSC, as well as through the universities, the essential human resource component is continually enhanced, adding to the efficiency of the market and to its reputational value.

What is important, in summary, is not so much individual 'success factors', such as taxation, but rather the holistic approach applied from the outset to the development and marketing of the Centre. This holistic approach, which itself echoes the evolving structure of the new global marketplace, and the constraint iterative process of change may be termed 'rolling innovation' and is the distinguishing feature of the IFSC and the principal determinant of its success.

Notes

1. A good outline of the theory is presented by Tobias Hoschka in *Cross-Border Entry in European Retail Financial Services: Determinants, Regulation and the Impact on Competition*, London: Macmillan – now Palgrave, 1993.
2. See, for example, *Financial Times* 'International Corporate Finance', 20 June 1997.

12
The Impact of CAR on Bank Capital Augmentation in Spain

Yener Altunbaş, Santiago Carbo and Edward P.M. Gardener

Abstract

This chapter reports on tests, using panel methods, of a new capital augmentation model on Spanish savings banks over the period 1987–1996. It is argued that this banking subsector and this time frame provide an interesting laboratory of the potential impact of regulation on bank capital augmentation. Early modelling work in this area is built on by, *inter alia*, including two previously omitted and key bank portfolio risks (liquidity and interest rate) and a new productive efficiency variable. The results indicate strong evidence of the impact of the new capital adequacy regulatory regime on bank capital augmentation. At the same time the model confirms the importance of bank profitability and productive efficiency in explaining capital augmentation.

12.1   Introduction

During the recent past there has been a great deal of policy attention and research focused on the impact on EU banks of the deregulation of banking structure and conduct rules: see, for example, Altunbaş and Molyneux (1996), Canals (1993), Cecchini (1988), COEC (1988) and Molyneux *et al.* (1996). Bank structure regulation covers areas like the functional separation of institutions, entry restrictions, and discriminatory rules against foreign banks and investors. Conduct regulations, on the other hand, encompass those regulations concerned with *inter alia* bank deposit and lending rates, fees and commissions, credit quotas, branching restrictions and reserve requirements. The development of the EU Single Market Programme in the 1990s, the approach of the single currency, and wider globalisation trends within the international financial system have all conspired to focus a great deal of contemporary policy and academic attention towards these key deregulating developments.

At the same time there has been an equally marked re-regulation of bank prudential (or supervisory) rules, especially those concerned with capital adequacy regulation (CAR). CAR is concerned practically with monitoring and constraining bank risk behaviour through relating a bank's risk exposures to its corresponding internal capital (net worth or 'own funds') position. Balance sheet ratios relating capital to the respective banking risks (essentially credit risk) have traditionally been used to regulate commercial bank capital adequacy.[1] The Basle (1988) scheme for international bank capital adequacy developed a new kind of risk assets ratio (RAR), which effectively became the prototype of modern (post-1988) commercial bank capital adequacy schemes across the globe.

Whereas deregulation stimulates a downward pressure, via the increased competition, on bank margins and profit, the corresponding re-regulation of capital adequacy exerts potential upward pressures. There are two main reasons for the latter. First, banks need to meet the new, usually stricter, CAR rules. Second, banks are also increasingly incentivised in this environment to meet new external, market-orientated tests of capital adequacy as the open market is empowered, via deregulation, with a greater role in internal bank resource allocation.

In this post-deregulation environment, bank productive and internal capital allocation efficiencies are increasingly prioritised by banks; maximising these efficiencies are necessary conditions for banks to achieve in order to maximise their corresponding shareholder value and capital adequacy positions. Improving bank productive efficiency is practically synonymous with cost minimisation: see, for example, Sinkey (1992). Recently, the competitive (from a cost saving perspective) managerial importance of bank productive efficiency, reducing X-inefficiencies, has been re-emphasized: see, for example, Berger *et al.* (1993). Internal capital allocation efficiency, on the other hand, refers essentially to the matching of a bank's internal capital to its corresponding risk exposures in order to maximise bank shareholder value: see, for example, Leemputte and Kearney (1990), Matten (1996), Parsley (1995) and Yang (1991).

The strategic importance of capital adequacy during this modern era of EU banking has been recently re-emphasized in a major empirical study for the European Commission (PACEC/IEF 1996). This latter study found[2] that EU banks ranked capital adequacy regulation as the single most important piece of Single Market legislation in terms of its impact on EU banking strategies. Despite the perceived strategic importance of capital adequacy, however, there is a paucity of work on the impact of capital adequacy on European banks.[3]

During the past decade or so the EU banking system has become a rather unique 'laboratory' for studying the impact of regulatory changes (both deregulation and re-regulation effects) on banks. This chapter focuses on the impact of the new CAR regime on bank capital augmentation. Capital augmentation is defined similarly to Kaufman (1992 p. 385) as bank capital growth: that is, increases in the amount of banks' capital resources available to absorb unexpected, or non-provisioned, losses. The Spanish savings banks sector during the period 1987–96 is the case study reported in this chapter.

The chapter is organised in the following way. Following this Section 12.1, Section 12.2 outlines the background to the specific case study and the methodology employed. Section 12.3 summarises some salient features of the statistical methodology. The data and empirical results are summarised in Section 12.4, which is followed by the conclusions in Section 12.5.

12.2   Background and model

The main research question addressed is whether the new CAR regime is effective in requiring banks to augment their capital if they fall below the regulatory minimum ratio requirement.[4] Of course, banks with inadequate regulatory capital may instead reduce their respective risk exposures in order to meet the regulatory standard. These changes in bank risk levels, however, are tracked and factored into the new form of RAR. The modern policy preference for the RAR form of capital adequacy regulation, theory and empirical evidence all appear to support the argument that a RAR form of capital adequacy regulation is likely to be more successful practically in monitoring and restraining excessive banking risk exposures compared with earlier, more simple ratio schemes: see, for example, Blanden (1993), Cantor and Johnson (1992), Cooper *et al.* (1991), Di Cagno (1990), Hall (1993), Lackman (1986) and O'Keefe (1993). Nissan (1995, p. 7) reported in his study of the new Basle capital adequacy ratios of the major banks of 29 countries between 1987 and 1992 that 'there was a perceptible trend toward more compliance between 1987 and 1992'.

From 1987–1992, the Spanish banking system was subjected to a marked deregulation, one whose comparative impact was more pronounced than in the majority of EU countries because of the previous (pre-deregulation) more regulated, and comparatively less competitive Spanish system (PACEC/IEF 1996).[5] At the same time, Spain instituted a much stricter capital adequacy system than hitherto in the wake of one of the severest banking crises (during 1978–1982) of any OECD country and the concomitant need to meet the new EU CAR rules by 1992. During this period in Spain, then, the specific liberalising effects of deregulation, together with the concomitant impact of stricter capital adequacy regulation, were apparently more pronounced than in most other EU countries.

Two other factors provide further support for using Spain as a useful case study 'laboratory' for present purposes. First, throughout the 1980s and early 1990s the option for Spanish banks to reduce their assets was constrained in the face of supervisory demands for improved capital adequacy since the growth of securitisation (credit intermediation via open financial markets) was still embryonic. This period was also a high growth phase for the Spanish economy and the financial system was seen as a key engine of overall economic development. Spanish savings banks operated a relatively simple asset structure during the study period 1987–96 and the opportunities to innovate around a stricter capital adequacy ratio were correspondingly constrained.

Second, the Spanish savings banks are also unquoted firms with a legal status similar to foundations; this means that these banks are not subject directly to the external tests and demands of the stock market.[6] Modern capital adequacy research has tended to focus much more directly on the impact of the external market on bank capital augmentation and banking performance generally: see, for example, Berger *et al.* (1995). The institutional features of the Spanish financial system in general, and the savings banks subsector in particular, then, provide a useful and rather unique kind of laboratory where the specific impact of CAR re-regulation on bank capital augmentation might be modelled more clearly, free of extraneous 'noise'.

Nevertheless, the model used does not obviate the impact and relevance of external market pressures on the savings bank performance and capital augmentation. This would be unrealistic since the evidence to date suggests that even unquoted banks cannot escape the discipline of external market tests of their comparative efficiency and performance (PACEC/IEF 1996). Indeed, this latter kind of discipline is generally an important policy aim of a banking deregulation. It is for this reason that variables like profit return on equity (ROE), managerial quality and productive efficiency comprise part of the explanatory variable set within the model reported in this note.

The earlier US groundwork on the impact of CAR on bank capital augmentation was carried out by students like Dietrich and James (1983), Mayne (1972), Mingo (1975) and Peltzman (1965, 1970); these studies often reached different and apparently conflicting results. Peltzman (1970), for example, found no regulatory effect on bank capital augmentation, whereas Mingo's results suggested a substantial effect. Dietrich and James, like Peltzman, bring into question the effectiveness of regulation on bank capital augmentation. Within this literature, CAR is modelled as an explanatory variable within a multiple regression model that estimates capital augmentation, the percentage growth in bank capital in a given year. Peltzman used aggregate data, but later US studies have generally employed individual bank data.

More recent US empirical work on bank capital changes has suggested that US regulatory capital-deficient banks augmented their capital ratios primarily by slowing down asset relative to capital growth: see, for example, Keeley (1988). Some of the more recent US work has been concerned with the role of bank regulation and its impact on capital and asset growth: see, for example, Cantor and Johnson (1992), Peek and Rosengren (1992, 1995) and Syron (1991). Much of this US work analyses the so-called 'capital and credit crunch hypothesis': other things being equal, poorly capitalised banks shrink their deposits and assets more rapidly than better capitalised ones.

The most recent and extensive review of the *extant* capital adequacy literature discussed the empirical difficulties in determining whether capital requirements are binding (Berger *et al*. 1995 pp. 418–19). One empirical problem is that the 'effective' regulatory capital requirement may include a kind of buffer above the mandatory regulatory minimum in order to allow a bank to exploit unexpected profitable opportunities and to cushion the effects of unexpected negative (resource draining) shocks. This buffer zone is known only to the regulators, and it may vary from bank to bank and from one period to another. This review found that the most recent US studies of the capital-to-asset requirements of the 1980s generally supported the view that regulatory CAR standards were binding on book or accounting measures of banks' capital-to-asset ratios: see, for example, Berger *et al*. (1995) and Keeley (1988).

Building from the Dietrich and James (1983) and earlier models, and extending these to reflect recent capital adequacy and market developments,[7] we estimate the following capital augmentation equation for Spanish savings banks:

$$\%dK_t = f\ (\text{ROE}, PK_t, LQ_t, dD_t, KR_t, IRR_t, NPL_t, MQ_t, OBS_t, CI_t,) \qquad (1)$$

where

$\%dK_t$ = percentage growth of bank capital (tier 1 and tier 2 capital) in a given year t

ROE = ratio of before-tax net income in year t to tier 1 capital in year t–1 (measure of bank profitability and cost of capital proxy)

PK_t = ratio of public sector securities held to total assets (measure of portfolio risk)

LQ_t = ratio of bank's cash accounts to total assets (liquidity indicator)

dD_t = deposit growth in year t (to capture any bank capital change associated with deposit growth)

KR_t = Basle-type (1988) RAR of actual bank capital to computed regulatory required (excluding any 'buffer zone' above this minimum) capital (measure of bank CAR compliance)

IRR_t = ratio of interest-sensitive assets to interest-sensitive liabilities (bank interest-sensitivity ratio or gap, measure of interest rate risk)

NPL_t = ratio of non-performing loans to total gross loans (additional measure of credit risk and (negative) measure of managerial quality)

MQ_t = ratio of bank's earning assets to total assets (measure of bank managerial quality)

OBS_t = ratio of off-balance-sheet business to total assets (proxy for innovation by management)

CI_t = ratio of total cost to total income (cost/income ratio, measure of bank productive efficiency)

This general empirical approach to bank capital augmentation is supported through the groundwork studies in this area by Dietrich and James (1983), Mayne (1972), Mingo (1975) and Peltzman (1970). The ROE, PK_t, LQ_t, dD_t and KR_t variables, for example, are similar to those employed by Dietrich and James (1983), Mayne (1972) and Mingo (1975). However, a significant extension (five new explanatory variables) of this earlier kind of US capital augmentation model is embodied in equation 1, together with two simplications related to the structure of this KR variable and the omission of a deposit insurance variable used in the early US studies.

ROE, the ratio of net income to lagged capital, is a proxy for the expected return on equity and, therefore, a bank's equity cost of capital; on *a priori* grounds it may be related positively or negatively with bank capital (Berger 1995). PK_t is a measure of portfolio (credit-related) risk; the higher is PK, the less risk from default associated with this portfolio, and hence less capital backing is desired. LQ_t captures the potential importance of liquidity in bank solvency appraisal: other things being equal, a higher LQ_t puts a corresponding reduced pressure on capital augmentation.[8] On the other hand, high LQ_t may reduce bank profitability and, therefore, increase regulatory pressures for capital augmentation. LQ_t is one of several new explanatory variables within our model that explicitly seek to recognize important banking risks that are not captured formally within the Basle-type (1988) RAR (modelled within our KR_t variable) but which still have a direct bearing on overall bank capital adequacy appraisal, both by management and supervisors. dD_t is intended to capture changes in capital associated with deposit growth.

The relationship between KR_t and $\%dK_t$ is the focus of traditional modelling in this area: see, for example, Dietrich and James (1983). KR_t is the ratio of a bank's actual (tier 1 and tier 2) capital in each year to the regulatory minimum; it is computed as a close approximation to the Basle-type (1988) RAR formula used by Spanish bank regulators. The higher this ratio, the less is the corresponding regulatory pressure for a bank to augment its capital (expected sign of KR is negative). On the other hand, a high KR ratio might also be highly correlated with a corresponding high ROE: see, for example, Berger (1995). In this latter case, the expected sign of KR would be positive: high profitability (ROE) augments capital via retained earnings and 'improves' KR (moves it towards unity and beyond). If this latter relationship holds, we would expect any contemporaneous regulatory pressure to augment capital to be picked up in other risk-related (and, therefore, capital ade-quacy-related) variables like LQ, IRR, NPL, MQ, OBS and CI. These latter variables also encompass key bank portfolio risks (especially liquidity, LQ, and interest rate risk, IRR) that are not covered directly within the Basle RAR model and, therefore, KR. Nevertheless, supervi-sors cannot and, of course, do not ignore these other important portfo-lio risks and wider aspects of management within their capital adequacy appraisals.[9] This extended model also recognizes the increas-ing strategic relevance of productive efficiency (proxied by our CI vari-able) to capital augmentation and overall value maximisation within the banking firm: see, for example, Molyneux *et al.* (1996).

Dietrich and James (1983), following earlier students, defined the KR variable as a negative inverse in order to permit a non-linear response to regulatory pressure. We found that this kind of transformation did not improve the model fit and, more importantly, did not appear necessary anyway within the 'relevant range' of response by individual banks to regulatory pressure when capital falls below the regulatory minimum (a KR of less than 1.0). In this relevant range, the assumption of a linear bank response function (one of two simplications[10] on earlier US work) appeared to be realistic for practical purposes.

The IRR variable is a proxy for bank interest rate risk which, like liquidity risk, is not captured within the RAR used to model KR. It is measured as the ratio of interest-sensitive assets to interest-sensitive liabilities, reflecting the interest repricing gap.[11] Spanish banks generally had high positive gaps throughout the study period. On the one hand, a positive gap may be more risky during the downturn of the interest rate cycle, suggesting a negative sign for IRR in our model for these periods. But IRR might also take a positive sign to reflect a kind of signalling effect: banks that have high positive gaps and deal strongly in interbank assets may also need to present corresponding strong capital positions to the market.

Banks that have a high volume of non-performing loans (high NPL values) may be expected to be under regulatory pressure to augment capital (expected sign of NPL is positive); on the other hand, such a bank may also have a corresponding low capital augmentation because of its reduced profitability (and so the expected sign of NPL is now negative). The expected signs of the MQ and OBS variables may also be argued on *a priori* grounds to be either positive or negative. High MQ may reduce regulatory pressure to augment bank capital (negative sign); a high MQ is also likely to be associated with a high rate of capital augmentation and good profitability, and so the expected sign of MQ would be positive. Similarly, a high OBS value could be argued to either reduce the need for capital augmentation, perhaps through regulatory avoidance activities or by economising on bank capital, or be associated with high rates of capital augmentation if it is an indicator of greater financial innovation by a bank and of corresponding higher profits.[12]

The final variable of the model is CI, the cost/income ratio. Given the strategic importance of bank productive efficiency and its relationship to overall bank performance and value, a positive or negative relationship might be argued on *a priori* grounds between CI and capital augmentation. The higher a bank's cost/income ratio, and the lower its productive efficiency, the less a bank's corresponding ability to augment its capital because of reduced profits. On the other hand, the higher a bank's cost/income ratio, the greater the regulatory pressure might be to improve the corresponding productive and capital alloca-tion efficiencies, and to augment capital.

12.3   Statistical methodology

The above model was tested using panel data. Panel data applications are steadily growing in various fields (for a survey, see Baltagi 1995) but their use in banking research appears to be still relatively infrequent. Most banking and capital adequacy studies use cross-sectional tech-niques based on aggregate data. However, significant differences in the number, structure and sizes of banks across countries and between regions offer considerable scope for the application of panel data analy-sis. Panel data techniques can improve the statistical analysis:

- by controlling for individual heterogeneity, panel data minimise bias in the results
- as balance sheet data are highly correlated among each other, panel data provide more information on variability, facilitate less collinearity among variables, increase degrees of freedom and, overall, can produce better statistical fits
- panel data are often able to explain the dynamics of change in a better way compared with time series and cross-sectional data analy-sis. Pooling of data opens up the possibility of observing simultane-ously differences in cross-sectional behaviour and through time for a given unit (firm). This should lead to more efficient estimation of common parameters: see, for example, Judge *et al.* (1980) and Owusu-Gyapong (1986).

In order to optimise statistical use of available data, the panel approach accounts for the combination of cross-sectional and time series effects:

$$y_{it} = \alpha + X_{it}\beta + u_{it}, \quad i = 1,\dots,N; \quad t = 1,\dots,T$$

0

$$u_{it} = \mu_i + v_i 0 \tag{2}$$

where, α is a scalar, β is $K \times 1$, X_{it} is the ith banking firm on K explana-tory variables, μ_i is the unobservable individual specific effect and v_i denotes the remainder of the disturbance.

Panel data models[13] may be grouped into fixed effects and random effects models. In the fixed effects model, μ_i are assumed to be fixed parameters to be estimated and the remainder disturbances stochastic with v_{it} i.i.d for all i and t. The fixed effects (FE) model may be a suitable specification if one is comparing the change across N banking firms and the model assumes that slopes are the same for all the firms, but the intercepts differ. The FE model is also called least squares dummy variable (LSDV) and may be given by:

$$y = \alpha\iota_{NT} + X\beta + Z_\mu + v \tag{3}$$

where Z is $NT \times (K + 1)$ and Z is the matrix of $NT \times N$. The individual coefficient terms (μ_i) are the firm specific dummy variables.

An important feature of the FE model is that it utilizes the variation of variables in each firm (unit) and ignores the variation among the industry means. As a result, the FE model wastes some information contained among the firm means and, therefore, may not be fully efficient. Improvements sought with use of the FE model led to the development of the RE (random effects) model. The RE model addresses the problem of missing information in the FE model by making assumptions about the distribution of μ_i. The RE specification treats the μ_i as random disturbances associated with the ith individual or group. The RE model may be written as:

$$y_{it} = X_{it}\beta + \eta_{it}0 \tag{4}$$

where, error term η_{it} is composed of two statistically independent components, one associated with cross-sectional units and another, v_{it}, is the remainder. The covariance matrix of error terms η_{it} is the block diagonal given by:

$$\begin{aligned}
\Omega &= V(\eta) \\
&= D(\sigma_\mu^2 J_T + \sigma_v^2 \iota_T + \sigma_\mu^2 J_T + \sigma_v^2 \iota_T + \sigma_\mu^2 J_T + \sigma_v^2 \iota_T)
\end{aligned} \tag{5}$$

where J_T is a $T \times T$ matrix with all elements unity. Generalised Least Square (GLS) may be used to estimate the RE model. The GLS estimator is efficient in comparison to LSDV or OLS estimators as it extracts information from between firms as well as within industry variation, and the GLS estimation ensures that v_{it} term is homoscedastic. The more general approach with more than two waves of data is to estimate the model on deviations of the variables from their means over time.

12.4 Data and results

Equation 1 was estimated using panel methods for the complete Spanish savings bank sector over the period 1987 to 1996.[14] The data used came from the banks' annual reports and accounts; supplementary data (where gaps existed) were obtained from the Bankscope database, a London-based bank credit rating agency. Table 12.1 summarises select descriptive statistics for the variables within the model for 1996. Capital augmentation (%dK) and ROE appeared both to be comparatively high; for the entire sample and over the complete time frame, KR on average exceeded unity. The positive interest rate risk gap (IRR variable) position of Spanish savings banks is also noteworthy; and so is the comparatively high cost/income ratio (CI).

Two dummy variables were used in the regressions. The first of these captured pre- and post-merger effects on capital augmentation where savings banks merged. During 1987–1996, the number of savings banks declined (especially during 1989/90 and 1990/91) from 78 in 1987 to 50 in 1996. These mergers may impact on capital augmentation: for example, they are often a vehicle for unlocking hidden value (increasing book capital) in a banking balance sheet.[15] The other dummy variable was used to distinguish between two capital adequacy regulatory periods in Spain, 1987–91 and 1992/93 onwards. The former period was a transitional one (during which 7.5 per cent was the minimum CAR) towards the new RAR system; from 1993 the banks were subject to the full EU (Basle-type) 8 per cent RAR requirement.

Table 12.1: Descriptive statistics of model variables in 1996

Variable	Mean	Median	St. Dev.	Min.	Max.
%dK	0.1415	0.1199	0.0656	0.0645	0.3698
ROE	0.2577	0.2426	0.0965	0.0450	0.7206
PK	0.0120	0.0043	0.0148	0.0000	0.0573
LQ	0.3810	0.3674	0.0895	0.1927	0.5510
dD	0.0981	0.0934	0.0489	0.0210	0.3227
KR	0.8317	0.7922	0.1699	0.5625	1.3487
IRR	1.1723	1.1321	0.2179	0.9059	2.3353
NPL	0.0065	0.0064	0.0046	0.0002	0.0210
MQ	0.9509	0.9528	0.0124	0.9270	0.9848
OBS	0.1300	0.1214	0.0403	0.0547	0.2299
CI	0.8695	0.8795	0.0448	0.7595	0.9774

Notes:
The other years' (1987–95) data are available on request.
The number of observations is 50.

Table 12.2: Distribution of banks according to KR_t variable

Summary data		Number of banks in each year			
KR	No. of banks	Year	KR		Total
<1	122		<1	1	>1	
1	9	1987	31	0	47	78
1>	478	1988	16	2	60	78
Total	609	1989	15	1	61	77
Group (KR_t)		1990	6	2	57	65
0–0.90	75	1991	4	0	52	56
0.90–0.96	34	1992	9	2	42	53
0.96–1.10	71	1993	0	0	51	51
1.10–1.30	146	1994	0	0	51	51
1.30–1.60	144	1995	0	0	50	50
1.60<	139	1996	41	2	7	50
Total	609	Total	122	9	478	609

Table 12.2 illustrates the distribution of banks in the panel recording KR variables greater than, equal to, and less than 1.0: a KR value of unity is where actual capital equates to the regulatory minimum for the respective year. For present purposes it is germane to note that 122 banks in the complete panel (22 per cent of the total sample observations in the panel) recorded KR values of less than 1.0. If we also allow (much more realistically) for the regulatory authorities adding on a kind of 'buffer zone' to the CAR minimum to allow for unexpected events (as suggested by Berger *et al.* 1995 p. 418) and we assume that this buffer raises the regulatory threshold KR value[16] from unity to, say, 1.60, then our sub-sample of banks potentially subject to regulatory induced capital augmentation pressure as a result of their recorded book KR values rises to 470 (around 77 per cent of the total sample). Table 12.2 also suggests that regulatory induced capital augmentation pressure in Spain was likely to have been greater in 1987, 1988, 1989 and 1996 when more banks recorded a KR value of less than unity.

Table 12.3 summarises the main regression results. Columns 1 and 2 show the separate panel results for the first regulatory sub-period 1987–91.[17] Column 1 estimates equation 1 using group dummy variables and period effects; it models a 'fixed effects' (FE) panel. Column 2, on the other hand, shows the random effects (RE) results (with no dummy variables) for the same panel. Columns 3 and 4 summarise the same two sets of panel results (FE model in column 3 and RE model in column 4) for the complete panel (1987–96).

Table 12.3: Panel regression results of capital augmentation on posited explanatory variables

Variables	Period 1987–91 (FE)	1987–91 (RE)	1987–96 (FE)	1987–96 (RE)
Constant	–3.6826*	–1.8773*	–2.3707*	–1.6361*
	(0.6241)	(0.4587)	(0.4591)	(0.3535)
ROE	0.6836*	0.8044*	0.73*	0.8222*
	(5.429)	(8.061)	(8.325)	(11.1160)
PK	0.8185***	0.553***	0.4703***	0.393***
	(1.621)	(1.738)	(1.684)	(1.805)
LQ	0.292	–0.3401***	–0.2018	–0.3293*
	(0.893)	(–1.687)	(–1.212)	(–3.064)
dD	0.1573	0.1155	0.2551*	0.177**
	(1.086)	(0.922)	(2.908)	(2.188)
KR	0.6618*	0.3535*	0.3454*	0.2710*
	(9.8290)	(8.636)	(9.757)	(10.236)
IRR	0.0843	–0.0123	0.0179	–0.0108
	(0.616)	(–0.179)	(0.369)	(–0.271)
NPL	–4.4364**	–2.8709*	–3.474*	–2.4718*
	(–2.752)	(–2.51)	(–3.419)	(–3.116)
MQ	0.0593	–0.7721***	–0.2849	–0.6302**
	(0.095)	(–1.803)	(–0.649)	(–2.045)
OBS	0.3462*	0.0582	0.1303**	0.0349
	(3.373)	(1.029)	(2.419)	(0.889)
CI	2.6707*	2.4474*	2.4368*	2.1788*
	(7.852)	(9.37)	(10.634)	(11.024)
R^2	0.5957	0.2597	0.4777	0.1878
N	354	354	609	609

Notes:
The absolute values of the t-statistics are in parenthesis.
Columns 1 and 3 summarise the fixed effects (FE) panel results; columns 2 and 4 summarise the corresponding random effects (RE) model results for these same panels.
 * Significant at 0.01 level;
 ** Significant at 0.05 level;
 *** Significant at 0.10 level.

The panel results confirm that the posited capital augmentation model performs well. The results (R^2 and explanatory variables) are markedly more significant than those of Dietrich and James (1983) and the earlier groundwork USA modelling work on capital augmentation. Unlike Peltzman (1970) and Dietrich and James (1983), our results accord with Mingo (1975) in that they imply that capital adequacy regulation does have a positive effect on bank capital augmentation. Nevertheless, as explained earlier, the capital augmentation model proposed in this study is not directly comparable with these earlier models since it has been extended and modified in several important ways.

All four sets of panel results confirm the apparent influence of the ROE, KR, NPL and CI variables on bank capital augmentation. The positive lagged ROE and dK relationship appears to support the kind of USA CAR and ROE book value story examined by Berger (1995) in a different context: increased earnings allow a corresponding increase in capital, and this relationship is particularly marked in the case of the Spanish savings banks which do not pay dividends. The positive sign and strong explanatory significance of KR suggests that a high KR value is strongly associated with a high rate of capital augmentation.

Similarly, the negative value and corresponding explanatory significance of NPL suggest that banks with a high NPL also produce low corresponding earnings and reduced capital augmentation. The strong explanatory performance and positive sign of the CI variable appear to support the view that a high cost/income ratio increases regulatory pressure to augment capital. Interestingly, this also seems to fit in with apparent Bank of Spain views in the early to mid-1990s that Spanish banks needed to improve their efficiency and corresponding profitability. The CI variable, then, clearly appears to be an important part of the capital augmentation story.

The individual significance of the other explanatory variables modelled is mixed. The significance (albeit relatively low) and positive signs of the PK (portfolio risk) and LQ (liquidity risk) variables might be suggestive of signalling behaviour: high PK and LQ values are consistent with good market standing by a bank, which increases its reputational capital and corresponding ability to augment capital. The significance of the dD (deposit growth) variable in the 1987–96 panel might imply increasing capital augmentation pressures in the second (1992–96) of our two regulatory periods, when the full EC CAR system became law in Spain.

The IRR (interest rate risk), MQ (management quality) and OBS (innovation) variables similarly produced mixed results in terms of their significance and predicted signs. As explained earlier, the high positive interest rate gap of our banks might be consistent with signalling behaviour. An empirical study by Angbazo (1997) also found that the net interest margins of USA money centre banks were not affected by interest rate risk and that the latter is consistent with the banks' greater concentration in short-term assets and off-balance sheet instruments. Our Spanish bank sample is very different, of course, from USA money centre banks, but the Spanish banks do have a high and growing concentration of their portfolio in short-term assets (positive gaps) over the study period.

The sign of the management quality (MQ) variable is difficult to explain; its negative sign and greater significance in the full panel (1987–96) might be reflective of a capacity (growth) limit coming into play. The OBS (innovation) variable suggests that higher innovation requires greater capital augmentation. This fits in with the new RAR capturing OBS growth rather than supporting innovation as primarily a (successful) regulatory avoidance activity in the case of Spanish savings banks.

Earlier on we suggested that the Table 12.2 data suggest that capital augmentation pressure by regulators might be expected to be stronger *a priori* in those years (1987, 1988, 1989 and 1996) when more banks were below a KR value of unity. The cross-sectional year-on-year regressions found that KR was most significant, in t-statistic terms, in each of the years for 1987–91, but especially in 1989 and 1990; from 1992 onwards, however, KR was not significant. Given the comparative smallness of the yearly cross-sectional datasets, however, these results appear much less robust statistically. As a result we focus on the respective (especially full) panel results (see Table 12.3).

12.5 Conclusions

This study has reported tests, using panel methods, of a new capital augmentation model on Spanish savings banks over the period 1987–96. It has been explained why this banking subsector and this time frame in Spain provide a rather unique 'laboratory' for exploring empirically the impact of capital adequacy regulators on bank capital augmentation. The model tested was built from earlier USA groundwork studies in this field, but it incorporated some significant extensions. These included an extension of the earlier models to incorporate the other (than relative credit risk) two basic portfolio risks of banking, namely interest rate risk and liquidity risk. Another important development was the inclusion of a productive efficiency variable to help explain capital augmentation. Theory, practical bank strategies, regulatory policies, and modern empirical evidence all support the inclusion of these variables within the capital augmentation story.

The model tested generally performed well, especially for the full panel (1987–96). The results confirm that the new capital adequacy regime appears to have a strong influence on capital augmentation. Bank profitability, non-performing loans and productive efficiency are also important factors in capital augmentation. In particular, and as one might expect, profitability and productive efficiency appear to be particularly important parts of the bank capital augmentation story.

Notes

1. Commercial bank capital adequacy focuses on 'banking book' business, the more traditional on-balance-sheet deposit and lending business of banks; balance sheet ratios have traditionally been used to appraise this kind of capital adequacy. Investment banking (or securities houses) capital adequacy, on the other hand, focuses on the 'trading book' where a variety of off-balance-sheet risk exposures are assumed, often for short periods of time. A different capital adequacy appraisal methodology is used for this kind of business that relates a bank's capital to the losses it might have to absorb in meeting its trading risk exposures if these positions had to be liquidated at short notice. One effect of deregulation and market developments is to draw closer together these two different bank regulatory regimes.
2. A postal survey covering around 25 per cent of all EU banks in terms of total bank assets, together with a series of 12 individual case studies spanning each EU country.
3. There are some noteworthy exceptions, like Cooper *et al.* (1991).
4. This is not to imply that a capital adequacy ratio operates in isolation of other important and related supervisory (or prudential regulatory) practices, like additional bank reporting requirements, assessing the accuracy of reserves, inspection and validation of banks' internal control systems: see, for example, Lemieux (1993). However, the specific concern of this chapter is with the link between the CAR and bank capital augmentation.
5. The Cecchini study also suggested that the potential gains from deregulating the Spanish banking sector were much higher than for the majority of EU countries (only Germany was close) (COEC 1988, Table 5.1.4, p. 91). These potential gains are broadly indicative for present purposes of the pre-deregulation competitive constraints within a banking system.
6. The Spanish stock market was also comparatively underdeveloped during the period (1987–96) of the current study.
7. This modelling was also preceded by a detailed field survey of the Spanish banking sector (see Carbo 1993).
8. Despite the apparent importance of liquidity in overall bank solvency appraisals (see, for example, Crouhy and Galai (1986) and Sealey (1983)) – only Mayne (1972) among the early US students in this field includes it within her explanatory variable set. Both the Spanish field survey (see note 7) and Basle 1988 capital adequacy framework confirm the pragmatic importance of bank liquidity within capital adequacy appraisal.
9. For example, the well-known CAMEL (Capital Adequacy Management Earnings and Liquidity) system exemplifies this wider aspect of bank capital

adequacy appraisal: see, for example, Sinkey (1992). Banks with low CAMEL 'scores', for example, are likely to have their 'buffer zones' raised above the regulatory minimum CAR.

10. Our other (second) simplification in relation to earlier capital augmentation models was to exclude the kind of deposit insurance variable used in the early US work. The practical argument is that there is no long tradition of bank deposit insurance in Spain since it was only introduced in the late 1970s. As a result, the opportunities for banks to substitute deposit insurance for capital adequacy were negligible. The field survey (see note 7) confirmed this point. We tested anyway for a deposit insurance variable (see also Carbo 1993) and found that it did not improve statistically the model reported in this chapter.

11. We used the same kind of interest rate risk ratio used by Hempel *et al.* (1994 p. 66): interest-sensitive assets are all short-term (90 day maturity or less) securities and all variable rate loans; transactions deposits, short-term time and savings deposits and borrowings comprise interest-sensitive liabilities.

12. This assumes, as stated earlier, that ROE and capital augmentation are positively correlated: see Berger (1995).

13. Panel data analysis makes feasible some important specification tests. For example, under the null hypothesis that individual effects are not significant, dummy variables in the FE model should equal the constant. To test this hypothesis, the residual sum of squares from the restricted model (OLS) and unrestricted model (FE) are compared using an F test. The second test examines whether unobservable or omitted individual specific variables are correlated with the explanatory variables: a Hausman and Taylor test is effected to test the orthogonality assumption and assessment of gain to be made from the adoption of the feasible generalised least squares (FGLS) technique over the FE model. A third test is of $_\mu^2 = 0$, under the assumption of non-existence of individual components by comparing the RE and OLS models. A fourth test is for temporal parameter stability: in order to test for temporal stability of slope parameters, restricted and unrestricted models are estimated and hypothesis testing is carried out of intertemporal parameter stability.

14. A total of 609 bank observations for the ten-year period.

15. Grullon, *et al.* (1997) consider that the need to improve capital ratios has been an important factor in the merger activity of US banks faced with declining capital levels since the late 1970s. The field survey work of Carbo (1993) confirms the strategic importance of improving bank capital within many Spanish bank mergers during our study period.

16. The point where regulatory pressure for capital augmentation becomes exerted.

17. The following sub-period (1992–96) panel is not shown separately since these results were affected by the reducing number of banks (via mergers) in that panel (see Table 12.2).

References

Altunbaş, Y. and P. Molyneux (1996), 'Cost economies in EU banking systems', *Journal of Economics and Business*, 48, pp. 217–30

Angbazo, L. (1997), 'Commercial bank net interest margins, default risk, interest-rate risk, and off-balance sheet banking', *Journal of Banking and Finance*, 21, pp. 55–87

Baltagi, B.H. (1995), *Econometric analysis of panel data*, Chichester, UK: John Wiley

Berger, A.N. (1995), 'The relationship between capital and earnings in banking', *Journal of Money, Credit and Banking*, 27, 2, pp. 431–56

Berger, A.N., W.C. Hunter and S.G. Timme (1993), 'The efficiency of financial institutions: a review and preview of research past, present and future', *Journal of Banking and Finance*, 17, pp. 221–49

Berger, A.N., R.J. Herring and C.P. Szego (1995), 'The role of capital in financial institutions', *Journal of Banking and Finance*, 19, pp. 393–430

Blanden, M. (1993), 'Basle bites', *The Banker*, July, pp. 74–94

Canals, J. (1993), *Competitive strategies in European banking*, Oxford: Clarendon Press

Cantor, R. and R. Johnson (1992), 'Bank capital ratios, asset growth and the stock market', *Federal Reserve Bank of New York Quarterly Review*, Autumn, pp. 10–24

Carbo, V.S. (1993), *The Impact of regulation on bank capital augmentations in Spain*, Ph.D. thesis, Bangor: University of Wales

Cecchini, P. (1988), *The European challenge in 1992: the benefits of a Single Market*, Aldershot: Gower Press

COEC (Commission of the European Communities) (1988), *European economy: the economics of 1992*, Brussels: Directorate-General for Economic Affairs, March

Committee on Banking Regulations and Supervisory Practices (1988), *International Convergence of Capital Measurement and Capital Standards*, Basle: Committee on Banking Regulations and Supervisory Practices, July

Cooper, K.J., J. Kolari and J. Wagster (1991), 'A note on the stock market effects of the adoption of risk-based capital requirements on international banks in different countries', *Journal of Banking and Finance*, 15, pp. 367–81

Crouhy, M. and D. Galai (1986), 'An economic assessment of capital requirements in the banking industry', *Journal of Banking and Finance*, 10, pp. 231–41

Di Cagno, D. (1990), *Regulation and banks' behaviour towards risk*, Aldershot: Dartmouth Publishing Company

Dietrich, J.K. and C. James (1983), 'Regulation and the determination of bank capital changes: a note', *Journal of Finance*, 38, 5, December, 1983, pp. 1651–58

Grullon, G., I. Owary and R. Michaely (1997), 'Capital adequacy, bank mergers and the medium of payment', *Journal of Business Finance and Accounting*, 24, 1, pp. 97–124

Hall, B.J. (1993), 'How has the Basle Accord affected bank portfolios?', Discussion Paper No. 1642, Harvard University: Harvard Institute of Economic Research, June, pp. 1–34

Hempel, G.H. and D.G. Simonson (1994), *Bank management: text and cases*, New York: John Wiley

Judge, G. *et al.* (1980), *The Theory and practice of econometrics*, New York: John Wiley

Kaufman, G.G. (1992), 'Capital in banking: past present and future', *Journal of Financial Services Research*, 5, pp. 385–402

Keeley, M.C. (1988) 'Bank capital regulation: effective or ineffective?', *Federal Reserve Bank of San Francisco Economic Review*, Winter, pp. 3–20

Lackman, C.L. (1986), 'The impact of capital adequacy constraints on bank portfolios', *Journal of Business Finance and Accounting*, 13, 4, pp. 587–96

Leemputte, P.J. and M.E. Kearney (1990), 'Where is value created in your retail business?', *Journal of Retail Banking*, Winter, pp. 7–18

Lemieux, C. (1993), 'The role of bank capital in a post-FDICIA world', in *Financial Industry Perspectives*, Bank Supervision and Structure Division, Kansas: Federal Reserve Bank of Kansas City, November, pp. 15–23

Matten, C. (1996), *Managing bank capital: capital allocation and performance*, Chichester: John Wiley

Mayne, L.S. (1972), 'Supervisory influence on bank capital' *Journal of Finance*, 3, 27, pp. 637–51

Mingo, J.J. (1975), 'Regulatory influence on bank capital investment', *Journal of Finance*, 30, 4, pp. 1111–21

Molyneux, P.,Y. Altunbaş and E. Gardener (1996), *Efficiency in European banking*, Chichester: John Wiley

Nissan, E. (1995), 'Capital adequacy in international banking 1987–1992: a survey', *International Journal of Development Banking*, 13, 1, January, pp. 3–9

O'Keefe, J.P. (1993), 'Risk-based capital standards for commercial banks: improved capital-adequacy standards?', *FDIC Banking Review*, 6, 1, Spring/Summer, pp. 1–15

Owusu-Gyapong, A. (1986), 'Alternative estimating techniques for panel data on strike activity', *The Review of Economics and Statistics*, LXVIII, 3, pp. 526–31

PACEC (Public and Corporate Economic Consultants) and Institute of European Finance (IEF) (1996), *A Study of the effectiveness and impact of internal market integration on the banking and credit sector: a summary report*, Brussels: European Commission DGXV

Parsley, M. (1995), 'The Rorac revolution', *Euromoney*, October, pp. 36–42

Peek, J. and E.S. Rosengren (1992), 'The capital crunch in New England', *Federal Reserve Bank of Boston New England Economic Review*, May–June, pp. 21–31

Peek, J. and E.S. Rosengren (1995), 'The capital crunch: neither a borrower nor a lender be', *Journal of Money, Credit and Banking*, 27, 3, pp. 625–38

Peltzman, S. (1970), 'Entry in commercial banking', *Journal of Law and Economics*, 8, October, pp. 11–50

Peltzman, S. (1965), 'Capital investment in commercial banking and its relation to portfolio regulation', *Journal of Political Economy*, 78, 1, pp. 1–26

Sealey, C.W. (1983), 'Valuation, capital structure and shareholder unanimity for depository financial intermediaries', *Journal of Finance*, 38, 3, pp. 1139–54

Sinkey, Joseph F., Jr. (1992), *Commercial bank management in the financial services industry*, New York: Collier Macmillan

Syron, R.F. (1991), 'Are we experiencing a credit crunch?', *Federal Reserve Bank of Boston New England Economic Review*, July, pp. 3–10

Yang, G. (1991), 'Pricing for profit', *The Bankers Magazine*, September–October, pp. 53–9

13

The Management of Foreign Exchange Exposures and Interest Rate Exposures in a number of UK and Swedish Firms 1985 and 1996

Göran Bergendahl

13.1 Background

Back in 1985 I participated in a conference on foreign exchange exposure management arranged by the *Financial Times*. At one coffee break a UK financial manager took me aside and asked for assistance. He said:

> We who are in the day-to-day routine work of international payments and international finance, never have any chance to reflect on totally new systems for liquidity transfers. But you, who are in the academic field, couldn't you listen to us and to others and consider the pros and cons of alternative ways of centralising and decentralising international activities? We never get access to systems of other firms. But you who are at a university, you should be considered as 'neutral' and you should be able to learn how others operate.
>
> Why couldn't you just interview twenty international treasurers and compare their experiences and tell us what is good and what is wrong? I don't believe that what is good for one firm must be good for others. But I do believe that each firm has had experiences that must be extremely valuable for the other ones. Of course, data and names must be kept confidential, but I am sure that all of us will be delighted to participate in such an investigation.

That was the igniting spark for this project. It happened to come at a time when I had had several long talks with Michael Earl at the Oxford

Centre of Management Studies. He had just finished a number of studies concerning the behaviour of UK British treasurers (Earl 1985). His theory was that most firms with international trade pass through several and similar stages concerning the organisation of their treasury management. Was he right or wrong? Are different firms really that alike?

Earl emphasized the use of exposures, that is, how firms measure their vulnerability to changes in exchange rates. Together with a colleague I decided to follow the route taken by Earl in order to investigate how business firms in the UK and in Sweden measured and managed foreign exchange exposures. We decided to make a comparison between UK and Swedish firms just because Sweden at that time had currency regulation and the UK did not.

Our purpose in 1985 was:

- to analyse how foreign exchange exposures (FEE) were measured and managed in a number of UK and Swedish firms
- to seek explanations for the different ways to manage FEE
- to suggest alternative ways to measure and to manage FEE.

Six UK and 20 Swedish firms were selected for personal interviews during 1985. We structured the interviews in five areas:

- choice of currency of denomination
- foreign exchange cash management
- currency risk exposure
- organisation
- stages of development.

The results of the interviews were presented in Bergendahl and Nyberg (1986).

When working on a project on international cash management ten years later, I recognized the rapid change that had taken place in exposure management. First, Swedish currency regulation had been removed. Second, the financial markets had expanded beyond anyone's imagination in 1985. Third, interest rate risk management had become a central issue. Stimulated by those experiences, a project was developed to renew the study of 1985. It is that project that is reported on in this chapter. The aim of this new project has been:

- to analyse the measurement and management of foreign exchange exposures in a set of English and Swedish companies
- to analyse the interaction between the management of foreign exchange exposures (FEE) and interest rate exposures (IRE) in these companies
- to compare the principles of foreign exchange exposure management of 1985 and 1996.

The study is based on interviews with approximately the same Swedish and UK firms as in 1985. However, one firm had gone bankrupt since then and others had changed their structures more or less completely. The consequence is that out of the 26 firms of 1985, 18 Swedish and five UK ones were interviewed once again in 1996. These firms were spread over a large number of sectors according to the structure given in Table 13.1. The interviews were structured into five more or less new areas:

- choice of currency of denomination
- international cash management
- currency risk exposure
- interest rate risk exposure
- organisation.

The study hopes to contribute to a better understanding of how different firms with different products and organisation choose different approaches to the management of foreign exchange risks and interest rate risks. The results from the interviews aim to shed new light on the changes in procedures, strategies and objectives.

Table 13.1: Firms interviewed by sector in 1996

Sector	No. of firms
Manufacture of fabricated products, machinery and equipment	10
Transport and communication	3
Construction	2
Manufacture of chemicals and petroleum	2
Manufacture of food, beverage and tobacco	2
Wholesale trade	2
Manufacture of pulp and paper products	1
Finance and insurance	1
Total	23

The study has two main sections: Section 13.2 presents the principles of exposure management, Section 13.3 gives an overview of how business firms handle exposure management in practice and finally, Section 13.4 gives the main conclusions of the study.

13.2   Exposure management in business firms

Business firms that operate in foreign countries are exposed to sudden and unexpected changes in exchange rates. Such changes may result in a purchased raw material becoming more expensive, products sold may generate less revenues, or the production in foreign subsidiaries may become less competitive. Consequently, such firms are exposed to foreign exchange risk. Even firms with no international activities may be hit by changes in exchange rates. Such a change may result in foreign competitors obtaining substantial cost advantages in the domestic market. Therefore, most firms are exposed to foreign exchange risk.

Foreign exchange exposures originate from trade and from financial activities. Exposures from trade start from the moment of signing purchasing contracts, of pricing final products, or of delivering tender offers; they terminate when the payments are settled. Financial activities generate exposures from the date when a loan is signed or a placement is made, and terminate when the last payment is over. This chapter is concerned with exposures as a way to measure the influence of currency risk on a firm. But future exposures in terms of production volumes or values of securities are also uncertain, which will enlarge the risk for losses.

Often the origin of a foreign exchange exposure is a period of delay in payment for goods and services. If goods were paid for at the moment of contracting and pricesetting, the sellers and buyers of goods and services would not be concerned about currency risks at all. If capital services like future instalments and interest payments were related to currency clauses, then no exposure risk would hit the borrower.

There are several kinds of foreign exchange exposures. One is transaction exposure, which concerns scheduled payments for goods and services. Another is translation exposure, which relates to the balance sheet and may be seen as a potential evaluation of assets and liabilities in the currency of the headquarters. A third one is economic exposure: this is a long-term measure that includes future earnings and net assets. There exist other formulations of exposures as well, such as commercial exposure and accounting exposure; see, for example, Donaldson (1987) and Kenyon (1990).

A company has a 'long' exposure in a certain currency and over a certain time period if the corresponding assets are larger than the liabilities or if revenues are larger than expenses. Inversely, the exposure is 'short'. In principle, the translation and the transaction exposures should be two different ways of estimating how a company is influenced by currency risk. Transaction exposure is a flow concept while translation exposure is a state concept. Transaction exposure estimates the trading risk starting from the moment of pricing and ending at the cash conversion (Kenyon 1990, chap. 8). Translation exposure, on the other hand, estimates the risk of losses to the net worth of the company as expressed in the balance sheet. In this way translation exposure may be an aggregate of trading risks that are not settled at the annual reporting date. However, it may also include the translation of fixed assets into the reporting currency. Thus it will consist of the net total of assets less liabilities specified per currency. However, this amount is an unrealized provisional sum estimated at each reporting date.

As transaction exposures are related to the time period between pricing and payment, they usually exist for short time periods only. It is only in the extreme cases of long-term contracts, like construction ones, that they have a life of a year or more. Translation exposures, on the other hand, are related to the balance sheets and may exist for a year or more. Economic exposure is often a long-term concept. It may go over several years in order to include future investments. It may be seen as a prolongation of the translation exposure, but is sometimes used as an after tax transaction exposure (see, for example, Puchon 1983 pp. 8.7–8).

The main difference between translation and transaction exposures is that a translation exposure relates to the balance sheet at a reporting date while transaction exposures will last over periods of time.

13.2.1   Transaction exposures

The transaction exposure is basic for business firms. It comes from a set of individual affairs where the income and the expenditures are denoted in different currencies. Figure 13.1 demonstrates just such a transaction exposure of an individual delivery of goods or services. The exposure originates from a price list or a tender offer and terminates when the transaction is settled in cash or on an account. The first phase of that exposure is initiated when at date A a price is offered in a

Figure 13.1: The transaction exposure of an individual sale

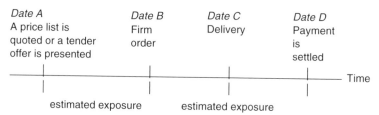

currency different from that of the expenditure. Such an offer may be given as a tailormade tender with specified quantities and dates for deliveries, but it may also be presented as a general price list without any specification of quantities. In both cases, the exposure will only be an estimation, as neither the size nor the time of the exposure may be known at date A.

The size and the time of the exposure for the seller is determined when at a date B the buyer places a firm order with the seller at the offered price. Then the exposed amount will stay over the date C, when the product is delivered, and up to date D when the buyer has settled the amount quoted in the order.

Many business firms act simultaneously as buyers and sellers on the international markets for both commodities and services. That implies that they have to manage both payables and receivables in a single foreign currency. Usually the payables precede the receivables. A firm that operates with a large number of payables and receivables may estimate at certain points in time the aggregated transaction exposure as a sum of contracted receivables less the sum of contracted payables.

It is obvious that the aggregated transaction exposure changes over time as it stems from the set of cash flows entering and leaving the firm at different dates. Consequently this aggregated transaction exposure may vary day by day, and often hour by hour. In practice, however, this kind of exposure is estimated at intervals only, often month by month. In doing so, the firm has to ignore the effect that comes from payments that are performed at dates inside such an interval. Consequently, the transaction exposure is defined currency by currency as a *gap* between receivables and payables. Such a gap is measured in terms of a net amount of payments that may generate uncertain cash flows in the home currency. Therefore, the aggregated transaction exposures may be given as a matrix with currencies on one axis and time periods on the other (Table 13.2).

Table 13.2: Aggregated transaction exposures (mil.)

Currency	25 January		25 February		25 March	
DEM	REC	2.3	REC	1.0	REC	0.5
	PAY	4.8	PAY	2.4	PAY	1.0
	NET	-2.5	NET	-1.4	NET	-0.5
GBP	REC	5.5	REC	3.0	REC	1.2
	PAY	0.2	PAY	0.1	PAY	0.1
	NET	5.3	NET	2.9	NET	1.1
USD	REC	10.2	REC	8.8	REC	3.2
	PAY	2.5	PAY	1.4	PAY	1.0
	NET	7.7	NET	7.4	NET	2.2

Notes: Net contracts at a given date, say, 1 January.
        REC = Receivables; PAY = Payables; NET = Net exposure that i, the gap).

Transaction exposure = The gap between contracted receivables and contracted payables, currency by currency.

The aggregated transaction exposures are supposed to provide the firm with an overview of the short-term risks for sudden changes in the exchange rates. That is, if the exchange rate in a foreign currency depreciates by a certain percentage, then the net income (NET in Table 13.2) will be reduced by the same percentage. Consequently, the net exposure will become a basis for actions to hedge contracted payments from losses that may be substantial to the firm.

13.2.2 Economic and translation exposures

Only a part of all outstanding financial obligations are due to be resolved at certain dates. Examples of this kind are inventories of raw material and finished products, production volumes that are expected to take place but are not yet contracted, and financial assets and liabilities that are to be sold at a certain date and at a price that is not yet determined. Usually this kind of exposure of non-contracted cash flows in a foreign currency is called an economic exposure. Consequently, this exposure measures the part of the value of the firm that depends on the future exchange rates. In the case where the economic exposure is measured at the end of the year, it may be called a translation exposure. The reason is that it is usually measured for accounting purposes and for a period that has passed. However, there are firms that forecast translation exposures in order to hedge assets and liabilities.

A special form of an economic exposure concerns cash flows in the currency of the headquarters but where the volumes depend on the exchange rates. Such an exposure may stem from competition from foreign companies. At a favourable exchange rate, these competitors may lower the price in the country of the headquarters and consequently force the local cash flow to diminish.

> *Economic exposure = The gap between receivables and payables that are estimated but not contracted measured currency by currency.*

In the treasury of a firm, individual exposures are aggregated as follows:

- the transaction exposure will measure currency by currency the contracted net inflow of funds per time period (usually measured month by month at a predetermined date). This measure is often used to estimate the immediate effect of changes in the exchange rates
- the translation exposure will measure currency by currency the values of assets and liabilities and will translate them into the currency of the headquarters. Usually such a translation is performed for accounting purposes at the end of the year but it may also be done more frequently. It is obvious that one per cent reduction of the translation rate will generate the same reduction of the corresponding asset or liability
- the economic exposure will measure currency by foreign currency the expected net inflow of funds per time period, as well as
- the flow of funds in the domestic currency that may be lost to a foreign competitor if the exchange rate is changed.

These definitions may vary slightly between different authors as well as between companies. For an overview see, for example, Donaldson (1987 chaps 4–8), Eiteman, *et al.* (1995 chaps 7–9), Kenyon (1990 chap. 8), Oxelheim (1985 Section 3.4), Oxelheim and Wihlborg (1987 chap. 3). As a consequence, a transaction exposure will measure the risks for changes in the expected group profit and loss account. On the other hand, a translation exposure estimates the risk for changes on the balance sheet and consequently a reduction in the equity. The use of the concept economic exposure stems from the risk for losses on non-contracted items on the profit and loss account as well as on the balance sheet.

Companies that ignore transaction risks but not translation risks seem to be interested mainly in a preservation of assets and less in the intraperiod flows. Transaction exposures would then be central to companies whose central activities are in trading. However, one can assume that most corporations fall into a third category, those who hedge certain transactions and at the same time want to protect their balance sheet positions (see for example, Puchon 1983 8.7.10).

Even if most companies fit into these three categories, one may suspect that their behaviour is different. Of central interest is to find out different and more or less systematic ways to measure exposures and then to use these measures for hedging. Interviews with treasury managers reveal that they are keenly interested in learning about how others manage their foreign exchange exposures. Major questions concern (George 1983 8.8.3):

1) How other firms define and measure exposures that result from both balance sheet positions and transactions?
2) How often and for how long a time period do they measure an exposure?
3) What are the experiences of more systematic procedures for foreign exchange exposure management?
4) Do companies with firm commitments or contracts hedge intraperiod transactions?
5) Do firms with stable balance sheet positions prefer to hedge translation exposures?
6) What effect do taxes and regulations have on the procedures the firms use for exposure management?

The basic controversy concerning economic exposures comes from trade, the reason being that these exposures may become uncertain for various reasons like:

a) Consider a sales contract that is signed in a foreign currency. Assume there is a risk that the customer will become insolvent and may go bankrupt so that it will be unable to meet the stipulated conditions. Consequently, the sales volume may be identified either as a transaction exposure or as an economic exposure.
b) A sales price has been offered but a contract has not yet been signed. Thus, there is a risk that the customer will not accept the conditions and that there will not be any inflow of foreign currencies. This risk may be called 'antenatal'. Certain companies may identify the esti-

mated sales volume as a transaction exposure, others may treat it as an economic exposure.

c) If sales prices are listed in a foreign currency, uncertain sales volumes will imply an uncertain inflow of foreign currencies. One may call this a situation of commercial risk and the exposure should be called economic.

d) Sometimes sales prices are listed but costs and competition will develop in such a manner that the price level will be changed without notice. Then the corresponding expected currency inflow (or outflow) is exposed to a price risk, which generates an economic exposure.

One can assume that:

- the insolvency (credit) risk
- the antenatal risk
- the commercial risk
- the price risk

in combination will result in foreign exchange exposures becoming uncertain. Therefore, all these risks should be estimated in terms of economic exposures.

Exposures fluctuate over time as sales revenues and purchase expenses vary. Payment conditions and float effects will also influence the exposures. Different industrial sectors demonstrate large variations in customs concerning conditions of delivery and pricing. Evidently it is an activity of precision as well as one of definition to determine a single firm's exposures at certain prespecified dates.

The insolvency risk is central to construction firms. Several of the firms in this sector have realized that there is a risk that a customer will never pay the total costs for plant or equipment. This implies a difference between the inflow of funds and what was stipulated in the contract. The question then is whether the planned schedule for payments should be introduced into a provisional exposure, which later has to be revised. However, in certain specific situations a change in exchange rates may be immediately compensated for by a change in the price level, so that the price risk is eliminated. In that case there is no economic exposure.

The antenatal risks are frequently observed by business firms. There are two kinds of situations where these risks are central. One concerns large-scale contracts for, say, road construction, a telecommunications system, or ship building. Such contracts seem to follow a similar development pattern, namely (see Kenyon 1981 p. 140):

a) the submission of a tender
b) the signing of the contract
c) the down payment
d) the cumulative cash collection
e) the final instalment.

The other situation with antenatal risks concerns agreements of general principles for medium-term delivery contracts. These contracts are often based upon a price list and stipulate a maximal amount of goods to be delivered over a certain specified time period. The customer is then allowed to suborder quantities when it suits him, as long as the producer has them available. This uncertainty of dates for suborders will result, in that an antenatal risk is directly combined with a commercial risk.

Antenatal risk for a tender means that the supplier is uncertain if or when the customer will accept the offer. This uncertainty has direct economic consequences for the supplier, as long as the offer is given in a foreign currency (other than the reporting one). On the other hand, such an offer in the currency of the supplier is often necessary for the customer in order to avoid a price increase.

Antenatal and commercial risks are sometimes interrelated. This is the case when a producer cannot present a tender unless he in his turn has chartered some kind of production capacity from a subcontractor. If the company fails to win the tender, then there is the (commercial) risk that there is no alternative use for the subcontractor.

Commercial risks concern the uncertain inflow, and sometimes outflow, of foreign currencies. For several companies this inflow will come in two steps. In the first step, the customer pays the subsidiaries in the local currency. In the second step, the subsidiaries pay either the producing unit or an invoicing centre. It is the second step that is of main interest to this study.

13.2.3   Interest rate exposures

Interest rate risk management is an issue whose importance to the corporate treasurer grows continuously. At one extreme, one treasurer may be so conservative that he attempts to eliminate any interest rate risk. The other extreme may be a treasurer who operates actively on the financial markets in order to arbitrage from interest rate fluctuations. Historically, interest rate risk management has been a topic reserved for bankers only. A bank has both assets and liabilities that depend directly on interest rate fluctuations. For a banker, it is an important issue to match fixed rate assets and fixed rate liabilities in a way that will eliminate the influence of market fluctuations. For a corporate treasurer, the interest rate risks come mainly from the liabilities both in terms of loans and equity. However, the return on certain assets, like inventory holdings, securities and liquidity resources may become, directly or indirectly, dependent on the level of interest rates. The source of an interest rate exposure is the mismatching of interest rate bases for associated assets and liabilities. In addition, these assets and liabilities may have different maturities and different patterns of cash flow.

Interest Rate Exposure = The gap between those interest rate incomes and interest rate expenses that are contracted.

Table 13.3 illustrates the interest rate exposures for an industrial firm. This firm has substantial short-term assets in three foreign currencies, DEM, GBP and USD. On the other side it has a large amount of long-term loans in USD. Consequently, it is exposed to both interest rate risks and foreign exchange risks. Table 13.3 demonstrates that the interest rate exposures for a single currency may be measured in terms of *gaps* for different buckets (time periods). For example, there is a long exposure of 3.6–2.5=1.1 USDm up to one month and a short exposure of 0.0–3.0=–3.0 USDm for the bucket of 6–12 months. However, observe that a 1 per cent reduction in the interest rate will generate larger effects for more distant buckets as a consequence of variations in the periods of exposure.

Asset and liability management (ALM), also known as balance sheet management (BSM), can be viewed as a process where the total assets and liabilities of a firm are controlled and managed simultaneously. In this way ALM integrates asset management (asset allocation) and liability management (liability choice). Asset management concerns the combination of different claims into a portfolio. Portfolio choice as an activity includes a 'direct control' of assets (liquidity placements and long-term investment) as well as an 'indirect control' (for example, pricing). Liability management includes subjects like capital structure.

ALM = Asset management + Liability management

Table 13.3: Interest rate exposures for a fictitious firm

	Time period of repricing (months)			
	0–1	1–2	2–3	3–4
Assets				
Securities				
DEM(m)	2.0	0.1	0.1	0.5
GBP(m)	4.1	0.1	0.2	2.0
USD (m)	3.6	0.5	0.0	0.0
Liabilities				
Loans, fixed-rate				
DEM(m)	1.5	0.1	0.1	0.0
GBP(m)	1.6	0.2	0.0	0.1
USD(m)	2.5	0.1	0.1	3.0
Interest rate exposures				
(Gaps)				
DEM(m)	0.5	0.0	0.0	0.5
GBP(m)	2.5	–0.1	0.2	1.9
USD(m)	1.1	0.4	–0.1	–3.0

The main objective for asset and liability management is to control the interest rate risks. For that purpose, a common procedure has been to estimate the gap between the interest rate exposures on the asset side and the same exposures on the liability side (see Table 13.3).

From the point of view of the balance sheet, the transaction exposure may be divided into two phases. The first one concerns the time period between the date (B) of the firm order and that (C) of delivery. That exposure has not yet been included in the balance sheet, but may be called an off-balance sheet exposure. The second phase of the transaction exposure relates to the time period between delivery (date C) and payment (date D). That currency exposure will then be included on the asset side of the balance sheet as short-term credits. This is the way in which the currency exchange risks and the interest rate risks are interdependent.

If we return to the fictitious firm analysed in Table 13.3, Table 13.4 will give a more detailed analysis of the exposures for that firm. The starting point is the interest rate exposures of Table 13.3, which are introduced in Table 13.4 as Items 1 Securities and 3 Loans, fixed-rate. We then assume that the firm has a stock of signed sales contracts valued to USD 1.2m at the moment when the exposures are measured. Furthermore, let us suppose that half of that amount concerns sales that have been delivered but have not yet been paid for (Item 2), and that the other half has not yet been delivered (Item 4). Therefore, the inter-

Table 13.4: Interest rate exposures and currency exchange exposures for a fictitious firm

| | Time period of repricing (month) | | | |
	0–1	1–2	2–3	3–4
Assets				
1. Securities				
DEM(m)	2.0	0.1	0.1	0.5
GBP(m)	4.1	0.1	0.2	2.0
USD(m)	3.6	0.5	0.0	0.0
2. Claims for goods delivered – USDm	0.3	0.2	0.1	0.0
Liabilities				
3. Loans, fixed-rate				
DEM(m)	1.5	0.1	0.1	0.0
GBP(m)	1.6	0.2	0.0	0.1
USD(m)	2.5	0.1	0.1	3.0
Off-Balance Sheet				
4. Claims for goods contracted but not yet delivered – USDm	0.2	0.3	0.1	0.0
Interest rate exposures and currency exposures				
5. Gaps				
DEM(m)	0.5	0.0	0.0	0.5
GBP(m)	2.5	–0.1	0.2	1.9
USD(m)	1.6	0.9	0.1	–3.0

est rate exposures for the fictitious firm may be revised and divided into different currency exposures as demonstrated under Item 5.

Up to now, the analysis of exposures has been given in terms of gaps for a set of four consecutive months. That technique demonstrates the rate at which assets, liabilities and off-balance sheet contracts mature or reprice. Therefore, it indicates the sensitivity to changes in market interest rates or currency exchange rates.

However, the gap analysis cannot balance short-term and long-term effects. Such a balance may be accomplished by expanding the gap analysis into an analysis of duration and volatility. The *duration* of a balance sheet element will provide the decisionmaker with a measure of the time-weighted average maturity resulting from the cash flows that are generated from such an element or a gap between elements. A special emphasis should be laid on exposures or gaps in foreign currencies. The longer the duration, the more sensitive is the company to a change in interest rates or exchange rates.

The analyses of gaps, duration and volatility are aimed at presenting the effect from a shift in interest rates or exchange rates over a period of one to about 12 months. That indicates a medium-term analysis. For a short-term analysis, however, these methods are not very precise, but may be replaced by a rather new method called value at risk (VAR).

The VAR method estimates the change in portfolio value, dP, as a random variable. It starts from the knowledge of the probability distribution for dP. A certain class of closed form VAR methods presumes a standard distribution for dP, an assumption that simplifies the analysis to one of estimating the mean m and the standard deviation s of that distribution. The VAR stands for the maximum loss that can occur within a certain confidence interval, say 90 per cent or 95 per cent. For example, a 95 per cent confidence interval will imply a maximum loss of

$$\text{VAR} = 1.65\ s + m$$

The longer the time period of study, the larger the mean m. That is the reason why VAR is computed for short time periods only for which m is small.

The interest rate exposures may be viewed as a set of discount bonds using the term structure of the interest rates. For example, the market value P_{DM} of the gaps in Deutschmarks (see Item 5, Table 13.4) may be estimated as:

$$P_{DM} = \frac{0.5}{(1+r)^{\frac{1}{12}}} + \frac{0}{(1+r)^{\frac{2}{12}}} + \frac{0}{(1+r)^{\frac{3}{12}}} + \frac{0.5}{(1+r)^{\frac{4}{12}}}$$

That leads to:

$$dP_{DM} = \left[-\frac{1}{12} \bullet \frac{0.5}{(1+r)^{1+\frac{1}{12}}} - \frac{4}{12} \bullet \frac{0.5}{(1+r)^{1+\frac{4}{12}}} \right] dr$$

Then, the percentage change in present value (dP/P) to a term structure shift in interest rate (dr) will become:

$$V_{DM} = \frac{\partial P}{P} \bullet \frac{1}{\partial r} = \frac{1}{P} \bullet \left[-\frac{1}{12} \bullet \frac{0.5}{(1+r)^{1+\frac{1}{12}}} - \frac{4}{12} \bullet \frac{0.5}{(1+r)^{1+\frac{4}{12}}} \right] =$$

$$\approx -\frac{1}{1+r} \bullet \frac{-\dfrac{1}{12} \bullet \dfrac{0.5}{(1+r)^{\frac{1}{12}}} - \dfrac{4}{12} \bullet \dfrac{0.5}{(1+r)^{\frac{4}{12}}}}{\dfrac{0.5}{(1+r)^{\frac{1}{12}}} + \dfrac{0.5}{(1+r)^{\frac{4}{12}}}} \approx -\frac{1}{1+r} \bullet D_{DM}$$

where D_{DM} stands for Duration (of DM) and V_{DM} for Volatility (of DM). For example, if $r = 0.08$ (8%) then the duration for Deutschmarks will become:

$$D_{DM} = \frac{\dfrac{1}{12} \bullet \dfrac{0.5}{(1.08)^{\frac{1}{12}}} + \dfrac{4}{12} \bullet \dfrac{0.5}{(1.08)^{\frac{4}{12}}}}{\dfrac{0.5}{(1.08)^{\frac{1}{12}}} + \dfrac{0.5}{(1.08)^{\frac{4}{12}}}} = 0.21$$

and $V_{DM} = -0.19$

The use of VAR for ALM gets even more complicated when the changes in different assets are not correlated. That happens, for example, when a change in market value of an asset in Deutschmarks (dP_{DM}) is not correlated to a subsequent change of an asset in US dollar (dP_{USD}). Consequently, one may expect that the VAR methods may become more widely used for the management of securities than for the management of entire assets and liabilities.

13.2.4   Points of departure for investigating business practice

A transaction exposure concerns *contracted* cash flows. It is a measure of the risk for losses in these flows from changes in exchange rates. The larger the exposure, the larger the risks will be. On the other hand, an economic exposure is assumed to concern the risks for exchange rate changes on *non-contracted* cash flows. (Observe that in certain studies the economic exposure is used as a union of all risks from changes in the exchange rates, then the transaction exposure forms a subset of the economic exposure.)

Transaction exposures are easy to identify, especially for firms with large volumes of payments entering and leaving the home country. For these firms it is a necessity to manage the transactions to a low risk and a low cost. Obviously, the transaction exposure ought to be the main emphasis for currency management. As transaction exposures concern contracted transfers, it would raise questions if such exposures were not hedged by use of forward or future contracts. Therefore, one would expect that most firms would hedge contracted currency exposures or interest rate exposures. On the other hand they may become irresolute as to where to hedge economic exposures.

Economic exposures concern expected transactions, expected price levels and expected dates. Consequently they are based upon options given to customers. On the other hand, such options are often more distant in time. Thus, this implies that many firms may take first things first and concentrate on transactions.

Translation exposures have usually been an issue for accountants when analysing contracted assets and liabilities. However, there have recently been firms that manage actively their balance sheet. For them a balance sheet exposure would give a better formulation than a translation exposure.

An interest rate exposure is another kind of balance sheet exposure. It concerns the risks that the values of assets and liabilities, and subsequently equity, will change as an effect of changes in the market interest rates. These risks have become more and more predominant during the last ten years.

Given this background it is not surprising if business firms have concentrated for many years on transaction and translation exposures in their day-to-day work. More complex issues like economic exposures and interest rate exposures may be difficult to understand and to make operational. Therefore, it would be relevant to hold a set of interviews in order to investigate how business firms measure and manage foreign exchange and interest rate exposures.

In this section we have presented three main ways to measure the exposure for foreign exchange risks and interest rate risks. They are:

- maturity gaps
- duration
- value at risk (VAR).

In the following section we will concentrate on the extent to which business firms make use of these risk measures.

Exposure management in UK firms has to a large extent been analysed by a number of researchers (see, for example, Donaldson 1987; Earl 1985; Edelshain 1992; Kenyon 1981, 1990). Earl observed that there is a lack of knowledge concerning how multinational companies (MNCs) 'perceive, measure and manage currency risks'. That has been the focus of his research in UK MNCs. Based on several searching interviews with UK executives, Earl concludes that 'what determines the rate of learning and evolution is probably the size and complexity of the MNCs FEE. Differences of approaches among MNC's seem to be explained by their product markets and their technology.' (Earl 1985 p. 46)

Earl's theory is challenging. It states that variations in exposure management come from differences in products, markets, technology and size. Kenyon has made a systematic classification of methods for the management of FEE. He finds (1981 p. 49) that there are broadly three classes of implements: 'those which avoid risk, those which hedge it and those which reduce the task of management'. As Kenyon views it, currency risk originates from a currency mismatch either between the selling price and the cost or between assets and liabilities. Risk might then be avoided by just using the same currency for price and cost. It might be hedged by the use of contracts. Netting is an example of a method that will reduce the risk.

Earl's theories on evolution and Kenyon's analyses of methods raise a set of additional questions about foreign exchange exposure management in business firms. Maybe their theories are relevant just to UK firms and not to Swedish ones? Could the difference in nationality between headquarters be so crucially important for the way of management; that Swedish firms operate in a different way to UK firms?

More than ten years have now passed since the study of 1985. During that period currency regulation has been eliminated in Sweden. That implies that both Sweden and the UK nowadays have well developed financial markets that would not result in any country differences in the use of exposure management. The last ten years have also demonstrated an increased emphasis on interest rate risks (see, for example, Eiteman *et al.* 1995 chap. 14).

The following analysis of business firms will show both how business firms measure different kinds of exposures in a regular manner, often month by month, but the analysis will also show how they avoid, reduce and hedge them as they are generated. This section has demonstrated the principles on how exposures may be *avoided* by a skilful choice concerning currencies of denomination, be *reduced* by the use of netting, or be *hedged* by signing forward contracts, future contracts, currency loans and currency options.

In theory, there has long been a controversy about whether it is good policy for a business firm to hedge its financial risks regularly or not. Those who favour regular hedging support the principle that a business firm should not take financial risks but should at least hedge contracted exposures. Those who do not hedge will often support a view that all risks will be matched in the long run. Eiteman *et al.* (1995 pp. 183–6) has presented an overview of the arguments for and against hedging and risk reduction (see Table 13.5).

His analysis leads to the two central tasks for exposure management in multinational firms:

- should a firm hedge its contracted exposures? In other words, should a business firm hedge its transaction exposures, its transla-

Table 13.5: Arguments for and against hedging

Arguments for hedging	Arguments against hedging
1. Reduction of risk will improve the planning capability.	1. Stockholders are more capable than management to diversify risk.
2. Reduction of risk will reduce the likelihood that the cash flow will fall below a necessary minimum.	2. Risk reduction is costly.
3. Management knows risks better than the stockholders.	3. Management is more risk adverse than stockholders.
4. Management is closer to the market and is in a better position than the stockholders to recognize disequilibrium and then to perform selective hedging.	4. At equilibrium, the expected net present value of hedging is zero. 5. Management is more oriented towards accounting costs than economic costs.

tion exposures, and its interest rate exposures? If so, the relevant instruments will be found in the markets for swaps, forward contracts, future contracts and interest rate contracts.
- should a firm hedge its economic and non-contracted exposures? If so, currency options and interest rate options will be the appropriate instruments.

There are no simple answers to these two tasks. The amount of hedging should depend on the price of hedging. In general, most transaction exposures of a reasonable size will be worthwhile hedging as the prices on the markets for forwards and swaps are relatively moderate. But the situation is quite different for the economic exposures, as the prices on the option markets are rather high. Consequently, each company might well develop a unique strategy to handle economic exposures. A general rule is that it will become too costly to eliminate all kinds of risks, as much of the profit from international business may come from the business of economic exposures. A comment by Parker (1995 p. 13) seems relevant here.

Financial innovation has been more concerned with risk reduction than any other subject. Derivatives are the capital market's way of moving risks around. Swaps, options, futures – all attempt to transfer risk much the way an insurance company can pass off its risks through reinsurance. A company wishing to eliminate nearly all risks can now do so in ways barely conceivable even a generation ago. With the possibility of managing risk near zero, the challenge becomes not how much risk can be removed but rather how much risks should be removed. The business of financial services is, in essence, the business of bearing risk for a price. Without risk in the product markets and capital markets of financial institutions, there is much less reason for their existence.

Given that background, it would be extremely fruitful to investigate differences between business firms' policies for international cash management, hedging and organisation of the treasury function. The interviews with the 23 firms were organised into five areas as presented in Section 13.1. The main research issues were given as follows.

- *Choice of currency of denomination.* Are products and services usually sold in the currency of the customer? How do the firms manage price lists and tender offers? Do they set time limits for these price lists and offers in terms of clauses?
- *International cash management.* How do the firms organise their systems for international cash management and netting? Which banks do they use and which service qualities do they demand from these banks?
- *Currency risk exposure.* Do the firms start from the netting system when they measure contracted (transaction) exposures? To what extent do they manage and hedge expected (economic) exposures?
- *Interest rate risk exposure.* How do the firms measure and manage interest rate exposures? To what extent do they hedge these exposures?
- *Organisation.* How do management principles influence the design of the treasury organisation?

Obviously different firms with different activities will generate different foreign exchange exposures and interest rate exposures. As mentioned in Section 13.1, the Swedish and UK firms analysed in this study were chosen in order to be representative of many different business activities. Obviously, that may be a reason why their foreign exchange exposures are different and why their procedures to manage and to measure them may vary. The analysis below will stress these variations.

As mentioned earlier, the 23 interviews performed were with almost the same Swedish and UK firms that were included in the study of

1985. A new interview guide has been set up, which lists a set of important questions (see Appendix). The analysis below will be based upon the answers given in those interviews.

13.3 Experiences from treasury departments

13.3.1 Choice of currency of denomination

Income and expenditures sometimes mismatch according to the currency of denomination. Goods may be produced in Sweden but sold in the USA, then the expenditure is in Swedish krona while the income will come in US dollars. That implies that the cash flows mismatch. Often the mismatch is not only in currencies but also in time. The expenditure (in Swedish krona) starts when production begins but the income will not take place until several weeks after the delivery of the finished goods.

Furthermore, the mismatch in currencies not only concerns income and expenditures but also assets and liabilities. For example, assets in terms of short-term credits may have been denoted in US dollars while liabilities in terms of bank loans may be in Swedish krona. This is the origin of balance sheet risks ('translation risks').

A reasonable assumption would then be that companies choose the currency of denomination primarily to avoid risk and secondly to match currency flows in order to reduce risk. In practice, however, these principles are difficult to apply.

First observe the difference between transactions with non-affiliated buyers and sellers, and those between divisions, subsidiaries or branches of the corporation. Transactions with affiliated units ought to be managed perfectly as regards the choice of currency. For non-affiliated buyers and sellers the situation is often one of tradition and negotiation. The emphasis below is therefore on the non-affiliated ones.

For a company located in a country with a strong currency (say DEM or USD) it may be tempting to invoice a non-affiliated company in that currency. However, such a tactic may be resisted by the customer if competitors offer more flexibility and are willing to invoice the customer in its own currency. Consequently, from the point of view of competition, it is an advantage to sell in the currency of the customer as well as to buy in the currency of the supplier.

At a first glance it looks as if the same reasoning would be possible for assets in and liabilities to non-affiliated organisations like banks, suppliers, and customers. Managers may try to reduce foreign exchange risk by concentrating assets into hard currencies and liabilities into soft currencies (see, for example, Jilling 1978 p. 149). However, the decisions to deposit or to borrow funds in a foreign currency may not only be based upon how strong or how weak that currency is. Other factors are also apparent, like the depth of the actual capital market, or the extent to which the company may invest in the country of that currency.

An analysis is given below that concerns five important aspects in the choice of denomination. They are:

1. the reasons for the mismatch
2. actions in affiliated organisations
3. risks generated by tenders and price lists
4. traditional currencies for different sectors
5. the geographical effect.

Most problems of mismatching stem from the different conditions under which a firm purchases raw materials and components and sells its products. In one firm, for example, 35 per cent of the raw materials are purchased from Germany according to price lists denoted in Deutschmarks. On the other hand, a large part of its final products is sold in US dollars and pound sterling as a result of negotiations using short-term and long-term tenders. Consequently, it is the mismatching between purchasing and sales in terms of currencies and conditions that generates a substantial part of the currency risk problems in MNCs.

As mentioned above, the management of transactions, assets and liabilities may be done with a much higher degree of flexibility among affiliated organisations than is the case when selling to separate customers. A usual procedure is to concentrate the foreign exchange management at the headquarters and to invoice and to pay subsidiaries in their local currency. Furthermore, any lending and borrowing between subsidiaries and the headquarters should be performed in the local currency.

A common approach is to invoice and to pay subsidiaries in their local currency in order to concentrate the currency risk management at the headquarters.

That gives a platform for a central management of costs and risks for currency exchanges. One manufacturing firm is an exception. That firm has decided that each production unit must invoice in the currency of the purchasing unit. At the same time, it has to hedge such an invoice and to cover the cost of hedging.

Most of the companies interviewed sell their products and services according to price lists. Those price lists are set for a period between three months and one year: the higher the inflation rate, the more frequent the price revisions. In addition, some of the companies present tender offers for larger projects. It is a common practice to set price lists in the currency of the customer, while tender offers are often denominated in a strong currency like US dollars or Deutschmarks (DEM).

Nowadays, only a few companies are willing to present tender offers in small currencies. If that is the case, and if a tender is supposed to be valid for a longer period than one month the tender will always be combined with a currency clause. Currency options are no longer used for tenders of that type. One company uses forward contracts to hedge tenders offers (which encourages the risk to sell currencies forward without being sure of matching it with an inflow in the same currency).

The choice of currency is especially important in the case of tenders for large projects. Most tenders are given in USD but other large currencies like pound sterling (GBP), Deutschmarks (DEM) and Japanese Yen (JAY) are used to a certain extent. On the other hand, general price lists are mostly given in the local currency. About 50 per cent of the companies work actively with price lists in both local and foreign currencies. These price lists are often set for one year ahead but may be revised when there is a rapid change in the inflation rate. A few other firms operate in markets where prices fluctuate daily and price lists are given in dollars, yen or sterling.

Price lists and tender offers generate substantial economic exposures to the firms. Those risks are difficult to hedge as currency options are found to be too expensive. Some firms use currency clauses in that case, but most firms rely on active management until a contract is signed.

The degree of variation is large. One industrial company sells 75 per cent of its products in terms of projects, another sells 55 per cent and a third sells 10 per cent. About 85 per cent of one company's export value is denominated in USD and 15 per cent in DEM. This may be an extreme example but USD is the main currency in most companies. For a few companies, it may take a long time from the date of a tender offer to the date when a contract is signed. For such long periods of tender risks, an offer in a foreign currency is mostly combined with a currency clause.

The choices of currency of denomination are sometimes dependent on the sector in which the firm operates. For example, the USD is the dominant currency for a company that sells minerals and mineral products and pound sterling is a currency often used by another company that exports machinery. In certain sectors, like paper and pulp, certain metals or oil, USD has been and still is the current currency. One treasurer said: 'We want to increase our assets in US dollars, because everything is oriented towards dollars.' USD has also been the main currency for trade with South America. The reason being that there is no stable currency in that area. For the same reason, the French franc is often used for sales to certain African countries.

Several firms state that they operate in 20–30 main currencies in order to meet the demand for selling in different geographical regions. Some of the others use the common international trade currencies, like USD. A few companies operate with a combination of both. UK companies sometimes use a combination of GBP and USD instead of only USD. Among the smaller Swedish companies interviewed, several use Swedish krona (SEK) as sales currency.

When discussing this subject further during the 1985 interviews, many of the companies said at that time that they tried to control which currencies to use. Sometimes a corporate finance department had discussions with the sales department about priorities between sales currencies. By using the foreign subsidiary's local currency the group could centralise the currency exposure in order to match payments and receipts. Swedish companies, being in a seller's market, often use SEK as a sales currency, in order to avoid currency exposures.

In 1985 the choice of currency was often open to negotiation and, in most cases, it is still so today. However, an MNC would find it easier to sell its products when the price was set in the currency of the customer. That is the main reason why most firms in this study operate in a large number of currencies instead of pricing in the currency of the costs.

13.3.2 International cash management

The task of selling products and services in a foreign country creates a set of problems different from those on the domestic market. On the international markets a firm has to accept longer credit times, larger floats and more costly transaction services. When there is a subsidiary in the foreign country, the use of the payments system will generally be more efficient than selling through an agent.

A majority of all foreign transactions are organised as bank payments without letters of credit or similar instruments. A procedure that is recommended is to direct these payments into currency accounts for the headquarters or into collection accounts for the subsidiaries. Then at predetermined dates, often once a month, the funds at the collection accounts will be transferred to the currency accounts of the headquarters. In most cases these transfers will take place over a netting system. Taxation systems, laws and regulations give a framework for a country to accumulate liquidity. Transaction costs may be reduced by aggregating payments denominated in the same currencies to a limited set of single transfers. However, such a concentration will expand the transaction exposures. Consequently, transfer costs may be reduced on behalf of currency risks or interest rate risks.

The majority of the firms interviewed receive and make several hundreds and, sometimes thousands, of international transactions per month. Most are performed electronically, but there are cases when cheques and even giros are used for such a purpose. Collection accounts are used in most of the countries and transfers to the headquarters are performed once or twice a month worldwide for the accumulated net amounts. Some of the firms use their own netting systems for these purposes but most of them make use of systems supplied by banks like Chase Manhattan, Chemical Bank, Citibank and Skandinaviska Enskilda Banken. Several firms include both affiliated and non-affiliated companies in their netting systems. The non-affiliated ones are large customers with a stable demand for which it is rather easy to forecast the transaction volumes.

In 1985, however, only some of the companies interviewed used bilateral netting and just a few used multilateral netting. At that time it was unusual to include external transactions in a netting system. One group used netting with its subsidiaries in the country of the parent company only. Seven of the companies operated a multilateral netting system. In most cases, netting was performed once a month. However, one firm did so twice a month, another firm every fourth week and a third firm once a week.

Today, high quality services, low costs and a low float are usually the objectives of netting. Certain firms with flows in many directions may net away 50–80 per cent of their transactions between countries. One firm estimates that the netting system will save them about 25 million SEK per year. One treasurer commented 'The netting procedure takes us 10 days per month. Consequently, we cannot do it more frequently than once a month.'

Most firms combine the use of one single bank (often Citibank or Skandinaviska Enskilda Banken) for international transactions with one or two banks in each country for local services. Almost all firms evaluate their banks regularly, often every third year, for quality of service and competitive prices, and change bank when these conditions are not met. Some comments were as follows:

We changed from Bank A to Bank B three years ago. Nowadays we use Bank B for 80 per cent of our transactions and the Postal Giro system for the remaining 20 per cent.

We have had 50 per cent of our Swedish services with Bank A and 50 per cent with Bank B. But last year we changed that to 70 per cent with Bank A and 30 per cent with Bank B. The main reason was that Bank A offered a much better service abroad.

We change bank every other year.

We change cash pool every third year.

Nowadays, most firms perform net transfers between countries month by month in terms of a netting system. They base such a system of international cash management on services from a network of banks. They rate those banks regularly and replace them when necessary in order to improve efficiency.

However, for a few companies netting is not a profitable approach. One company almost balances its surplus and deficits in each country. Consequently, that company makes very few transfers from the subsidiaries to the headquarters. Another company in the financial sector borrows liquidity locally during certain days of a month. Another one with a surplus of liquidity renews its portfolio positions at least five times a year. That company has established an internal bank in order to obtain an efficient portfolio management.

Today, very few firms make active use of lead and lag. However, in 1985, there was still a number of firms that used lead and lag in order to reduce the currency risk exposures both from internal and external transactions. But the awareness of a good payment discipline was growing and one treasurer stated that 'We want to keep a good reputation among our suppliers by paying in time.' Furthermore, in 1985 many of the companies used lead and lag regularly for group internal payments. A couple of firms actively controlled lead and lag from their headquarters. For them it was an easy way to handle short-term liquidity problems within the group, even if it would not have any effect on the total exposure. Today such a procedure belongs to history.

Most firms perform a regular rating of existing and potential banks in order to ensure that they get the best possible services for their money. Most firms put a stronger emphasis on service quality than on low price alternatives. It is a common practice to use one bank (say Citibank) for international transactions and another one (say SE-Banken) for their local services. One firm may change bank every other year in case the service qualities have not been satisfactory.

13.3.3 Currency risk exposure management

Most fund transactions are non-cash. That implies that a transaction is an action to clear a debt and the corresponding claim. Consequently, any transaction exposure may be treated as an expected future balance sheet exposure or a translation exposure in the near future.

An economic exposure concerns transactions that are not yet contracted. For example, tender offers generate substantial economic exposures for the firms involved, but may take a small part of the overall economic activity. Often those exposures last for long time periods. Currency options would then become suitable instruments for hedging economic exposures of this type. However, these exposures are usually very costly to hedge as the market for long-term currency options is rather thin. One construction firm declares: 'The customer has to cover the currency risk. We cannot possibly use long-term currency clauses, and currency options are too expensive.' Another construction firm states that 'it is too expensive to hedge everything. If we do so we take away the possibility to earn money.'

One would expect that a modern treasury unit regularly hedges contracted currency risks and interest rate risks. On the other hand it would be an issue whether or not to hedge expected but non-contracted economic exposures.

In 1985, the majority of the companies that were interviewed were hedging their transaction exposures according to the following principles:

- estimate future transaction exposures for a relevant set of time periods
- plan to net as much as possible of these exposures
- then, the residual (net) exposure can either be forward contracts, local borrowing, etcetera, or it can be left open to be exchanged in the spot market

- hedge a certain percentage (say, 50–75 per cent) of these exposures month by month, one year ahead.

Obviously, most companies at that time actually hedged both transaction ('contracted') exposures as well as economic ('estimated') exposures. Two of the treasurers expressed it as follows:

> We forecast transaction exposures a year in advance based upon a multilateral netting system. Then we cover about 50 per cent of these amounts in order to allow for changes in the sales volumes.
>
> We don't have any cash management system. Every morning we cover 80 per cent of our new sales. On average we aim at 70 per cent cover, but in certain currencies we cover 100 per cent.

Just a few companies were concerned about translation exposures except for the closing of the accounts. But there were treasurers that measured their exposures regularly in order to reduce balance sheet risks. One of them expressed it as follows: 'We measure the translation exposure every quarter of the year. We may then use it when we choose the currency of the loans that we take in order to buy a foreign company.'

Today, most firms hedge their transaction exposures centrally at headquarters. However, at least one headquarters does not consider that it is exposed to substantial transaction risks but leaves that exposure unhedged. Another firm instructs each subsidiary and division on how to hedge its own net exposure. Such a hedge may be done either with its local bank or with the treasury. Then, the headquarters estimates the remaining exposure for the end of each month and hedges the relevant part of them.

Several firms include estimated but non-contracted transactions in their transaction exposures. On the other hand, they seldom hedge 100 per cent of such an exposure just because it is not completely contracted. Some firms admit that they only hedge 50–70 per cent of the exposed values just to preserve flexibility in case any estimated sales are not realized. One firm performs a regular hedging on the translation exposure 'in order to preserve the net capital intact'.

Most firms measure their transaction exposures once a month and at least three months ahead. Two firms indicate that their estimations go up to six months, and two others aim at a nine-month planning horizon. For those cases, the transaction exposure is actually converted into one of economic exposure, as most transactions are estimated but not confirmed. About eight of the firms stated that they hedged their transaction exposures to 100 per cent four months ahead. Beyond those four months they made a proportional hedging, with a proportion of 40–60 per cent for several cases. The majority of the firms used forward contracts as the control instrument for hedging. Between eight and ten firms confirmed a simultaneous use of options for that purpose. Four firms stressed the use of currency loans for hedging. About nine firms used translation exposure as a basis for hedging and about six firms used economic exposure for that purpose.

The insolvency risk is emphasized by one particular firm. This firm sells equipment regularly in USD and on a long-term basis. The construction phases for such equipment are financed by export credits (also in USD), which become due at a predetermined sequence of dates. The instalments from the customer are then scheduled in order to correspond to those dates. However, those payments are sometimes halted or delayed, an effect that has to be considered when estimating the translation exposure. The company has tried to consider these insolvency risks in their translation exposure by replacing the uncertain claims on customers by the market values of the equipment.

One firm says that 'delivery contracts are difficult to handle. You cannot estimate when you will get the payments and how large they will be.' Another firm has a similar view: 'The tender's period is a difficult one. You do not know where the raw material will come from.'

Several companies are greatly concerned with antenatal risks for large-scale investments. One construction company operates with tender periods, that is the time period between the date when the tender is given and the one when a contract is signed. This company has not yet tried to hedge the antenatal risks. Another firm, usually with a tender period of six months, has used currency options for hedging. A third firm with contracts in the range of five–ten years has not yet used hedging for the tender period.

Several companies have stressed the currency risk of tenders for medium-term deliveries. Four of the companies have used currency clauses to avoid the currency risk. In principle, this gives the same result as if the seller had used its reporting currency for invoicing. One customer would not accept this practice unless he could get compensation in terms of lower prices. Consequently, such clauses will only transfer currency risks into commercial risks.

Two companies produce services in foreign countries. At a certain date, a tender might be given in local currency (LC). Production capacity might have been chartered from a subcontractor at the same time (and in LC). If the tender is not accepted, there is a risk that the services from the subcontractor cannot be efficiently utilized, even if the production costs in the reporting currency (RC) are avoided.

Let us assume that the tender is accepted. The company will then receive long positions in LC over several time periods. On the other hand, a rejection of the tender will result in that some of the costs, for the subcontractor (including term contracts) cannot be avoided. Consequently, there will then be a short position in LC. In one company, there is a need to cover the long (net) position in LC in case the tender is accepted. Currency options are one instrument to achieve such a cover. The other of the two companies has chosen to avoid some of the antenatal risks by signing optional contracts with subcontractors. Then, as in Table 13.2, the cumulative cash flow to the subcontractor will not be initiated before a contract has been signed. In that case it is only the net position between the two cash flows (A–B) that are open in LC.

Several of the companies make regular one to three-monthly forecasts of the inflow of currencies directly from customers and indirectly from subsidiaries. These forecasts are then used to determine the size of hedging. Most companies centralise their foreign exchange exposure management by letting the subsidiaries pay the headquarters or the invoicing centre in LC.

A majority of the investigated firms base their hedging of transactions exposures on data from their netting systems.

Commercial risks prevent the companies from making detailed and precise forecasts for periods longer than one month. As a consequence it is difficult to carry out an exact hedging strategy. Several companies have emphasized these problems of long-range planning.

A controversial issue for the treasurers is to what extent they should hedge economic exposures in terms of expected but not contracted volumes of foreign currency. Comments are as follows:

We would like to be flexible. That means that we hedge 30–60 per cent of the annual flow of foreign currencies.

We must cover the equity in our foreign subsidiaries by loans in the same currency. For that purpose we take short-term credits which we renew regularly.

We hedge currency exposures three months ahead. Longer economic exposures are covered by using interest rate swaps.

13.3.4 Interest rate risk management

An interest rate risk is a risk that the market values of assets and liabilities for a company will change when the interest rates fluctuate on the financial markets. An increase in a market rate will reduce the value of an asset and expand the value of a liability as long as those values are based upon a fixed interest rate. One would, therefore, expect that a treasury unit may regularly estimate and manage interest rate risks in terms of maturity gaps, duration or VAR.

In 1985 almost no firms analysed and hedged interest rate risks. An exception was one trust company which had just started a programme to manage efficiently its assets and liabilities. In 1996 that situation has changed completely. Several firms have established so-called asset and liability committees (ALCOs) which include members from both the executive office and the treasury. Asset and liability management (ALM) has become the usual name for the activities performed by those committees.

A few firms have installed computer systems and established management procedures in order to handle ALM efficiently on a regular basis. ALM has been used mainly for the management of risk, but there is a growing interest among banks to use it for the management of return as well. Some firms operate with foreign exchange exposure management in parallel with ALM. These two activities are interrelated to a certain extent, as changes in market interest rates interact with changes in foreign exchange rates.

A usual procedure of ALM is to group assets and liabilities into buckets (gaps) with almost the same length of time until repricing. For example, one bucket may be assets with fixed rates less than one month ahead. A second one may be assets that will be repriced one to three months ahead. One firm reports that it makes use of ten such buckets, while another one operates with six. Several firms estimate bucket by bucket their interest rate exposures as the mismatched volumes of assets and liabilities. That activity, called gap management, was illustrated in Table 13.3 and Table 13.4. It is utilized in order to hedge bucket by bucket the exposure. In this way, an interest rate risk on the asset side is accepted so long as it is matched by an interest rate risk on the liability side to the same size.

Nowadays, many firms measure and manage their interest rate exposures in terms of 'Gap Management'. Just a few firms use concepts like 'Duration', 'Volatility', and 'Value at Risk (VAR)' for that purpose.

In addition to this elementary form of interest rate risk management, there are a few firms that balance the joint risks from different buckets in terms of the duration of its assets, its liabilities and even its equity. As before, duration stands for the time of repricing weighted with regard to the interest on these assets or liabilities. In theory, there are a set of principles to reduce the interest rate exposure. They attempt to:

i)   reduce the gap between assets and liabilities bucket by bucket;
ii) balance the duration of the assets with the one of the liabilities;
iii) aim at a specified duration of the equity formulated as a weighted difference between the duration of the assets and the one of the liabilities.

These three approaches will result in substantial differences in policy. For example, principle ii will allow for a matching of long-term assets and short-term liabilities, which is not possible with principle i. Principle iii will aim at a given return on equity (ROE), while that return will fluctuate with the market rate when using principle i or principle ii.

Three main 'instruments' are available in order to reduce these risks:

• to negotiate the conditions of loans and placements
• to swap fixed-interest assets or liabilities with floating rate ones
• to hedge fixed interest assets and liabilities by the use of off-balance sheet instruments.

Two of the firms have explained that they aim at an equal balance between fixed rate and floating rate assets. Another one has an objective of 35 per cent fixed rate assets. One firm has declared that its objective is to preserve a duration on equity of about five–seven years. Another one reduced risk by prohibiting any repricing date more than one year ahead.

Firms with internal banks demonstrate a more active use of ALM than others. They often measure short-term risks by the use of VAR and long-term risk by duration. Just a very few firms attempt to control simultaneously interest rate exposures and foreign exchange exposures. But most of the firms are convinced that such a joint exposure management will become necessary in the future, independent of whether the UK or Sweden joins EMU.

13.3.5   Organisation

In this study we analyse the management of currency exposures as a part of international financial management in a firm. In a small and medium-sized firm these activities will take place inside its accounting department. In a larger firm, however, these tasks are often performed inside a specific treasury department or financial department. A department called Corporate Treasury will often handle such important tasks as:

- formation of capital structure
- international cash management
- liquidity management
- currency exposure management
- interest rate risk management
- bank relations.

The formation of capital structure includes topics like issues of equities in different countries and in different currencies, and the choice of long-term and short-term lending. International cash management covers transactions of payments including the control of costs for transfer, currency exchange and float losses. Liquidity management concerns the control of cash surplus on collection accounts as well as placements in short-term financial instruments. Currency exposure management includes all activities for controlling and reducing currency risks. Interest rate risk management concerns choices between borrowing and placements in fixed rate versus floating rate alternatives. Finally, bank relations concerns the interaction with one or several banks in order to carry out in practice the above mentioned activities.

A treasury function may be organised in different ways. A standard approach is to form a special department for these activities. This may be done either as a 'cost centre' or as a 'profit centre', depending on whether the treasury function is supposed to make a profit out of its transactions. Another approach is to organise the treasury function as a special subsidiary, which may be treated as an 'internal bank'. The control of the treasury function may be formalised in terms of a 'financial policy document'. Such a document will then include a set of rules specially designed for currency issues and for interest rate policies. A currency policy may include:

- currencies the company is dealing with and ways to measure currency exposures
- types of currency risks
- the time period for currency management
- the financial impact of the policy
- restrictions because of currency exchange controls
- acceptable deviations from the policy
- the responsibility for each organisational level within the finance function
- a general policy for the company's handling of currency risks.

Most of the Swedish companies interviewed did not have a written policy for exposure management in 1985 and several companies did not have one yet in 1996. Among those who do have it nowadays, the policy is signed by the managing director or by the treasurer. It is often expressed in general terms, and tangible statements that express the policy are not used at all. A few companies have formed their policy in terms of maximum and minimum limits for the amount that has to be hedged, or as expressions in general terms about the exposure balance. Some groups let their treasury department form the group policy and implement it within the rest of the group; such a policy is more oriented towards a control of financial tasks on other organisational levels than on the treasury level. Finance committees, which are responsible for daily operations, are used in a few companies especially for interest rate risk management. The firms specify the objectives of treasury management as:

- to maximise return on financial management
- to minimise risks caused by variations in currency exchange rates and interest rates
- to minimise the costs of payments, domestically and internationally
- to co-ordinate all inflow and outflow of liquidity
- to provide the departments and subsidiaries with financial services that are competitive
- to handle issues of taxes and regulations in an efficient way.

Many MNCs do not allow their subsidiaries to hedge currency risks or interest rate risks on the market. Instead that has to be done through internal contracts with treasury. This is based upon a belief that central co-ordination will generate better terms on the money market than activities with local banks. A disadvantage of such a principle is that there will be little incentive to utilize local conditions. The manager of one subsidiary has expressed these fears as: 'We have had enough of centralisation. It takes away the competence. And people will lose interest in being efficient managers.' In certain companies it is up to the subsidiary to find out if the local bank may provide it with better conditions than the treasury function. If so, they are allowed to use the local services.

The interviews demonstrated significant differences between UK and Swedish companies in formulating a policy for foreign exchange exposure and how to control its management. Today, all the UK companies interviewed, and the majority of the Swedish ones, have formulated a written policy agreed by the board. In some cases such a policy is made operational in tangible terms, within frames and limits to be used in the daily operations. In others, the corporate finance department operates with a finance committee which makes the decisions on a day-to-day basis. Compared to the situation in 1985 there has been a dramatic change in 1996; in 1985 only a very few companies had formulated a written policy.

13.4   Conclusions

Over the period 1985 to 1996 the financial markets have expanded beyond imagining. At the same time most firms have become much more cautious in the control of international payments and foreign exchange exposures. Their strategies have become: to avoid risks where applicable; to reduce risks as much as possible; and to hedge the remaining risks when economically viable.

An efficient currency denomination is of primary importance in order to avoid foreign exchange risks. An MNC will eliminate these risks by selling its products in the currency of its costs. However, just a few firms implement such a policy successfully. When that is the case, those firms have decentralised their production country by country in order to serve the local markets from a local production unit. One firm of this kind was found in the food sector, another one in the sector of transportation and services. However, most companies interviewed have become international just in order to make use of the economies of scale in production. Consequently, they have concentrated their production into a few units and countries. For those firms to become competitive, they have to sell their products either in the currencies of their customers or in a currency that is competitive for that particular sector. For example, oil and petroleum products are mostly sold in USD.

Two main forms of sales strategies are available for those firms that cannot sell their products in the currency of costs: they are tender offers and price lists in foreign currencies.

Tender offers are usually concerned with long-term construction projects. However they may also include long term delivery contracts. Three of the Swedish firms and two of the UK ones were heavily involved in such construction projects that had their origins in a series of tenders. At certain stages of these processes they had been able to use currency options in order to hedge for currency risks. However, in most cases they had to balance their currency risks to their profit margins. That had become very tricky in those cases where the tender periods lasted for a year or longer. A general strategy for these firms has been to set a time limit for the tender after which an unfavourable development in the exchange rate could be prevented by a currency clause.

Price lists in foreign currencies are generated by most of the companies interviewed. Most firms declare the price lists as valid for a calendar year even though there are a couple of firms that change their price lists as often as once a quarter. However, most firms reserve the right to revise the price lists in the case of an extreme escalation in costs.

The sales currencies that dominate these firms are the US dollar, pound sterling, the French franc, the Deutschmark, the Dutch guilder, the Belgian franc, the Italian lira and the Japanese yen. However, the Deutschmark is the main currency of purchasing contracts.

In 1985 many firms estimated their expected flows in terms of transaction exposures. In so doing they included not only contracted flows but also long-term expected flows. Today, most firms concentrate on short-term transaction exposures. These companies have observed that if they hedge long-term economic exposures, they will actually take on the risk of contracting future exchange operations for transactions that are uncertain. Tender offers and price lists generate economic exposures that are costly to cover. Even if currency options became suitable instruments, they could only be used in those limited cases when the expected size and date of a contract is relatively well known. However, most of the companies have found options too costly to use in this respect.

Some companies have launched a strategy to estimate month-by-month the probability of signing contracts in different currencies. They cover the expected sales volume by use of forward contracts. The risks they take will then depend on how well they may estimate the probability of signing contracts.

Today netting is a generally accepted procedure, which it was not ten years ago. The controversy is about how often to perform a netting. Firms with thousands of payments per month cannot estimate their net transactions more than once a month. A large percentage of the firms declared that they were able to net away as much as 50–60 per cent of the values to be transacted. In many cases third party transactions were included into those net values.

In 1985 the banks dominated the payment systems and the foreign exchange markets in a way which they do not do today. The firms of today regularly evaluate their actual and potential banks in order to obtain more efficient and less risky transactions. Certain banks, like Citibank, dominate the payment systems, while others specialise in the financing activities.

By 1996 business firms had become more aware of the interest rate risks to which they were exposed. As many as 20 of the firms have declared that they regularly analyse interest rate risks in terms of maturity gaps. A couple of the firms estimate the duration for different groups of assets and liabilities. For example, one firm aims to keep the duration of equity in the range of five–seven years. Three firms stress that they concentrate on short-term interest movements, for which VAR would become a proper instrument. A few firms had actually started to install ALM systems. However, the strategies behind the use of these systems had not yet been well developed.

Finally, the controversy between those in favour of hedging and those against hedging has not yet been solved. However, many treasurers state that they have taken the position not to speculate. On the other hand they may well hedge expected exposures in spite of the fact that such actions may well expand the currency risks. So even if they support the four arguments for hedging given in Table 13.5, a new controversy has emerged over whether or not to hedge economic exposures. That issue has not yet reached a satisfactory conclusion.

Appendix

Personal interviews: guide

Foreign exchange exposure management project

Purpose

The aim of the project is:

a) to analyse the measurement and management of foreign exchange exposure in a set of UK and Swedish companies
b) to analyse the interaction between the management of foreign exchange exposures (FEE) and interest rate exposures (IRE) in these companies
c) to compare the principles of foreign exchange exposure management of 1985 and 1996.

The study will be based on interviews with about 25 Swedish and UK firms. The study should contribute to a better understanding of different methods to be used for managing foreign exchange risk. It will also explain how firms with different products and different structures choose different approaches.

The following paragraphs list the five sets of questions that were presented to the firms.

1. Choice of currency of denomination

Which currencies are used for tenders?
Which currencies are used for the purchasing of raw material?
Which currencies are used for internal transactions?
Which currencies are used for internal loans?

2. International cash management

How are the cash management systems operated?
Do you use several banks? If so, why?
Are the bank services efficient? Do the prices correspond to the costs?
What are the gross and the net amounts of transactions?
How often do you perform netting and payments for transactions?
Do you include both affiliated and non-affiliated companies?

Where and how do you accumulate liquidity?
Do you have separate systems and procedures for internal and external payments?
What is the use of lead and lag?
Can you give a short overview of the currency streams?

3. Currency risk exposure

Which are the measures of currency exposure?
Which are the elements of these exposure measurements?
Are tenders included in these exposures?
How can you use these exposures to reduce risk?
How frequently do you measure these exposures?
From where do you get data for these measures and which data do you use?
Do you use alternative strategies to reduce currency exposures? Why?
What do you use the currency exposure for?

* Follow up?
* Short-term operation activities?
* To determine the extent of forward cover?

Do you cover 50 per cent, 70 per cent or 100 per cent of the exposure?

4. Interest rate risk exposure

Which measures do you use? Do you manage short-term or long-term?
Which policy do you follow?
How does this policy interact with the foreign exchange risk management?
What are the proposals for future changes of the management of FEE and IRE?

5. Organisation

Is the organisation of FFE and IRE centralised or decentralised?
What influence does the organisation structure have on the currency risk management?
In what way does your financial department participate in the management of different exposures?
What emphasis does the management put on the management of FFE and IRE?
To what extent are you willing to take risks in order to obtain a better return?
When and why has there been a change in policies?

Note

Special thanks go to those representatives of UK and Swedish firms that have devoted their time to my interviews as well as to the Nordbanken for financial support. Thanks also go to Dr Gert Sandahl and my colleagues of the Department of Business Administration, University of Gothenburg, who have given constructive comments to an earlier version of this chapter.

References

Bergendahl, G. and M. Nyberg (1986), *Foreign exchange exposure management: an analysis of the practice in 26 British and Swedish firms*, FE-Report 265–1986, Department of Business Administration, University of Gothenburg
Donaldson, J.A. (1987), 'Corporate currency risk: a reappraisal', *Financial Times Business Information*, London
Earl, M. (1985), 'A stage model of measuring and managing foreign exchange exposure', *The Treasurer*, March
Edelshain, D. (1992), *British corporate currency exposure and foreign exchange risk management*, Ph.D. thesis (unpublished), London Business School, Sussex Place, Regents Park, London
Eiteman, D.K. *et al.* (1995), *Multinational business finance*, Reading, Mass: Addison-Wesley
George, A.M. (1983), 'Currency exposure management', in A.M. George and I.M. Giddy, *International finance handbook*, vol. 2, New York: Wiley-Interscience
Jilling, M. (1978), *Foreign exchange risk management in US multinational corporations*, UMI Research Press
Kenyon, A. (1981), *Currency risk management*, London: Wiley
Kenyon, A. (1990), *Currency risk and business management*, Oxford: Basil Blackwell
Oxelheim, L. (1985), *International financial market fluctuations*, Chichester, England: Wiley
Oxelheim, L. and C. Wihlborg (1987), *Macroeconomic uncertainty*, Chichester, England: Wiley
Parker, G. (1995), 'Dimensions of risk management: definition and implications for financial services', in W.H. Beaver and G. Parker, *Risk management: problems and solutions*, New York: McGraw-Hill
Puchon, G. (1983), 'Defining and measuring currency exposure', in A.M. George and I.M. Giddy, *International finance handbook*, vol. 2, New York: Wiley-Interscience

14
Fat Tails and the Effect on Optimal Asset Allocations

André Lucas and Pieter Klaassen *

Abstract

In investment management problems one often uses scenarios to determine optimal strategies and to quantify the uncertainty associated with these strategies. Such scenarios are mostly based on the assumption of normality for variables like asset returns, inflation rates and interest rates. Financial economic time series often display leptokurtic behaviour, implying that the assumption of normality may be inappropriate. In this chapter we use a simple asset allocation problem with one shortfall constraint in order to uncover the main consequences of non-normal distributions on optimal asset allocations. It is found that the probability of shortfall plays a crucial role in determining the effect of fat tails on optimal asset allocations. Depending on this probability, the presence of fat tails may lead to either more aggressive or more prudent asset mixes. We also examine the effect of misspecification of the degree of leptokurtosis. Using distributions with an incorrect tail behaviour may lead to portfolios with a minimum return that is up to 418 basis points below the minimum return imposed in the model. In value-at-risk calculations, this implies that the true value-at-risk may deviate by more than 4 per cent (as a fraction of the invested notional) from what an incorrectly specified model suggests. This illustrates the importance of using scenario generators that exhibit the correct tail behaviour.

14.1   Introduction

In asset allocation problems, we often employ scenario analysis to obtain insight into the consequences of alternative strategies. As

Bunn and Salo (1993) argue, scenario analysis is a very useful tool for evaluating the performance of asset allocation strategies and for assessing the risk associated with these strategies under a range of different conditions. In the asset allocation context one is usually concerned with the future possible development of economic quantities such as asset returns, inflation rates, interest rates, and so on. In order to describe these developments, that is in order to generate scenarios, frequent use is made of the normal or lognormal distribution.

The use of the normal distribution has several advantages. First, the normal distribution is easy to use and produces tractable results in many analytical exercises. Second, all moments of positive order exist for the normal distribution. Third, the normal distribution is completely characterised by its first two moments, thus establishing the link with mean–variance optimisation theory. Finally, the normal distribution arises as the limiting distribution of a whole class of statistical testing and estimation procedures and, as such, plays a central role in empirical modelling exercises.

The normal distribution, however, also has several disadvantages. These are especially relevant in the asset allocation context. As the tails of the normal distribution decay exponentially towards zero, large realisations are extremely unlikely. This seems to contradict empirical findings on asset returns, which state that these returns generally exhibit leptokurtic behaviour, that is, fatter tails than the normal distribution (see, for example, de Vries (1994) for a recent review of some stylised facts). This phenomenon need not be important if one is only interested in, for example, expected returns. If one is also interested in measures that describe the uncertainty or the risk that is associated with a given strategy, however, the precise shape of the tails of the distribution may matter a great deal.

This chapter describes the effect of fat tails on asset allocation problems. The sensitivity of stochastic programmes such as asset allocation problems to the underlying distribution has been addressed in more general terms in, for example, Dupacová (1990) and some of the references cited therein. The results in these papers can be used to obtain a qualitative assessment of the effect of fat tails by computing bounds for and approximations of the effect of leptokurtosis on optimal asset allocations. In this chapter we follow a more direct line of research. We consider a simple one-period asset allocation problem with a shortfall constraint to illustrate the main issues involved when fat tails are allowed. In this way we obtain a quantitative assessment of the effects, thus providing valuable insight. The shortfall constraint is added to incorporate the idea that the investor wants to put a (probabilistic) upper bound on the maximum loss that is allowed.

The chapter results in two main implications. First, the probability of shortfall plays a decisive role in determining the effect of fat tails. If the shortfall probability is moderately large, say 5 per cent, then the existence of fat tails results in more aggressive asset allocations. By contrast, if the shortfall probability is small, say 1 per cent, then leptokurtic behaviour leads to the choice of more prudent asset allocations. The optimal asset mixes vary considerably over the degree of leptokurtosis. As a second implication of this chapter, we find that misspecifying the degree of leptokurtosis may lead to both overly aggressive and overly prudent asset allocations. In particular, if scenarios are based on the normal distribution and if reality is fat-tailed, the optimal asset allocation may be far too prudent if the shortfall probability is moderately high (5 per cent). Analogously, the asset mix based on normality is much too aggressive if a shortfall probability of 1 per cent is used and if reality is leptokurtic.

The chapter is set out as follows. In Section 14.2 we present the asset allocation problem under study and the class of probability measures that is used and in Section 14.3 we give some general characterisations of the effect of fat tails on the problem at hand. Section 14.4 presents an empirical application of the model in Section 14.2 using historical returns on four Dutch asset categories, namely cash, stocks, property and bonds. We discuss the effect of misspecifying the degree of leptokurtosis of the scenario generator in Section 14.5 and Section 14.6 concludes, indicating interesting lines for future research.

14.2　The model

We consider a one-period model with n asset categories. In period one, the investment manager is given an amount of one dollar which can be invested in any of these asset categories. The manager is not allowed to hold short positions. The objective of the investment manager is to maximise the expected utility of his terminal wealth subject to a shortfall constraint. The shortfall constraint states that with a sufficiently high probability $1 - \psi$ (with ψ being a small number), the return on the portfolio will not fall below the shortfall return r^{low}. Formally, the sketched asset allocation problem is given by

$$\max_{x \in \Re^n} \ E_m \left[U \left(\sum_{i=1}^n x_i(1+r_i) \right) \right]$$

$$s.\,t. \quad P\left(\sum_{i=1}^n x_i(1+r_i) < 1 + r^{low} \right) \leq \psi, \tag{1}$$

$$\sum_{i=1}^n x_i = 1,$$

$$x_i \geq 0.$$

The amounts or fractions invested in each of the n asset categories are denoted by $x_1, \ldots, x_n$, while the (stochastic) return on asset category i is denoted by r_i. Shortfall constraints as in (1) can also be found in, for example, Leibowitz and Kogelman (1991) and Leibowitz *et al.* (1992). We assume that the utility function of the manager $U\,(\cdot)$ is concave and monotonically increasing.

The operator $E_m\,(\cdot)$ in (1) is the expectation operator of the manager with respect to the probability measure of the asset returns P_m. By letting this measure depend on the manager's discretion, we are able to study the effect of discrepancies between the measure used by the manager, P_m, and the true probability measure of the asset returns, P_t, say. The probability measure P_m can be thought of as the distribution used by the manager to generate future scenarios. As such, P_m can be called the scenario generator. Discrepancies between P_m and P_t can thus be interpreted as the use of a misspecified scenario generator by the manager for generating future states of the world.

Frequently, the scenario generator P_m is taken to be the normal or lognormal distribution. The aim of this chapter is to study the effect of fat tails on the solution of the problem in (1). Therefore, we need to introduce a class of probability measures that allows for fat tails, while simultaneously yielding to tractable derivations. The class of Student t distributions meets these requirements. The probability density function of the n-dimensional multivariate Student t distribution is given by

$$f(r; \mu, \Omega, v) = \frac{\Gamma((v+n)/2)}{\Gamma(v/2)\cdot\ \pi v \Omega^{\frac{1}{2}}} \cdot \left(1 + \frac{(r-\mu)'\Omega(r-\mu)}{v} \right)^{-(v+n)/2} \tag{2}$$

with $\Gamma\,(\cdot)$ denoting the Gamma or generalised factorial function, $r = (r_1, \ldots, r_n)'$ denoting the vector of stochastic asset returns, $'$ denoting transposition, and, μ, Ω^{-1}, and v denoting the mean, the precision matrix, and the degrees of freedom parameter of the Student t distribution, respectively. The Student t distribution nests the normal distribution for asset returns in the sense that (2) reduces to the normal density with mean μ and covariance matrix Ω if $v \to \infty$. The degrees of freedom parameter v determines the degree of leptokurtosis. v has to be strictly positive. The smaller v, the fatter are the tails of the Student t distribution. The first two moments of the Student t distribution play an important role in the subsequent analysis. These moments are given by $E(r) = \mu$ and $E((r - \mu)(r - \mu)') = v\Omega/(v - 2)$ and they require $v > 1$ and $v > 2$, respectively. Figure 14.1 displays several Student t distributions for the univariate case $n = 1$. The distributions are scaled in such a way that they all have the same mean and variance. It is clearly seen that for lower values of v, the tails of the distribution become fatter and the distribution becomes more 'peaked' near the centre $\mu = 0$.

In order to distinguish the scenario generator from the true probability measure, we add subscripts to the parameters in (2). We assume that the scenario generator P_m is characterised by μ_m, Ω_m, and v_m, and that the true distribution P_t is characterised by μ_t, Ω_t, and v_t.

In order to use the scenario generator P_m, we must first specify its parameters. We assume that v_m is chosen by the manager on *a priori* grounds. For example, it is common practice to base scenarios on the normal distribution, implying that v_m is usually set equal to infinity. Given the degree of leptokurtosis imposed by the manager, we further assume that the manager follows the usual strategy of matching the first two moments of the scenario generator to those of the observed data. In the present setting this amounts to matching the mean and variance of P_m to that of P_t. Note that we abstract from the fact that we usually only have limited knowledge of the parameters of P_t, because we only observe a historical time series of finite length. By abstracting from the effect of finite observed samples, we are able to fully concentrate on the effect of leptokurtosis. Given the above strategy of matching P_m to P_t, we obtain $\mu_m = \mu_t$ and

$$\frac{v_m \Omega_m}{v_m - 2} = \frac{v_t \Omega_t}{v_t - 2} \Leftrightarrow \Omega_m = (1 - 2v_m^{-1}) \cdot \frac{v_t \Omega_t}{v_t - 2} \tag{3}$$

As v_m is set by the manager and the mean μ_t and covariance matrix $v_t \Omega_t/(v_t - 2)$ are derived from the data, we have determined all the parameters of the scenario generator P_m.

Figure 14.1: Student t distribution for various values of the degree of freedom parameter ν

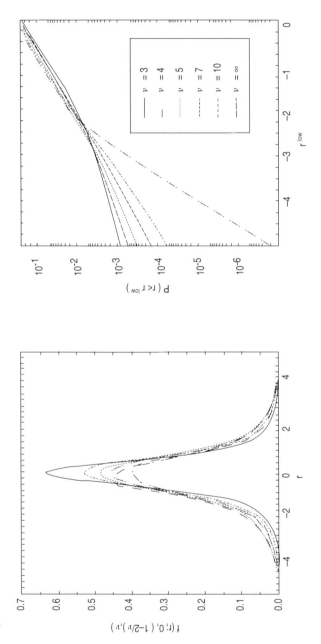

14.3   Theoretical effects of fat tails

The scenario generator plays a prominent role in the objective function and the shortfall constraint. We discuss the effect of varying v_m on each of these in turn. We start with a discussion of the shortfall constraint. Decreasing v_m has two effects on this constraint. First of all, the tails of the distribution become fatter, resulting in a larger probability of extreme events for fixed precision matrix $\Omega^{-1}{}_m$. As can be seen in (3), however, the precision matrix is not independent of v_m. As v_m decreases, the (eigenvalues of the) precision matrix increase. As a result, the distribution becomes more concentrated around the mean μ_m, compare Figure 14.1. It is easily verified from the right panel in Figure 14.1 that the composite effect on the shortfall constraint of altering v_m critically depends on the shortfall probability ψ. For $\psi = 0.001$, the quantiles of the Student t distribution are ordered from left to right for increasing values of v, that is, for decreasing degrees of leptokurtosis. This implies that for sufficiently small values of ψ, the shortfall constraint becomes less binding if v_m is increased. The reverse holds if we consider sufficiently large values of ψ, for example, $\psi = 0.1$.

It is interesting to present the break-even shortfall probability for the normal distribution, that is, the value of ψ as a function of v such that the shortfall constraint for that value of v is as binding as the shortfall constraint of the corresponding normal distribution. The values are given in Figure 14.2. This figure indicates that the critical shortfall probability ranges from $\psi = 1.8$ per cent for $v = 3$ to $\psi = 3.6$ per cent for $v = 10$. For values of ψ below these critical levels, the effect of fat tails on the shortfall constraint dominates the effect caused by increased precision. Again, the reverse holds for values of ψ above the critical level. In the empirical study in Section 14.4 we use $\psi = 1$ per cent and $\psi = 5$ per cent in order to illustrate both settings.

We now proceed with the effect of v_m on the objective function in (1). Let μ and ω^{-1} denote the mean and precision of a univariate $(n = 1)$ Student t random variate Y with v degrees of freedom. Then it is easy to prove using the monotonicity and concavity of $U(\cdot)$ that for a fixed value of v $E(U(Y))$ is a non-increasing, concave function of $\sqrt{\omega}$. The intuition is straightforward. If ω is larger, then, other things being equal, both high and low values of Y become more likely. Due to the concavity of $U(\cdot)$, the high values of Y are weighted less heavily than the low values, causing a decrease, or at least a non-increase of $E(U(Y))$.

One of the nice properties of the multivariate Student t distribution in (2) is that linear combinations of r also follow a Student t distribu-

Figure 14.2: Critical shortfall probability ψ for the Student t distribution with v degrees of freedom (benchmark is the normal distribution)

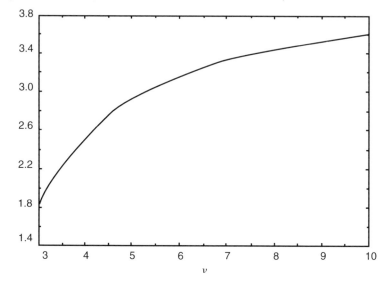

v

tion. In particular, $p = \Sigma_{i=1}^{n} x_i (1 + r_i$ has a univariate $(n = 1)$ Student t distribution with degrees of freedom parameter v_m, mean $\mu_{p,m} = x' (1 + \mu_m)$, and precision $\omega^{-1}/_{p,m} = (x' \Omega_m x)^{-1}$, where $x' = (x_1, \ldots, x_n$. As mentioned earlier in this section, decreasing v_m has two opposite effects: first, the tails of the t distribution become fatter, and second, the precision of the t distribution is increased through the specification of Ω_m in (3). As shown above, the increase in precision leads, other things being equal, to an increase in utility. The effect of the increased fatness of the tails, however, is much more difficult to qualify *a priori*. The effect largely depends on the precise form of the utility function. For example, if $U(p)$ is linear in p, then varying v_m has no effect on E_m $(U(p)) = U(\mu_{p,m})$. By contrast, if the utility function is sharply curved, the effect of v_m will be more pronounced, as extreme positive realisations of p will then be weighted less heavily than extreme negative realisations. So the effect of v_m on the objective function largely depends on the curvature of the utility function. The more curved the utility function, the larger the effect.

An illustration of the theoretical effects mentioned in this section and a quantitative assessment of the precise impact of fat tails on the asset allocation problem in (1) is given below.

14.4   An application to Dutch asset classes

The example in this section is based on a model of Dert (1995) containing four Dutch asset categories: cash, stocks, property and bonds. For cash we observe the return on short-term deposits denominated in Dutch guilders. For stocks, property and bonds we have the total returns on an internationally diversified stock portfolio (Robeco), property portfolio (Rodamco) and bond portfolio (Rorento), respectively. The yearly returns are observed from primo 1956 to ultimo 1994, see Dert (1995 p. 110).

In order to fit the scenario generator to the data, we compute the mean and variance of the return series. Let x_1, ..., x_4 denote the amounts invested in cash, stocks, property and bonds, respectively, and let the corresponding returns be denoted r_1, ... r_4. Then r has mean

$$\begin{matrix} cash & stocks & property & bonds \\ (0.0602, & 0.1024, & 0.0767, & 0.0638)', \end{matrix} \qquad (4)$$

standard deviation

$$\begin{matrix} cash & stocks & property & bonds \\ (0.0245, & 0.1677, & 0.0812, & 0.0816)', \end{matrix} \qquad (5)$$

and correlation matrix

	cash	stocks	property	bonds	
cash	1.00	−0.16	−0.06	0.19	
stocks	−0.16	1.00	0.33	0.43	(6)
property	−0.06	0.33	1.00	0.52	
bonds	0.19	0.43	0.53	1.00	

It is seen from the values of the means, the standard deviations and the correlations, that bonds are dominated by property. Therefore, we drop bonds from the remaining analysis. Unreported experiments indeed show that when bonds are incorporated in the analysis, they never enter the optimal asset mix.

As mentioned in the previous section, we consider two values for the shortfall probability ψ, namely $\psi = 1$ per cent and $\psi = 5$ per cent. We also report the results for several values of the shortfall return r^{low}, namely $r^{low} = 0$ per cent, − 5 per cent, − 10 per cent. So for example the combination $(\psi, r^{low}) = (1$ per cent, 0 per cent) means that the manager requires an asset mix that results in no loss with a 99 per cent probability. Similarly, the combination $(\psi, r^{low}) = (5$ per cent, $- 5$ per cent) means that the manager is satisfied with an asset mix that results in a maximum loss of 5 per cent with a 95 per cent probability.

For the utility function, we only discuss the linear case in this chapter. We have performed some experiments with different utility functions exhibiting more curvature, for example, piecewise linear, but the qualitative results presented below remain unaltered.

In order to concentrate fully on the effect of leptokurtosis, we abstract from the fact that the parameters in (4) through (5) are estimated using a finite instead of an infinite number of observations. We also abstract from the fact that one generally uses a finite number of scenarios. So we study the effect of varying v_m in a context with an infinite number of observations and an infinite number of scenarios. Results obtained in this context, however, can be directly extended to situations with a finite number of scenarios and/or observations.

Using the GAMS optimisation package, we computed the optimal values of x_i satisfying the shortfall constraint in (1) for several values of $v_m = v_t$. The results are presented in Table 14.1.

An obvious effect in Table 14.1 is that the optimal asset mixes become more aggressive if the shortfall constraint is relaxed. This can be done by increasing the allowed shortfall probability ψ or by lowering the required shortfall return r^{low}. If we concentrate on the effect of v_m, we note the difference between the 5 per cent and the 1 per cent shortfall case. We first discuss the 5 per cent case. Increasing the fatness of the tails of the scenario generator then leads to more aggressive asset allocations. The optimal asset mixes contain less of the relatively safe cash and more of the risky assets stocks and property. The effect is more pronounced if the required shortfall return r^{low} is lower.

Although the result that fat tails lead to more aggressive asset mixes may seem counterintuitive at first sight, it is easily understood by the results of the previous section. Decreasing v_m while keeping the variance fixed has two opposite effects. First, the probability of extreme events increases, leading to more prudent asset allocation strategies. Second, the precision of the distribution increases, leading to more certainty about the spread of the outcome and, thus, to a more aggressive strategy. For a shortfall probability of 5 per cent the latter of these two effects dominates. By contrast, if we consider the case of a 1 per cent shortfall probability, we see the opposite. Decreasing v_m now leads to more prudent asset mixes. Again the effect is more pronounced if the required shortfall return r^{low} is lower.

Table 14.1: Optimal asset allocations

v_m	$r^{low} = 0\%$			$r^{low} = -5\%$			$r^{low} = -10\%$		
	Cash	Stock	Prop.	Cash	Stock	Prop.	Cash	Stock	Prop.
				Shortfall probability of 5%					
3	42.1	25.0	33.0	0.0	47.8	52.2	0.0	84.2	15.8
5	51.3	20.6	28.0	12.4	38.8	48.8	0.0	67.4	32.6
7	52.9	19.9	27.2	14.9	37.6	47.5	0.0	64.4	35.6
10	53.6	19.6	26.8	16.1	37.1	46.8	0.0	63.0	37.0
∞	54.5	19.1	26.3	17.5	36.4	46.1	0.0	61.3	38.7
				Shortfall probability of 1%					
3	80.0	7.2	12.7	51.3	20.6	28.0	29.6	30.8	39.6
5	79.6	7.4	13.0	51.0	20.8	28.2	29.2	31.0	39.9
7	77.7	8.3	13.9	49.4	21.5	29.1	27.0	32.0	41.0
10	76.3	9.0	14.7	47.9	22.2	29.8	25.0	32.9	42.1
∞	72.9	10.6	16.5	44.2	24.0	31.8	19.9	35.3	44.8

Note: This table contains the optimal asset allocations (as percentages of the amount invested) for the problem (1) for alternative values of the degree of leptokurtosis used by the manager in the scenario generator ($v_m = v_j$).

14.5 The effect of misspecification of fat tails

After having demonstrated the effect of v_m on the optimal asset mixes in the previous section, we now turn to a second important issue. The scenario generator P_m used by the manager is used to describe the real distribution of the asset returns, P_t. In the present context, the manager would do best by matching μ_m, Ω_m, and v_m to μ_t, Ω_t, and v_t, respectively. For one reason or another, however, the manager can fail to match all the parameters of the scenario generator to those of the true data generating mechanism. In particular, there can be a mismatch between the true degree of leptokurtosis (v_t) and the degree of leptokurtosis used in the scenario analysis (v_m). The most obvious example is the use of scenarios based on normality when the real data are not normally distributed. This can have important effects for the feasibility and efficiency of optimal asset mixes. These issues are investigated below.

Let x_m denote the optimal strategy of the investment manager using a scenario generator with key parameter v_m. The appropriate values of x_m can be found in Table 14.1. We now want to compute the effect of using x_m when the data actually follow the distribution P_t instead of P_m. In particular, we are interested in the effect of a discrepancy between v_m and v_t on the shortfall constraint. We can quantify this effect in at least two different ways. First, we can use the strategy x_m while keeping the required shortfall return r^{low} in (1) constant and compute the actual shortfall probability $\psi^\star$ under the true probability measure P_t. Alternatively, we can use the strategy x_m while keeping the required shortfall probability ψ constant and compute the corresponding shortfall return $r^{\star,low}$. Both approaches are followed below.

First consider the case of fixed r^{low}. We then compute

$$\psi^\star = P_t\left(\sum_{i=1}^{3} x_{m,i}(1 + r_i) \leq 1 + r^{low} \right),\qquad(7)$$

where $x_{m,i}$ is the optimal asset allocation to category i for v_m, see Table 14.1. It turned out that different values r^{low} produced similar results. Therefore, we only present the case with $r^{low} = 0$ per cent. The results are given in Figure 14.3.

The left panel in Figure 14.3 gives the results if the optimal strategy is computed with $\psi = 5$ per cent. The first thing to note is that, as expected, the true shortfall probability $\psi^\star$ is equal to ψ if the investment manager uses the correct distribution, that is, $v_m = v_t$. Second, if

Figure 14.3: True shortfall probability for several combinations of ν_m and ν_t.
Note: The numbers in the figures denote the true shortfall probability ψ^* under the probability measure with ν_t degrees of freedom when using a strategy based on a scenario generator with ν_m degrees of freedom. The nominal shortfall probabilities are $\psi = 5$ per cent and $\psi = 1$ per cent. So for example for $\psi = 5$ per cent the use of a normal scenario generator ($\nu_m = \infty$) if reality is leptokurtic ($\nu_t = 4$) leads to a true shortfall probability ψ^* of about 4 per cent which is 100 basis points below the nominal level of 5 per cent.

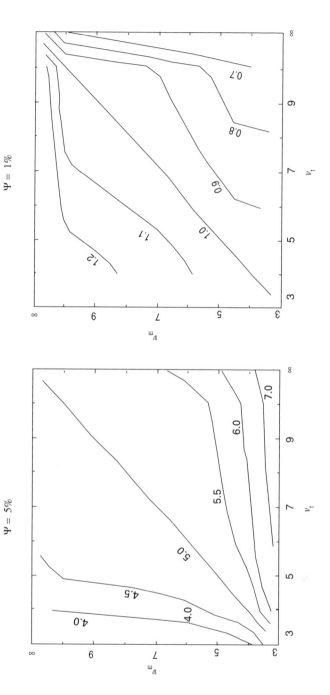

the investment manager uses a distribution that has thinner tails than reality, then he is conservative in the sense that the shortfall constraint in (1) is not binding. This holds even though the manager may believe the constraint to be binding based on his (misspecified) scenario generator. As a result, efficiency could be gained by using the correct degree of leptokurtosis. By contrast, if the manager uses a distribution with fatter tails than reality, the shortfall constraint is violated.

If we consider the case $\psi = 1$ per cent, the results are reversed. If a thin-tailed scenario generator is used, for example the one based on normality while reality is leptokurtic, then the shortfall constraint is violated. Moreover, if $v_m < v_t$, the shortfall constraint is not binding. Note that although the absolute difference between ψ^* and ψ is of a smaller order of magnitude for $\psi = 1$ per cent than for $\psi = 5$ per cent, the relative differences are approximately equal for different combinations of (v_m, v_t).

We now turn to the effect on the shortfall return r^{low} for fixed ψ. We compute the required shortfall return $r^{*,low}$ such that

$$P_t\left(\sum_{i=1}^{3} x_{m,i}(1 + r_i) \le 1 + r^{*,\,low} \right) = \psi. \tag{8}$$

The difference $r^{*,low} - r^{low}$ in basis points is presented in Table 14.2.

The qualitative results are similar to those in Figure 14.3. For high values of ψ, using a scenario generator that has thin tails compared to reality produces a conservative strategy, while the opposite holds for small values of the shortfall probability ψ. The impact of using a normal scenario generator if reality is fat-tailed is quite substantial. Consider the case of a postulated required minimum return r^{low} of -5 per cent. So with a maximum probability of ψ, the manager is willing to take losses up to 5 per cent. If $\psi = 5$ per cent, the true shortfall return can be as much as 232 basis points above the postulated level, implying a shortfall return of -2.7 per cent instead of -5 per cent with a probability of 95 per cent. So exploiting the fat-tail property in this case can lead to more aggressive asset allocations and, therefore, efficiency gains for a given level of shortfall. Alternatively, consider the case $\psi = 1$ per cent. Using a normal scenario generator for a reality with $v_t = 3$ now leads to a violation of the shortfall constraint. While the manager believes his maximum loss with a 99 per cent probability is 5 per cent, his actual loss given that probability may be 159 basis points higher, that is 6.6 per cent. In this case a correct assessment of the degree of leptokurtosis will lead to a more correct assessment of risk

Table 14.2: The effect of misspecification of v on the required shortfall return

v_m	$r^{low} = 0\%$			$r^{low} = ms5\%$			$r^{low} = -10\%$		
	v_t 3	7	∞	v_t 3	7	∞	v_t 3	7	∞
	Shortfall probability of 5%								
3	0	-136	-161	0	-248	-292	0	-354	-418
7	111	0	-20	203	0	-36	293	0	-52
∞	126	19	0	232	36	0	335	51	0
	Shortfall probability of 1%								
3	0	21	73	0	41	139	0	60	202
7	-24	0	53	-43	0	101	-62	0	148
∞	-86	-60	0	-159	-112	0	-232	-163	0

Note: This table contains the changes in basis points in the actual shortfall return ($r^{*,low}$) with respect to the required shortfall return (r^{low}) imposed in the model. This change is a result of a discrepancy between the degree of leptokurtosis used by the manager in the scenario generator (v_m) and the 'true' degree of leptokurtosis of the data (v_t). The asset allocation problem is described in the text and in Table 1. Given the asset mix of the manager (based on v_m), we compute the shortfall return $r^{*,low}$ under the true distribution P_t such that the shortfall constraint is just satisfied, see (8).

and to the exclusion of infeasible strategies. All these effects are even more pronounced if the manager is, *a priori*, willing to take higher losses, that is if r^{low} is even lower.

The above results have obvious and important consequences for value-at-risk analyses. Using a distribution with an incorrect tail behaviour may lead to portfolios with a minimum required return $r*,^{low}$ that can be as much as 418 basis points below the minimum return r^{low} imposed by the model. In value-at-risk calculations, this implies that the true value-at-risk may deviate by more than 4 per cent (as a fraction of the invested notional) from what an incorrectly specified model suggests. Put differently, the value-at-risk may be more than 40 per cent off the mark. This illustrates the importance of trying to get the tail behaviour of one's scenario generator right.

14.6 Concluding remarks

In this chapter we investigated the effect of leptokurtosis or fat tails on optimal asset allocations and shortfall constraints using a simple asset allocation problem under a shortfall constraint. The chapter has resulted in two major conclusions. First, a correct assessment of the fat-tailedness of asset returns is important for the determination of optimal asset allocations. If scenarios are used based on the normal distribution, the resulting allocations may either be inefficient or infeasible. Both effects can be quite substantial. As a second conclusion, it appears that the shortfall probability set by the investment manager plays a crucial role for the effect of leptokurtic asset returns. If the shortfall probability is set sufficiently high, using normal scenarios for leptokurtic asset returns leads to overly prudent and, therefore, inefficient asset allocations. By contrast, if the shortfall probability is sufficiently small, the use of normal scenarios leads to infeasible strategies if reality is fat-tailed.

Several interesting topics for future research remain. The effects of leptokurtosis in multi-period asset allocation problems have to be addressed. Especially the effect of fat tails on problems with recourse seems an interesting direction for future research. It is also interesting to study the quantitative effect of leptokurtosis in situations where one only uses a finite number of observations and a finite number of scenarios.

Notes

* We wish to thank Guus Beender, Frank Bronwer, Cees Dert and especially Bart Oldenkamp for helpful discussions.

References

Bunn, D.W. and A.A. Salo (1993), 'Forecasting with scenarios', *European Journal of Operational Research*, **68**, pp. 291–303

Dert, C. (1995), *Asset liability management for pension funds: a multistage chance constrained programming approach*. Unpublished Ph.D. thesis, Erasmus University, Rotterdam

de Vries, C.G. (1994), 'Stylised facts of nominal exchange rate returns', in F. van der Ploeg, (ed.), *The Handbook of international macroeconomics*, Cambridge, Blackwell, pp. 348–89

Dupacová, J. (1990), 'Stability and sensitivity-analysis for stochastic programming', *Annals of Operations Research*, **27**, pp. 115–42

Leibowitz, M.L., and S. Kogelman (1991), 'Asset allocation under shortfall constraints', *Journal of Portfolio Management*, Winter, pp. 18–23

Leibowitz, M.L., S. Kogelman and L.N. Bader (1992), 'Asset performance and surplus control: a dual shortfall approach', *Journal of Portfolio Management*, Winter, pp. 28–37

Index

All terms in the index relate to banking and Europe unless otherwise stated.

AIB   211
Amazon book shop   71, 72, 80, 85
American Express (Amex)   10, 89, 92
Amsterdam financial centre   197
Asia financial centres   197–8
assets and bank numbers 1988–95
   32–5
assets and fat tails (leptokurtosis)
   application to Netherlands assets
      280–2
   asset allocation theories   272–87
   fat tails effects   278–9, 283–7
   modelling   274–7
ATMs (automated teller machines)
   transaction fees   98
Austria
   bank costs 1988–95   27, 29, 30
   bank mean X-inefficiency levels
      1988–95   40, 41
   bank numbers and assets 1988–95
      32, 34, 35
   bank scale economies 1988–95
      38, 39
   EFTPOS terminals 1990–95   88
automatic clearing house (ACH)
   payments   11–12

bank cards see cards
Bank of Boston   12–13
Bank of Ireland   211
Bank of Scotland   4, 5
BankScope database   26
Banque Nationale de Paris (BNP)
   186
Banque Paribas   12
Barclays Bank   4, 5, 7, 66
Barnes and Noble   79
Basle capital adequacy ratios   214,
   215, 219
Belgium
   bank costs 1988–95   27, 29, 30

bank interest margins 1984–95
   113
bank mean X-inefficiency levels
   1988–95   40, 41
bank numbers and assets 1988–95
   32, 34, 35
bank scale economies 1988–95
   38, 39
bank spread 1984–95   113
EFTPOS terminals 1990–95   88
entrepreneurial return   123
IFSC activities   208, 209
regional development policies
   188–9
regulation effects of EU market
   114–23
regulation methodology statistics
   130–2, 134
Big Bang   166
book shops
   Amazon book shop   71, 73, 74, 80,
      85
   Barnes and Noble   79
   distribution channels   79–80
Boston Net Service   12
branches   14, 16
British Petroleum (BP)   181
British Telecom   177–8

Canada
   IFSC activities   208, 209
capital adequacy regulation (CAR)
   213–28
   Basle capital adequacy ratios   214,
      215, 219
   definition   214
   historical development   213–15
   Spanish savings banks   216–27
   USA   217, 226
Cardiff financial centre   185–6

cards
  American Express (Amex)   10, 89, 92
  co-branded payment cards   89–90, 95–6, 101
  Diners Club   10
  EFTPOS terminals 1990–95   88
  electronic purses   10–11, 68–70
  Eurocard   92
  fees   90–101
  fraud   67
  Internet payments   9–12
  MasterCard   7, 9, 11, 65, 66, 68, 89, 94
  payment methods   65–9
  prepaid cards 68–9
  pricing systems   90–101
  retailer cards   89–90, 92–4
  security and crime   67
  Sweden   87–101; fees   90–4
  UBank Check Card   94–5, 101
  USA: card fees   94–5, 101; co-branded payment cards   95–6
  Visa   7, 9, 11, 66, 68, 89, 94
cash management *see* exposure management
charges *see* costs
Chase Manhattan   256
Chemical Bank   186, 256
Chemical Bank Home Loans   186
cheques
  electronic cheques   11–12, 69–70
  paper cheques   64–5
  transaction fees   98
chip cards   67
Cisco   71, 73, 74, 80, 85
Citibank   256, 257, 258, 268
Citicorp   83–4
co-branded payment cards *see* cards
Coca Cola   208
communications and financial centres   198–9
companies *see* multinational companies (MNCs)
Compaq   3
competition
  financial centres   196–7
  general trends   46–9
  Germany   110

IT and competition   46–61
price competition   48, 51–61
relationship banking   51–61
Spain   139–61: diversity and specialisation   154–7; groups of competitors   148–54; product mix indicators   141; product mix measures   142–8
costs
  card fees   90–101
  cheque transaction fees   98
  data processing costs   3
  effects of technological changes   19–20
  EFTPOS transaction fees   98–9, 100
  employee costs   4–7, 58
  EU banks 1988–95   26–31
  methodology   20–6: Fourier Flexible (FF) functional form   21–4; stochastic cost frontier approach   24–6
  outsourcing   49–51
Countrywide Pasadena   8
credit cards *see* cards
crime *see* security and crime
cross-border transactions   202–3
currency management *see* exposure management
customers and relationship banking   51–61
cyber wallets   10–12
Cyberbank   10
Cybercash   70

data processing costs   3
debit cards *see* cards
Dell Computers   73, 74, 85
Denmark
  bank costs 1988–95   27, 29, 30
  bank mean X-inefficiency levels 1988–95   40, 41
  bank numbers and assets 1988–95   32, 34, 35
  bank scale economies 1988–95   38, 39
  EFTPOS terminals 1990–95   88
  IFSC activities   208
deregulation *see* regulation

Deutsche Telecom   8
Digicash   11, 70
Diners Club card   10
Directives (EU)
    Second Banking Directive   107
    Undertakings for Collective
        Investment in Transferable
        Securities (UCITS) Directive
        203
Direct Line Insurance   8
Discover   15
distribution of services
    book shops   79–80
    definitions   72–4
    distribution channels   8–9, 78–83
    electronic mortgage systems   83–5
    forms of distribution   74–5
    general factors   76–8
    market effects on distribution   75
    retail financial services   81–3
    virtual communities   75–6
downsizing and relationship banking
    48, 52, 60–1
Dublin Docks Development Authority
    211
Dublin International Financial
    Services Centre (IFSC)   201–12

economies of scale 1988–95   38–9
EFTPOS
    EU terminals 1990–95   88
    transaction fees   98–9, 100
electronic banking   7–9, 15–16
electronic cash payments   10–11, 70
electronic cheques   11–12, 69–70
electronic mortgage systems   83–5
electronic payment systems *see*
    payment systems
electronic purses   10–11, 68–70
electronics *see* information
    technology
employees
    customer relations   59
    downsizing effects   60–1
    training   59
    UK bank employee numbers and
        costs   4–7, 58
Eurocard   92
European Union (EU)

bank costs 1988–95   26–31
banking survey 1996 (PACEC/IEF)
    214–15
EC Internet regulation   14
EFTPOS terminals 1990–95   88
regional development policies
    188–9
Second Banking Directive   107
Undertakings for Collective
    Investment in Transferable
    Securities (UCITS) Directive
    203
see also member countries
Europey   9
exposure management   232–70
    company policies   247–52
    currency of denomination   252–5
    currency risk exposure
        management   258–62
    economic and translation exposure
        238–42
    foreign exchange exposure   235–6
    hedging   249–51, 258–62, 268
    interest rate exposure   242–7
    interest rate risk management
        262–4
    international cash management
        255–8
    netting   256–7, 268
    organisation of treasury function
        264–6
    transactions exposure   236–8

failure of banks   16
fat tails (leptokurtosis) *see* assets and
    fat tails
fees *see* costs
FICS Group   12
financial centres   193–200
    Asia   197–8
    Cardiff financial centre   185–6
    characteristics   194–7
    communications   198–9
    competition   196–7
    Dublin International Financial
        Services Centre (IFSC)   201–12
    future trends   199–200
    globalisation   198, 204–5
    historical development   197–8

financial centres (*continued*)
  location 195–6
  London financial centre 166–8
  offshore financial centres 194,
    204–5
  Scotland 174
financial flows *see* UK: regional
  financial flows
Financial Services Act 1986 13–14,
  16, 166, 167
Financial Services Technology
  Consortium (FSTC) 11
Finland
  bank costs 1988–95 27, 29, 30
  bank mean X-inefficiency levels
    1988–95 40, 41
  bank numbers and assets 1988–95
    32, 34, 35
  bank scale economies 1988–95
    38, 39
  EFTPOS terminals 1990–95 88
First Boston 83–4
foreign exchange exposure *see*
  exposure management
Fourier Flexible (FF) functional form
  21–4
France
  bank costs 1988–95 27, 29, 30
  bank interest margins 1984–95
    113
  bank mean X-inefficiency levels
    1988–95 40, 41
  bank numbers and assets 1988–95
    32, 34, 35
  bank scale economies 1988–95
    38, 39
  bank spread 1984–95 112
  EFTPOS terminals 1990–95
    88
  entrepreneurial return 123
  IFSC activities 209
  regional development policies
    188–9
  regulation effects of EU market
    114–23
  regulation methodology statistics
    130–2, 134
fraud *see* security and crime
fund managers, UK 177, 186–7

General Agreement on Tariffs and
  Trade (GATT) 203
Germany
  bank competition 110
  bank costs 1988–95 27, 29, 30
  bank interest margins 1984–95
    113
  bank mean X-inefficiency levels
    1988–95 40, 41
  bank numbers and assets 1988–95
    32, 34, 35
  bank scale economies 1988–95
    38, 39
  bank spread 1984–95 113
  co-operative banks costs 20
  EFTPOS terminals 1990–95 88
  entrepreneurial return 123
  Haus banks 53–5
  IFSC activities 208, 209
  regional development policies
    188–9
  regulation effects of EU market
    114–23
  regulation methodology statistics
    130–2, 134
giro transfers 64–5
globalisation and financial centres
  198, 204–5
Greece
  bank costs 1988–95 27, 29, 30
  bank mean X-inefficiency levels
    1988–95 40, 41
  bank numbers and assets 1988–95
    32, 34, 35
  bank scale economies 1988–95
    38, 39
  EFTPOS terminals 1990–95 88
GTE 9

Haus Banks 53–5
hedging 247–51, 258–62, 268
Heinz 208
Hewlett Packard 11
Holland *see* Netherlands

IBM 9, 208
ICI 181
IFSC (Dublin International Financial
  Services Centre) 201–12

information technology (IT)
  bank competition and IT 46–61
  effects on banking generally 2–3
  effects on relationship banking
    51–61
  effects on UK banks 3–7
  outsourcing 49–51
Intel 3
interest rate exposure *see* exposure
  management
Internet
  general trends 2–3
  payment systems 9–12, 69–70:
    electronic cash payments
    10–11, 70; electronic cheque
    payments 11–12, 69–70;
    secure electronic transaction
    standards (SET) 9–10, 11
  regulation 13–15
Intranet 12
Intuit 83
investment in UK *see* UK: regional
  financial flows
Ireland
  bank costs 1988–95 27, 29, 30
  bank mean X-inefficiency levels
    1988–95 40, 41
  bank numbers and assets 1988–95
    32, 33, 34, 35
  bank scale economies 1988–95
    38, 39
  Dublin Docks Development
    Authority 211
  Dublin International Financial
    Services Centre (IFSC) 201–12
  EFTPOS terminals 1990–95 88
  Irish Bankers' Federation (IBF)
    210
  Irish Development Agency 207
Italy
  bank costs 1988–95 27, 29, 30
  bank interest margins 1984–95
    112
  bank mean X-inefficiency levels
    1988–95 40, 41
  bank numbers and assets 1988–95
    32, 33, 34, 35
  bank scale economies 1988–95
    38, 39

  bank spread 1984–95 113
  EFTPOS terminals 1990–95 88
  entrepreneurial return 123
  IFSC activities 208
  regional development policies
    188–9
  regulation effects of EU market
    114–23
  regulation methodology statistics
    130–2, 134

Japan
  bank costs 20
  IFSC activities 208, 209
Javawallet 10

leptokurtosis *see* assets and fat tails
Lloyds TSB 4, 5, 7, 186
London
  financial centre 166–8
  pension funds 178–81
Luxembourg
  bank costs 1988–95 27, 29, 30
  bank mean X-inefficiency levels
    1988–95 40, 41
  bank numbers and assets 1988–95
    32, 33, 34, 35
  bank scale economies 1988–95
    38, 39
  EFTPOS terminals 1990–95 88

M&G Midland and General Trust
  Fund 187
Manchester financial centre 174
MasterCard 7, 9, 11, 65, 66, 68, 89,
  94
Microsoft 3, 7, 9, 83
Microsystems 10
Midland/HSBC 4, 5
Mondex 11, 68–9
Morgan Stanley Dean Witter Discover
  15
mortgages
  electronic mortgage systems 83–5
multinational companies (MNCs)
  cross-border transactions 202–3
  exposure management 232–70:
    company policies 247–52;
    corporate treasury function

multinational companies (MNCs)
(*continued*)
264–6; currency of denomination
252–5; currency risk exposure
management   258–62; economic
and translation exposure
238–42; foreign exchange
exposure   235–6; hedging
249–51, 258–62, 268; interest
rate exposure   242–7; interest
rate risk management   262–4;
international cash management
255–8; netting   256–7, 268;
transactions exposure
236–8

National Provident Institution
186
National Westminster Bank   4, 5, 7
Netherlands
Amsterdam financial centre   197
assets and fat tails   280–2
bank costs 1988–95   27, 29, 30
bank interest margins 1984–95
113
bank mean X-inefficiency levels
1988–95   40, 41
bank numbers and assets 1988–95
32, 33, 34, 35
bank scale economies 1988–95
38, 39
bank spread 1984–95   113
EFTPOS terminals 1990–95   88
entrepreneurial return   123
IFSC activities   208, 209
regulation effects of EU market
114–23
regulation methodology statistics
130–2, 134
netting   249, 256–7, 268
Netscope   9
Norwich Union   187

offshore financial centres   194,
204–5
Dublin International Financial
Services Centre (IFSC)
201–12
outsourcing   49–51

Parent Soup virtual community   76
payment systems
automatic clearing house (ACH)
payments   11–12
cards   65–9; Sweden   87–101
cheques   64–5
cyber wallets   10–12
electronic purses   10–11, 68–70
giro transfers   64–5
Internet   9–12, 69–70: electronic
cash payments   10–11, 70;
electronic cheque payments
11–12, 69–70; secure electronic
transaction standards (SET)
9–10, 11
UK   3–4, 6
pension funds, UK   176–81, 186–7
personnel *see* employees
plastic cards *see* cards
Portugal
bank costs 1988–95   27, 29, 30
bank mean X-inefficiency levels
1988–95   40, 41
bank numbers and assets 1988–95
32, 33, 34, 35
bank scale economies 1988–95
38, 39
EFTPOS terminals 1990–95   88
PRC Advanced Systems Inc.   83
prepaid cards *see* cards
prices
card fees   90–101
price competition   48, 51–61
Prudential   83

Quelle   8

Rabobank   11
regional development policies
188–9
regional financial flows *see* UK:
regional financial flows
regulation
capital adequacy regulation
(CAR)   213–28: definition
214; historical development
213–15; Spanish savings
banks   216–27; USA   217,
226

deregulation effects   2, 108–14, 213–15
effect of EU unified market   114–23
general bank regulation   16–17
historical background   106–8
Internet regulation   13–15
methodology   125–36
Second Banking Directive   107
Spanish savings banks   216–27
UK: Financial Services Act 1986 13–14, 16, 166, 167; Securities and Investments Board (SIB) 13–14
USA: capital adequacy regulation (CAR) , 217, 226; Internet regulation 14–15; Securities and Exchange Commission (SEC) 14
relationship banking   51–61
Rennie Mae   83
retailer cards *see* cards
Royal Bank of Scotland   4, 5, 13

SAIC   9
Salomon Brothers   16
savings banks *see* Spain
scale economies 1988–95   38–9
Scotland
    financial centres   174
    pension funds   178–81
    regional financial flows   183
SE-Banken (Skandinaviska Enskilda Banken)   256, 257, 258
Second Banking Directive   107
Securities and Exchange Commission (SEC)   14
Securities and Investments Board (SIB)   13–14
security and crime
    cards   67
    corporate networks   12–13
    electronic cheque payments 11–12
secure electronic transaction standards (SET)   9–10, 11
Security First Network Bank (SFNB) 71–2, 75, 81, 85
services and relationship banking 56–61

services distribution
    book shops   79–80
    definitions   72–4
    distribution channels   8–9, 78–83
    electronic mortgage systems 83–5
    forms of distribution   74–5
    general factors   76–8
    market effects on distribution   75
    retail financial services   81–3
    virtual communities   75–6
Skandinaviska Enskilda Banken (SE-Banken)   256, 257, 258
smart cards *see* cards
Sofinco   8
Spain
    bank capital adequacy regulation (CAR)   216–27
    bank competition   139–61; diversity and specialisation 154–7; groups of competitors 148–54; product mix indicators 141; product mix measures 142–8
    bank costs 1985–94   20
    bank costs 1988–95   27, 29, 30
    bank interest margins 1984–95 113
    bank mean X-inefficiency levels 1988–95   40, 41
    bank numbers and assets 1988–95 32, 33, 34, 35
    bank scale economies 1988–95 38, 39
    bank spread 1984–95   113
    EFTPOS terminals 1990–95   88
    entrepreneurial return   123
    regional development policies 188–9
    regulation effects of EU market 114–23
    regulation methodology statistics 130–2, 134
    savings banks: capital adequacy regulation (CAR)   216–27; costs 1985–94   20
staff *see* employees
stochastic cost frontier approach 24–6

subcontracting *see* outsourcing
Sweden
 bank costs 1988–95   27, 29, 30
 bank mean X-inefficiency levels
  1988–95   40, 41
 bank numbers and assets 1988–95
  32, 33, 34, 35
 bank scale economies 1988–95
  38, 39
 cards   87–101: fees   90–4
 EFTPOS terminals 1990–95   88
 exposure management   232–70:
  company policies   247–52;
  currency of denomination
  252–5; currency risk exposure
  management   258–62;
  economic and translation
  exposure   238–42; foreign
  exchange exposure   235–6;
  interest rate exposure   242–7;
  interest rate risk management
  262–4; international cash
  management   255–8;
  organisation of treasury
  function   264–6; transactions
  exposure   236–8
 IFSC activities   208, 209
Switzerland
 IFSC activities   208

technology *see* information
 technology
telephone banking   51–2
trade
 General Agreement on Tariffs and
  Trade (GATT)   203
 World Trade Organisation (WTO)
  203
training and relationship banking
 59
treasury management *see* exposure
 management
TSB Group   186
Tullett and Tokyo   12

UBank Check Card   94–5, 101
Undertakings for Collective
 Investment in Transferable
 Securities (UCITS) Directive   203

United Kingdom
 bank costs 1988–95   27, 29, 30
 bank employee numbers and costs
  4–7
 bank interest margins 1984–95
  113
 bank mean X-inefficiency levels
  1988–95   40, 41
 bank numbers and assets 1988–95
  32, 33, 34, 35
 bank scale economies 1988–95
  38, 39
 bank spread 1984–95   113
 Big Bang   166
 card fraud   67
 EFTPOS terminals 1990–95   88
 entrepreneurial return   123
 exposure management   232–70:
  company policies   247–52;
  currency of denomination
  252–5; currency risk exposure
  management   258–62;
  economic and translation
  exposure   238–42; foreign
  exchange exposure   235–6;
  interest rate exposure   242–7;
  interest rate risk management
  262–4; international cash
  management   255–8;
  organisation of treasury
  function   264–6; transactions
  exposure   236–8
 Financial Services Act 1986
  13–14, 16, 166, 167
 fund managers   177, 186–7
 IFSC activities   208, 209
 Internet regulation   13–15
 London financial centre   166–8
 Manchester financial centre
  174
 payment systems   3–4, 6
 pension funds   176–81, 186–7
 regional financial flows   164–89:
  distribution of institutional
  investment   172–81; effects on
  regions   181–9; household
  expenditure on investment
  172–6; theory of regional
  financial flows   168–71

regulation effects of EU market
114–23
regulation methodology statistics
130–2, 134
Scotland: financial centres 174;
pension funds 178–81;
regional financial flows 183
Securities and Investments Board
(SIB) 13–14
Wales: Cardiff financial centre
185–6; pension funds 178–81;
regional financial flows 181–9
United States of America
automatic clearing house (ACH)
payments 11–12
bank branches 14
bank capital adequacy regulation
(CAR) 217, 226
bank costs 20
card fees 94–5, 101
co-branded payment cards 95–6
electronic mortgage systems 83–5
IFSC activities 208, 209

Internet regulation 14–15
regional development policies
187–8
Securities and Exchange
Commission (SEC) 14
US Bancorp 94–5, 101

Verifore 10
Verisign 9
Virgin Direct 187
virtual communities 75–6
Visa 7, 9, 11, 66, 68, 89, 94

Wales
Cardiff financial centre 185–6
pension funds 178–81
regional financial flows 181–9
Wells Fargo 74
workers *see* employees
World Trade Organisation (WTO)
203

x-inefficiency levels 1988–95 40–1